POETS'
RIDDLES

Edward Le Comte

POETS'
RIDDLES

*Essays in Seventeenth-Century
Explication*

National University Publications
KENNIKAT PRESS • 1975
Port Washington, N.Y. • London

Manufactured in the United States of America

Published by
Kennikat Press Corp.
Port Washington, N.Y. • London

Library of Congress Cataloging in Publication Data

Le Comte, Edward Semple, 1916—
    Poets' riddles.

    (National university publications)
    Includes bibliographical references and index.
    1. English literature—Early modern, 1500-1700—
Addresses, essays, lectures. 2. English literature—
Explication. I. Title.
PR433.L38   820'.9   74-77656
ISBN 0-8046-9065-0

Contents

Acknowledgments

Permission has kindly been granted by the copyright holders for me to make use of articles previously published, as follows: "New Light on the 'Haemony' Passage in *Comus*," *Philological Quarterly*, 21 (1942), 283–98; "The Ending of *Hamlet* as a Farewell to Essex," *English Literary History*, 17 (1950), 87–114, The Johns Hopkins University Press; " 'That Two-Handed Engine' and Savonarola," *Studies in Philology*, 47 (1950), 589–606; "Supplement," ibid. 49 (1952), 548–50; "Marvell's 'The Nymph Complaining for the Death of her Fawn,' " *Modern Philology*, 50 (1952), 97–101, The University of Chicago Press; "Jack Donne: From Rake to Husband," pp. 9–32 of *Just So Much Honor: Essays Commemorating the Four-Hundredth Anniversary of the Birth of John Donne*, edited by Peter A. Fiore, copyright © 1972 by The Pennsylvania State University.

Preface

These seventeenth-century studies, commencing with two essays on *Hamlet* (which I date 1601) and one on Donne's marriage (which I date 1602), all employ the technique of close reading, backed by research, for the purpose of resolving a difficulty. In some cases—as with the celebrated "two-handed engine at the door" in "Lycidas"—there is universal agreement that there is a difficulty. In other cases the difficulty may not really be there, but has been thought to be. With Donne's marriage the problem is one of reconciling a letter of his with a document in juridical Latin the very handwriting of which induces a Gorgonian freeze in the novice and gives even the expert pause. The other explications range from one line of poetry to one poem.

Of the seven essays two are new and have not been published before. The others have been revised. I started to write the earliest—that on the magic plant haemony in *Comus*—as an M.A. candidate at Columbia University thirty-five years ago.

Evidently I am drawn to cruxes the way others are drawn to crossword puzzles or cryptograms or palimpsests. The school I went to was old by American standards (founded in 1709) and old-fashioned even when I was a student there.

The grammar school had grammar (what grammar school still does?), and I delighted in construing sentences, making diagrams on a blackboard. In the high school or preparatory school, I had, besides French, four years of Latin and three of Greek. If one "faked" a translation or offered just a general impression or was airy about the precise meaning of a word, one had one's knuckles rapped in one way or another. After more Latin and Greek at Columbia College, it was more or less inevitable that if I were to be drawn to an English author it would be Milton (Landor was too minor), or if I did a doctoral dissertation it would have something to do with the classics.

A prime inspiration at college was that most brilliant and erudite of source studies John Livingston Lowes's *The Road to Xanadu*. In my first year as a graduate student, I was fired with zeal to do a "Road to Xanadu" for lines 629–41 of *Comus*. In one of the acknowledged sources of the masque, I thought I found a clue. The result was duly filed with the Columbia Library in 1940 and was published, in shortened form, in *Philological Quarterly* in 1942. The interest of these two years is that in between, in 1941, came out A.S.P. Woodhouse's extremely influential article "The Argument of Milton's *Comus*" (*University of Toronto Quarterly*), which, as John G. Demaray has lately put it, "unknowingly started a new movement dedicated to complex readings of Milton's masque." I, however, cannot complain of lack of attention to my more confined exposition. Thomas P. Harrison, Jr., published a sequel to it in 1943. It was found convincing by Cleanth Brooks and John Hardy in their New Criticism edition of the Minor Poems, 1951, but also by the more academic Rosemond Tuve in 1957 (and Kester Svendsen in 1956). Robert M. Adams attacked it in a 1953 article that became part of his widely read book *Ikon: John Milton and the Modern Critics,* 1955. John M. Steadman also begged to differ, going off on his own in a major article, "Milton's *Haemony*: Etymology and Allegory," *Publications of the Modern Language Association,* 1962. There have been smaller

notes and numerous editions these thirty years, right up to
Woodhouse's word on the problem—and Douglas Bush's—in
the Columbia *Variorum Commentary*, II (1972), 931–38.
Obviously, I have had some updating to do.

The same *Variorum* says, on page 691, apropos of a still
more famous crux, "Whatever doubts may be left respecting
the source proposed, one of the most valuable examinations
of the problem and of many previous inquiries is provided by
E. S. Le Comte." This was a 1950 article on "Lycidas,"
130–31, a couplet which has begotten scores of interpretations and a hundred notes. (See the *Variorum* bibliography
through 1970, II, 1103–05.) I tried for a triple harmony: of
source, of Milton's expressions elsewhere, and of what the
reader of 1638 could reasonably be expected to make of the
lines. The letters I received from Miltonists were encouraging.
E. M. W. Tillyard, for notable instance, wrote: "Many thanks
for your offprint on 'that two-handed engine.' I find it most
convincing, though we can't be certain that there was not
someone as well as Savonarola to supplement the Scriptures.
I congratulate you on having cleared away so much rubbish."
This meant something, since this eminent critic, unlike others
from whom I heard, had published an interpretation of his
own, Appendix F of his *Milton* (1930). It takes an objectivity
(if not magnanimity) that not everyone can come up with to
find merit in an interpretation different from one's own. My
article is reflected in the three notes on l. 130 in the edition
put out in 1952 by Mr. and Mrs. Tillyard, *Comus and Some
Shorter Poems* (Harrap's English Classics). Much water has
gone under the bridge since—of the writing about "that two-
handed engine" there is no end—and I, striving for the open-
mindedness of Tillyard, find a 1971 *English Language Notes*
piece by Philip Rollinson very interesting (and a sequel to it
by Karl Felsen which I have read in manuscript). But otherwise I have not seen much progress. One novelty that I suggested in passing, only to reject, was taken up by J. Milton
French. Another that I threw out as a joke to a class of
graduate students at Columbia developed, with due but

embarrassing acknowledgment, into seventeen pages in
Studies in Philology in 1962. In addition, there has been
some portentous nonsense that deserves to be scotched.

In 1948 I went down from Berkeley to the Huntington
Library to look up some rare references. There William
Haller, who had been my best teacher of Milton, introduced
me to Louis B. Wright, who had resigned from the Huntington to be the director of the Folger Shakespeare Library in
Washington, D.C. Dr. Wright politely asked me what I was
working on. I answered, in one word, *"Hamlet."* "You're not
the first," he responded. *That* I was laboriously aware of,
having spent months finding out, or endeavoring to find out,
whether what I wanted to say had been said before. It
apparently had not been (proving the inexhaustibility of
Hamlet), though the theory to which I was contributing
detail had a leading proponent in J. Dover Wilson—the theory
of some cause-and-effect relationship between the second
earl of Essex, the queen's ill-fated favorite, and Shakespeare's
tragedy. The result, as embodied in what is now Part 1 of my
article, seemed strange even to me. However, something
insisted—and still does—that the last seventy lines of the play
have, especially in their theatrical imagery, a continuous
ambiguity worth calling attention to and accounting for. But
it was all too outré for the two consultants of *PMLA*, where I
had hoped it would be published. One dated the play 1600
(which knocked out my hypothesis). The other looked
askance, as if I belonged to the lunatic fringe and would soon
prepare a sequel announcing that Queen Elizabeth (another
indecisive personage, like her once dear earl) had herself
penned *Hamlet* as a disguised autobiography (perhaps with
the assistance of Christopher Marlowe, who recovered from
that tavern brawl and went underground). On receipt of these
disparagements I decided to proclaim sanity by adding Part 2,
a vigorous refutation of Part 1. In Part 2 I used every argument against my own exposition I could think of. Disarm
the opposition by anticipating it? Was that sanity—or
schizophrenia? I sent the now very long piece to another

learned journal and in due course there came back, with the manuscript, the question, "If Le Comte doesn't believe his own theory, how can he expect anybody else to?" Eventually I found hospitality in *English Literary History*. "The Ending of *Hamlet* as a Farewell to Essex" even received a good press in *Shakespeare Survey* 5 and 9. It remains a curiosity outside the larger modern critical interests, but following the scent was fun.

Some of the above-mentioned articles, plus the new one with which this book commences, "Hamlet's Second Utterance: Forty-Three Interpretations," may give the impression that I like to make complications. I deny this, and the last two pieces here are on the other side, the side of simplicity and common sense. One of them is new, "New Objections to a Pre-Restoration Date for *Samson Agonistes*" and seeks to dispose of a gratuitous conjecture that has muddied up Milton studies since 1949. The other, "Marvell's 'The Nymph Complaining for the Death of her Fawn,' " was welcomed by Ronald S. Crane into *Modern Philology* in 1952, he, like me, being weary of those subtle minds that read in meanings that there is no particular reason to believe are there. The "haemony" passage urges allegory upon us because *Comus* is an allegorical and didactic poem (masques are inherently symbolical). Marvell's poem is nothing of the sort, seems sufficient unto itself on the surface. The literal should always be tried first and abandoned only when it does not work out or suit the form and tradition. In my view, the annotators on the crux "Amnon's murther" in Dryden's *Absalom and Achitophel*, 39, have gone demonstrably astray in supposing a reference to Sir John Coventry's mutilation, since Coventry did not die of his sliced nose. They should rather look for someone that Monmouth killed—and there was such a person, a night watchman, as I pointed out in *Notes and Queries* in 1963. But this note, though it appeared in the bibliographies, got lost in the shuffle (or common sense is no fun), and the latest authorities still go on babbling about Coventry as if they'd never heard what "murder" means.

The Marvell article did not settle anything, either. Rather, it started something, a hornets' nest or mare's nest. More than a dozen articles have appeared since, beginning with "A Reply" by Karina Williamson, 1954. (The two pieces are reprinted in the Penguin Critical Anthology on Marvell, 1969.) That is not the least of the joys of literary criticism, arguing different points of view. I am glad for the present opportunity to leap into the fray again and have, however temporarily, the last word. From a 1957 book of mine I have reprinted, as an appendix, a parody of the New Criticism that is not so out-of-date as one might hope.

E. Le C.

State University of New York at Albany

I

Hamlet's Second Utterance: Forty-Three Interpretations

Every editor knows his obligation to gloss Hamlet's first line, "A little more than kin, and less than kind". But what about Hamlet's second line? Some of the best academic editions have no note,[1] and even those that furnish two or three interpretations are slighting the rich possibilities, even probabilities.

The first line came in response to the king's "But now, my cousin Hamlet, and my son. . . ." The second answers Claudius's question, "How is it that the clouds still hang on you?" "Not so, my lord; I am too much i' the sun" (I.ii.67).

There being a quibble on "sun"–"son" that is pointed up by the Second Quarto spelling "in the sonne,"[2] the meanings subdivide as follows:

A. "sun"

1. "I am beamed on–favored–too much by your grace."[3] On the surface–unless delivered sarcastically–this is a courtierly response. Underneath, it is a barb carrying the message, "Stop trying to curry favor with me."

2. "I am too much out of doors"[4] (I do not frequent the Court).

3. "I am disinherited." The usurper has "popp'd in between the election and my hopes" (V.ii.65) of the throne.

3

Whereas we say, "I am out in the cold," the Elizabethans, as Dr. Johnson noted, had a proverb for dispossession that is found in *King Lear* (II.ii.167ff.): "Good king, that must approve the common saw,/Thou out of heaven's benediction com'st/To the warm sun."[5]

4. "I have descended 'from an exalted, or honourable, state or occupation to a low or ignoble one.' "[6] Laborers work in the sun, the better-born only under unfair compulsion—Orlando, Prince Ferdinand.

5. "I, in mourning, find your sunny court gaiety oppressive."[7]

6. "The sun is shining upon my face, and I must needs turn away my eyes, to try to conceal that I have been weeping."[8]

7. "Highly visible is my position as a dissenter."

8. "I see all too clearly, uncloudedly. I see through you, hypocrite that you are." This gets ready for, "O my prophetic soul! My uncle!" (I.v.40).

9. "I am too much in the presence of royalty"—*le roi soleil* (sarcastic and/or straight). The association of monarchs with the sun is as old as Ikhnaton. When Lady Leicester put on too many airs, Queen Elizabeth I told her "that as but one sun lighted the east, so she would have but one Queen in England."[9]

10. "I am aware that I am a prince in the spotlight—it puts a strain on me, everybody watching me."[10] Compare 159, "But break, my heart, for I must hold my tongue!"

11. "I, the principal actor in this play, have a long and strenuous part ahead of me." *Hamlet* is about acting, in every sense of the word, and Shakespeare anticipated the modern self-consciousness of, for instance, Pirandello (not to mention Tom Stoppard) with such a remark as Cleopatra's "I shall see/Some squeaking Cleopatra boy my greatness/I' the posture of a whore" (*Antony and Cleopatra*, V.ii.218ff.).

12. "I am too much in the way: a mote in the royal eye."[11]

13. "It is so bright and dazzling here that I cannot see reality." The first two scenes contrast. It is, however

paradoxically, the first scene, of midnight darkness and the Ghost, to which Hamlet must go for the truth.

14. "I am but too mature." The fourth of the Seven Ages of Man is Early Maturity and is dominated by the sun (in the fourth position in the Ptolemaic universe), the most perfect of the planets and the ripener of lovers of honesty and virtue. Jaques, in his review, presented at this stage "a soldier . . . jealous in honour, sudden and quick in quarrel" (*As You Like It*, II.vii.149), which Hamlet is or must be.[12]

15. "I know that *you* have me under all too close observation."

16. "On the contrary, I am not mourning for my father enough."

17. "I recall all too well the glory of my father's reign and achievements." The comparison will be a sun god, "Hyperion to a satyr" (140), "Hyperion's curls" (III.iv.56).

18. "I am not ambitious." "Who doth ambition shun,/ And loves to live i' the sun" (*As You Like It*, II.v.39).

19. "I am distracted, sun-struck." Although "sun-struck" is a word not on record before the nineteenth century, the *coup de soleil* had long been recognized. Burton's *Anatomy of Melancholy*[13] supplies the appropriate quotations. Capivaccius said, "If the brain be hot, the animal spirits will be hot, and thence comes madness." Rhasis warned against "long abode in hot places, or under the sun." "Fear . . . the heat o' the sun" (*Cymbeline*, IV.ii.258). Compare Isaiah, 49:10. In 1606 Shakespeare was to show what happened to unsheltered Lear: "My wits begin to turn" (III.ii.67).

20. "I am dried up, withered" ("How weary, stale, flat, and unprofitable" . . . 133).

21. "Amidst the prevailing flattery and deceit I do not pretend but make apparent my thoughts and feelings."[14]

22. "Are you trying to tell me that Elsinore *has* any sun?" (Sarcasm on the climate).[15]

23. "I hate life; I am but too much alive." Macbeth: "I 'gin to be aweary of the sun" (V,v,49).

24. "I am more careless and idle than I ought to be[16] —as on vacation" (I desire to return to my studies at Wittenberg).

25. "I am exposed to too much feeling."

26. "I am unmarried and have lost my family." This fits with the same interpretation of Beatrice's (at least as being single) "I am sun-burnt" (*Much Ado about Nothing,* II.i.333).[17]

27. "Like Icarus, I was flying high, but now my wings have melted and I have plummeted." "The sun, that sear'd the wings of my sweet boy," is a quotation that is not alone as an early allusion to the myth that so befits the "overreaching" Renaissance (*3 Henry VI*, V.vi.18–25; cf. *1 Henry VI*, IV.vi.54ff.;vii.16).[18]

28. "I must remain here stationary, like the earth, under your–the sun's–control." Compare 112–17, including the astronomical language.[19]

29. "I abhor the thought of generation, whether yours or mine"–the sun being the generative principle or power. "For if the sun breed maggots in a dead dog. . . ." "Let her not walk i' the sun: conception is a blessing but not as your daughter may conceive" (II.ii.182,186).

30. "Hitherto obscured, I shall yet (you will find) be showing my true mettle." Compare Prince Hal's soliloquy on himself as sun breaking through clouds (*1 Henry IV*, I.ii.219ff.). This was common rhetoric. Anthony Bacon wrote of Essex: "Our Earl, God be thanked, hath with the bright beams of his valour and virtue scattered the clouds and cleared the mists that malicious envy had stirred against his matchless merit."[20]

31. "Whatever you say, I in my hostility will contradict you." (George Eliot in *The Mill on the Floss* [VI. vi. 2nd par.], remarked on Hamlet's "frankest incivility.")

B. "son"

1. "I am more of a son to you than I want to be"[21] (reverting to the first exchange, "A little more than kin," etc.).

2. "Stop throwing the word 'son' at me." Hamlet puns defensively–or aggressively.

3. "That you have made me your stepson is all too much on my mind."

4. "I have too much of the son-successor and public staging without possession of my rights."[22]
5. "I do not want two fathers."[23]
6. "I fear there will be a son (and heir) born of my mother's union with you."
7. "I am around you—my stepfather—too much."
8. "I have my relation as son to my true father on my mind."
9. "I do not want father–domination."[24]

C. "sun"-"son" without clear dominance

1. "I have conception on my mind" (Gertrude and Ophelia). This is the prelude to numerous sexual references, beginning with the first soliloquy.
2. "I was in the shadow of my (glorious and life-giving) father, but now I am not. I am on my own."[25]
3. "My word play shows that I am attempting a forced cheerfulness."[26]

In sum, with his second utterance the riddling Hamlet has surpassed himself—and certainly anyone else that one can think of.

NOTES

1. G.B. Harrison (ed.), *Complete Works* (New York, 1952); W.A. Neilson and C.J. Hill (eds.), *Complete Plays and Poems* (Boston, 1942); Cyrus Hoy (ed.) *Hamlet* (New York, 1963).
2. The First Quarto does not have Hamlet's first two remarks. One translation by August Wilhelm von Schlegel works in both words: "Das nicht; mir scheint als Sohne zu viel Sonne."
3. However put (I am doing my own phrasing, or paraphrasing, except where direct quotation is specified), this seems to be the favorite interpretation: e.g., the edition of *Hamlet*, ad loc., by J.Q. Adams (Boston, 1929); Tucker Brooke and Jack R. Crawford (New Haven, 1947); Willard Farnham, Penguin edition (1957); Edward Hubler (New York, Signet, 1963); put first among several by [Brinsley] Nicholson (1867) in the H.H. Furness *Variorum* edition (New York, Dover reprint, 1963), second by Hardin Craig, *Complete Works* (New York,

1961), and the only interpretation in such books as Martin Holmes, *The Guns of Elsinore* (New York, 1964), p. 68, and G.R. Elliott, *Scourge and Minister* (New York, 1965), p. 11, n. 7. (I quote Shakespeare in this and the next essay from the Oxford text of W.J. Craig.)

4. Direct quotation from Hardin Craig, listed by him first of four and unique to him.

5. See *OED*, s.v. "God," 5c and citations in Furness. Meaning *b* (of two) in *Complete Works*, ed. Irving Ribner and G.L. Kittredge (Waltham, Mass., 1971).

6. Favored by J. Dover Wilson, *What Happens in "Hamlet"* (Cambridge, 1951), p. 33, who is quoting (my single quotes) P.L. Carver, "'Out of Heaven's Blessing to the Warm Sun,'" *MLR*, 25 (1930), 478–81. Carver is giving what he regards as the correct interpretation of the proverb of 3 above (n. 5 above), but it seems to me we are in the presence of another interpretation, which I go on to expand.

7. [Henry Norman] Hudson and Nicholson in Furness; Edward Dowden (ed.), *Hamlet* (London, 1899); Levin L. Schücking, *The Meaning of "Hamlet"* (Oxford, 1937), p. 73.

8. Up to the second comma I am quoting, then paraphrasing, George Newcomen, "A New Interpretation of a Line in *Hamlet*," *The Academy and Literature* (London), 46 (1894), 538. Newcomen cites "vailed lids" (70) and "the fruitful river in the eye" (80).

9. Robert Lacey, *Robert, Earl of Essex* (New York, 1971), p. 31.

10. This is evidently the interpretation favored by the *OED*, under the noun "sun," 4b–"exposed to public view." Cf. George Steevens in the eighteenth century in the Boswell-Malone *Third Variorum* (London, 1821), VII: "Meaning probably his being sent for from his studies to be exposed at his uncle's marriage as his *chiefest courtier*, etc."

11. Quotation from [Howard] Staunton in Furness.

12. Sir Walter Raleigh said, "The fourth [belongs] to the Sun, the strong, flourishing, and beautiful age of man's life." *The History of the World* (1614), bk. 1, ch. 2, sec. 5, p. 31, quoted in Samuel C. Chew, *The Pilgrimage of Life* (New Haven, 1962), p. 165.

13. Everyman's Library, I, 378–79.

14. Suggested to me by Gerald B. Spillane of Great Barrington, Mass. This is a good place to mention that some of the hitherto unrecorded interpretations I offer arose from classroom discussions with my undergraduate students in Shakespeare at the State University of New York at Albany, but I failed at the time to note who said what and so can make only a general acknowledgment, in the spirit of my own great teacher, Mark Van Doren, who said in the acknowledgments of his now classic *Shakespeare* (New York, 1939): "No one unless I tell him, and I hereby do, will appreciate my debt to those students of Columbia College with whom I annually read and discuss the complete works of Shakespeare."

15. Also suggested by Mr. Spillane.

16. Direct quotation up to this point from Alexander Schmidt, *Shakespeare-Lexicon* revised and enlarged by Gregor Sarrazin (New York, 1902), II, 1154. "Leading an easy, aimless life, like one who suns himself": Richard Grant White (ed.), *Comedies, Histories, Tragedies, and Poems* (Boston, 1911).

17. See the long discussion by [Joseph] Hunter in Furness. Revived by H.D.F. Kitto, *Form and Meaning in Drama* (London, 1959), p. 259; Eleanor Prosser, *Hamlet and Revenge* (Stanford, 1967), p. 126, n. 20.

18. Suggested by French and Italian translations that translate back as "too near the sun": "Me voici trop près du soleil"; "Troppo son io vicino al sole." (Suggestive of other meanings is one of Schlegel's versions: "Ich habe zu viel Sonne.")

19. Suggested to me by the discussion of 112–17 in M. M. Mahood, *Shakespeare's Wordplay* (London, 1968), p. 115.

20. Letter to Dr. Hawkins in Walter Bourchier Devereux, *Lives and Letters of the Devereux, Earls of Essex* (London, 1853), I, 392.

21. Hardin Craig; Ribner & Kittredge.

22. I quote [Thomas] Caldecott in Furness, except for a change of "son and successor" to a compound.

23. "He finds himself to be the son of three people": O.B. Davis in the Avon edition (New York, 1964, with *Much Ado about Nothing* and *Richard III*).

24. Suggested to me by the remarks about "the two paternal attributes ... fatherliness and tyranny" in Ernest Jones, *Hamlet and Oedipus* (New York, 1955), p. 154.

25. "With his 'youthful' and filial characteristic, the Sun is associated with the hero, as opposed to the father, who connotes the heavens." J.E. Cirlot, *A Dictionary of Symbols* (New York, 1962), p. 302. "The clouds" that "hang" represent the father.

26. Suggested by Coleridge's "Play on words either [due] to 1. exuberant activity of mind, as in Shakespeare's higher comedy; [or] 2. imitation of it as a fashion, which has this to say for it—'Why is not this now better than groaning?' " J.C. Levenson (ed.), *Discussions of "Hamlet"* (Boston, 1960), p. 14.

A forty-fourth interpretation I reject as not appropriate at this stage of the play: I have become absorbed in religion—I have the Savior on my mind" ("the Sun of righteousness"—Malachi 4.2–Son of God association, as in Donne's "A Hymn to God the Father").

II

The Ending of *Hamlet* as a Farewell to Essex

A number of scholars, of whom the best known is the late Dover Wilson, have believed that the inspiration for the character of Hamlet "came to Shakespeare from the career and personality of the most conspicuous figure in England during the last decade of the sixteenth century, namely the brilliant, the moody, the excitable, the unstable, the procrastinating, the ill-fated Earl of Essex."[1] The identification is of course only partial, and it does not, I take it, seek glibly to pluck the heart of Hamlet's mystery. It simply furnishes, at most, a basis for that mystery (if there *is* a mystery) by suggesting that the dramatist, along with thousands of his contemporaries, was fascinated by a particular case of enigmatic human nature, more complex than anything to be found in treatises on melancholy,[2] and that in some degree, which it will be the business of part 1, the pro side, of this paper more particularly to define, *Hamlet* is a memorial to Essex.

However, as this is to enter the realm of conjecture, honest and balanced consideration demands a statement of cons as well. Rather than risk the confusion of a paper that would be at war with itself on every page, I have kept the two sides separate. Part 1 will present a brief review of some old points and make some new ones in behalf of the Hamlet-Essex theory, especially as it can be related to the ending of the play, where it has hardly been applied and yet where it most neatly works. In part 2 I have concentrated the principal objections and alternatives that occur to me.

PART 1

One *starts*, at any rate, with facts. First, even those who treat of Shakespeare as if he had lived in a vacuum, have to admit that once, in the chorus to act V of *Henry V*, the dramatist went very far out of his way to make a direct and extended reference to Essex, wishing "the general of our gracious empress" a speedy and successful return from Ireland and alluding to his popularity:

> How many would the peaceful city quit
> To welcome him!

This was in 1599: Essex's tragedy and Hamlet's were soon to be enacted. Equally undeniable is the link between Shakespeare and Essex provided by Southampton, who, because of his part in the same rebellion for which Essex was beheaded, was in the Tower when *Hamlet* was written,[3] and remained there until James freed him. Third, there is overwhelming evidence that plays *were* taken topically, as by the queen herself, when she said, "I am 'Richard the Second,' know ye not that?"[4] The Essex conspirators would have had her so, apparently, since they paid forty shillings to have Shakespeare's play performed on the eve of the rebellion.[5] As it turned out, they might more appropriately have attended a performance of *Hamlet,* had that play as we have it been in existence, with its unsuccessful rebellion and its hero who cannot make up his mind. For on Sunday, February 8, 1601, hundreds of Londoners personally witnessed the indecisions of Robert Devereux, who, given a native hue of resolution, might well on that day have become king of England.[6]

To come to the play itself, it has been pointed out a number of times in what an uncanny way the family situation of Robert Devereux fits Shakespeare's changes—for are we not to call such a change as the poisoning his, since we do not know it to have been made by anyone else?—in the old Amleth story. At least according to purveyors of scandal, the earl of Leicester seduced Robert's mother, poisoned his father (by "an Italian *Recipe*" which induced "an extreame Flux"),[7] and then married—this is fact—the widow. We thus have a situation as near to that of *Hamlet* as "The Murder of Gonzago," for if the reputed history involves an earl rather than a king (it is hardly fair at this point, and at this point only, to cite the 1603 Quarto, where the king and queen are duke and duchess), and is without the blood relationship (which derives from the saga) between murdered and murderer, the play within a play lacks the adultery theme and does not give us fratricide either.

There were those in the audience who would recall this notorious scandal—as does Camden[8] in his *Annals*—if they had occasion to, but of course it was ancient history. The association of Hamlet with Essex would have come rather from current history and from correspondences between the two characters. The correspondences are probably sufficiently summed up in the words from Dover Wilson with which this article began, except that there is another adjective to add: "woman-hating."[9] The earl cursed the very femininity of the queen herself. "The Court is a prey to two evils—delay and inconstancy; and the cause is the sex of the sovereign."[10] Nothing that Hamlet says to Ophelia or his mother is so savage as Essex's outburst when, during his final estrangement from the queen, someone ventured to speak in his presence of "Her Majesty's conditions." "Her conditions! Her conditions are as crooked as her carcase!"[11] The fact remains that, whether we are thinking of Amleth or of Essex, Shakespeare has transmuted a crude original hero as well as a crude original plot. Hamlet is nobler in every way than the historical Essex, and we today are left to wonder how his contemporaries could so have overrated and taken to their hearts this spoiled child of fortune, whose vanity and ineptitude abundantly come through in the accounts, but not his charm. Yet there can be no denying his sway over the idealizing poets, and he may well have been the original of Spenser's Sir Calidore, "Courtesie,"[12] though Chapman was nearer to his character in equating him with Achilles. The latest biographer, free of any interest in equating him with anyone, provides a provocative description.

His way with the ladies of the Court was as legendary as the sway he held over their Queen. Somewhat careless of his appearance, a somewhat awkward dancer whose tall frame stooped with his head thrust forward as he moved, silent and contemplative at mealtimes, his behaviour hinted at poetic depths which slicker courtiers lacked. His long brooding sulks, which in later years were to infuriate Elizabeth beyond recall, fitted exactly into the fashionable conventions of pastoral melancholia. His furrowed brow and furious eyes could exert a Byronic attraction. And when he smiled his beauty was irresistible.

But the once great lover, "the glass of fashion and the mould of form," had a physical reason for turning against the sex and lapsing into religious melancholia, if, as conjectured, he suffered toward the end of his life from the tertiary stage of syphilis, "one manifestation of which can be nervous disorder. The sufferer loses co-ordination, behaves erratically and eventually degenerates into total lunacy. Preceding that collapse are bouts of insanity whose fury and unpredictability correspond closely to the fits to which the Earl of Essex became increasingly prone after 1596."[13]

Leaving the question of character and pathology, there is something to be said regarding the personal appearance of Hamlet and Essex. It has been asserted that the earl affected black in his liveries—this on the basis of a poem of 1590:

Young Essex, that thrice-honourable earl;
Y-clad in mighty arms of mourner's dye,
And plume as black as is the raven's wing.
. . . .

His staves were such, or of such hue at least,
As are those banner-staves that mourners bear;
And all his company in funeral black.

It would seem, however, that this is going too far back in the
earl's life, for the evidence of a poem of 1595 (not quoted by
those who quote the above, though it comes from the same
poet, Peele) cuts the other way;[14] besides, both are descriptions of special ceremonious occasions. But, and this is my
point, Essex in his last days—the Essex whom, by a theory I
am going to introduce, Shakespeare was particularly thinking
of—did, like the doomed man he was, wear black. During his
trial,[15] as well as on the day of his well-witnessed[16]
execution,[17] he was dressed all in black.[18]

We must put ourselves in the place of the audiences in
those troubled days of 1601 and 1602, when shadows had
fallen on the glory of Gloriana. In the second scene of
Hamlet they see an actor accoutered like Essex, and they
begin to find out that this is a play which deals with the
question of succession to the Crown—that question which
was vexing all England, and Scotland as well, and to which
the aged, ailing queen would give no answer. Did not
"Denmark" become England readily enough, and the Danish
court the English, which had its full share of factions and
spyings and conspiracies?[19] What were they thinking, these
original audiences, by the fourth act, when they found, too,
that this was a play with a rebellion in it, just such a rebellion
as had taken place on the streets of London a few months
before and wrought the downfall of a popular candidate for
the throne? Of course, the rebellion is not assigned in the
play to Hamlet; that would be going too far, and Shakespeare
had other purposes. However, as John E. Hankins[20] observed,
the cry of the populace, "Laertes shall be king, Laertes
king!" is not very appropriate, since "in the play there has
been nothing to show that Laertes aspired to the throne. We
learn from his advice to Ophelia that his family is not of
royal blood, and we are told that Hamlet, the lineal heir, is
very popular with the public (IV.vii.18)." Yet, on further

consideration, we are all the nearer to the late event here, for Essex had scarcely a claim to royal blood either.[21] Moreover, he, like Laertes, was talked and negotiated out of carrying through his original intention to seize the throne when he might have done so, Queen Elizabeth, like Claudius, not being adequately guarded on that fatal day.

The Essex theory is, in short, a potent instrument of interpretation, and the problem is to use it restrainedly. We must not see Essex everywhere, but only in certain places, and as for the other dramatis personae, the more of them we attempt to identify, the more ingenious and improbable we become.[22] I should deny, because it seems to me that the context does not in the least encourage it, what many see as the one reference to Essex and his rebellion, "the late innovation" of II.ii.356.[23] But looking elsewhere, the minimum suggestion would be that there are more allusions to Essex in the play than modern readers have suspected.

William Camden, in his *Annals, or, the Historie of . . . Elizabeth,*[24] tells a romantic story apropos of the visit of the duke of Biron to the queen in September,[25] 1601.

> Whereas certaine *French* writers have delivered, that amongst other things of those which were condemned, she shewed the Earle of *Essex* his skull in her private Chappell, or (as others write) fastened upon a pole, to *Biron* and the *Frenchmen*, it is a ridiculous vanity, for it was buried together with his body.[26]

We are to recall not only Hamlet taking up the skull of Yorick, but Hamlet's words to that skull: *"Now get you to my lady's chamber,* and tell her, let her paint an inch thick, to this favour she must come; make her laugh at that" (V.i.212–15). I believe we may have a case of cause and effect here, but it seems impossible to guess which is cause, and which effect, whether the popular play gave rise to the story, or is capitalizing on it.[27]

Coming now to the ending of the play, I wish first to add a point to the association, grounds for which have already been

given, of Claudius with Leicester. The last scandal of
Leicester's life was that he died from a poisoned draft which
he had meant for another—namely, his wife, of whom he was
jealous. According to the scandalmongers, the countess
exchanged this poison for his medicine.[28] What other
comment can there be on this than Laertes'

> He is justly serv'd;
> It is a poison temper'd by himself. [V.ii.341–42]

But it is four lines further on that the real ambiguities
begin, and continue through seventy lines to the end.

> I am dead, Horatio. Wretched queen, adieu!

In two ways the second half of this line is rather odd. In the
first place, in the play the "wretched queen" is dead: why
does the dying Hamlet say "adieu" to her? Are they not
going to the same place (to put it theologically, as this play
would)? When Romeo hears that Juliet is dead, his thought is
that by dying he will join her,[29] not be separated from her:
he therefore bids farewell to life, but not to her. This is the
normal pattern. In drama we are used to the dying saying
farewell to the *living* or survivors saying farewell to the dying
and the dead, but I can think of no instance, except the
above, where the dying bid adieu to the dead. The second
oddity is this word "queen" itself. Up to now Hamlet has
invariably addressed the queen as "mother."[30] That word
"mother" is indeed the motive and the cue for Hamlet's
passion. Only here does he say "queen," and not, I
conjecture, without topical reason. Let it not be supposed
that I am contending the queen is Queen Elizabeth at any
other point in the play, even though the psychoanalysts have
found Hamlet to be in love with his mother and though
Queen Elizabeth was old enough to be Essex's mother. It is a
nonce identification, like that cry which rings out twice at
the end of *Macbeth*: "Hail, King of Scotland!" To see a
passing compliment to King James in those words is not to

claim that Malcolm is King James. Of course, in *Hamlet* Shakespeare is not indulging in any compliment to the present ruler:[31] rather, in "wretched" he is taking the view that Elizabeth lived to regret her favorite's death, a romantic view, eloquently vouched for by William Browne,[32] as well as by Lytton Strachey. And certainly it is fact that she was wretched from the ills of old age, if not from a broken heart.

The point is that from here on, now that the plot is over and the time for ceremonious leave-taking has come, Hamlet is, by my postulation, at least as much Essex in Shakespeare's mind as he is Hamlet, and the first sign is this impression that it is a living queen who is being addressed here. But the main clue is in the persistent imagery of the stage and of the theater that marks the ending of the play and makes it self-conscious, an imagery which seems to have struck none of the commentators. It begins with the very next lines:

> You that look pale and tremble at this chance,
> That are but mutes or audience to this act,
> Had I but time,—as this fell sergeant, death,
> Is strict in his arrest,—O! I could tell you—
> But let it be. Horatio, I am dead;
> Thou liv'st; report me and my cause aright
> To the unsatisfied.

We are first put in mind of the theater, and then—after a curious and surely not purposeless allusion to death as a sergeant-at-arms—the theme of the faithful friend's telling Hamlet's story aright and so redeeming a wounded reputation—that theme is struck, and further insisted on when Hamlet wrests the poisoned cup away.

> O God! Horatio, what a wounded name,
> Things standing thus unknown, shall live behind me.
> If thou didst ever hold me in thy heart,
> Absent thee from felicity awhile,
> And in this harsh world draw thy breath in pain,
> To tell my story.

In the words of John Chamberlain,[33] writing February 21, 1600–01, Essex defended himself at his trial in such a manner "that a man might easily perceive that, as he had ever lived popularly, so his chief care was to have a good opinion in the people's minds now at parting." He did not know that to forward that good opinion he would have after his death the greatest possible panegyrist. Yet, a few months earlier, in a letter to the queen, he had prophesied correctly, though with undue bitterness: "They print me and make me speak to the world, and shortly they will play me upon the stage."[34]

The ending of *Hamlet* is full of word play, of ambiguities and puns which have remained locked because no one has applied the key. We must look again at the line,

> Absent thee from *felicity* awhile.

Guilpin in *Skialetheia* satirized Essex as "Faelix" (or "Felix").[35] The reason for this appellation is not far to seek. We have only to recall Spenser's similar pun on "Devereux" in *Prothalamion,*[36]

> Joy have thou of thy noble victorie,
> And endlesse happinesse of thine owne name
> That promiseth the same . . .

where, as R. E. Neil Dodge points out, "Devereux" is taken as equivalent to *"devenir heureux* or simply *heureux."* Shakespeare was thus neither the first nor the second poet to pun felicitously on the name! (Most *in*felicitously, according to our taste, but we have to remember how different the Elizabethan view was, that Shakespeare could play on words in deadly earnest, that Lady Macbeth could say, "I'll gild the faces of the groom withal;/For it must seem their guilt," that King Henry IV angrily dismisses Worcester with the words, "You have good leave to leave us," that both Romeo and Juliet die with a double-entendre on their lips.)

The "war-like volley" of "young Fortinbras" is heard saluting "the ambassadors of England," whereupon Hamlet says,

I cannot live to hear the news from England,
But I do prophesy the election lights
On Fortinbras: he has my dying voice.

Here we have Shakespeare going to great because dra-
matically inappropriate lengths to relate "the news from
England" to the election lighting on Fortinbras. The question
seems unprecedented, but I ask it: why the connective
"but"? In the play, the news from England has nothing to do
with Fortinbras: that news is simply "that Rosencrantz and
Guildenstern are dead." Why should Hamlet with almost his
last breath, at this climactic point in the drama, be showing
any interest in those trivial false friends whom he hoisted
with their own petard, "not shriving-time allowed"? Can it be
that Shakespeare wants to connect Fortinbras and England
for good current reasons? Fortinbras, this prince from
another country, may here stand for James VI of Scotland,[37]
soon to be James I of England, with whom Essex was in
secret correspondence, whose unfortunate ally Essex (as well
as Southampton) was. The name Fortinbras—"Strong-arm"—
seems ridiculous to us when we think of the later James, but
it superlatively fitted the James who was supposed to have
overpowered with his own bare hands a would-be assassin on
the day of the Gowry conspiracy, August 5, 1600.[38] It was a
conservative prophecy, then, this of Hamlet's and Shakespeare's, but it was made at a troubled time when no one
could be sure who would be the next ruler, and all were
anxious.

After those four last words of Hamlet, "The rest is
silence," which happen to be foreshadowed at the beginning
of that same letter of the earl's from which I have already
quoted, "Before . . . he that sends this enjoins himself eternal
silence . . . ,"[39] Horatio pronounces his benediction:

Now cracks a noble heart. Good-night, sweet prince,
And flights of angels sing thee to thy rest!

Malone long ago pointed out that there is an echo here of Essex's twice-uttered prayer on the day of his execution: "Lift my soul above all earthly cogitations, and when my life and body shall part, send Thy blessed angels to be near unto me, which may convey it to the joys in Heaven"; and again: "I pray . . . it would please the Everlasting God to send down His angels to carry my soul before His Mercy Seat."[40] As for "Good-night, sweet prince," Miss Winstanley notes that shortly after the execution the ballad-mongers had a broadside ready entitled "Essex' Last Good-night," every stanza of which ended with the refrain "good-night"![41]

After exclamations have been exchanged on the dismal sight, Horatio says,

> . . . Give order that these bodies
> High on a stage be placed to the view;
> And let me speak to the yet unknowing world
> How these things came about . . .

For this business of putting bodies on a stage there is no precedent nor parallel in the Elizabethan drama.[42] Nor is there anything in the Hamlet saga to account for it.[43] I suggest that Shakespeare is playing with words here, beginning with the word "stage," which can mean, yes, a platform or "scaffold" (as the blundering First Quarto calls it[44]), but which can also mean the stage of the Globe Theater and be a continuation of the play's consciousness of itself, of the dramatist's references to his own creative art. (In fact, a glance at a concordance or Schmidt's *Lexicon* will show that Shakespeare never uses the word "stage" elsewhere in any other concrete sense than the stage of a theater.)

"Stage" is the first pun, and "world" is the second.

> . . . Let me speak to the yet unknowing world
> How these things came about.

Scholars have seen a reference to the Globe Theater at II.ii.386. I suggest that there is a second allusion here. Dekker in fact made the identical pun:

How wonderfully is the world altered! And no marvel, for it has lyen sick almost five thousand years: so that it is no more like the old *Theatre du munde,* than old Paris Garden is like the King's Garden at Paris. What an excellent workman, therefore, were he that could cast the *Globe* of it into a new mold.[45]

But there is hardly need to quote Dekker when we have Jaques's "All the world's a stage" following upon the duke's words about "this wide and universal theatre" in *As You Like It*, II.vii.137ff., the punning point of which was recaptured by Fleay in 1886.[46]

Thus, Shakespeare says again that a tarnished reputation will be refurbished, here and now, in *Hamlet.*

> So shall you hear
> Of carnal, bloody, and unnatural acts,
> Of accidental judgments, casual slaughters;
> Of deaths put on by cunning and forc'd cause,
> And, in this upshot, purposes mistook
> Fall'n on the inventors' heads; all this can I
> Truly deliver.

These lines fit the dramatic situation with almost mathematical exactitude, but they do not do badly for the Essex rebellion either.[47] The original defense of the Essex party was that their "purposes" had been grossly "mistook," that they had not been guilty of any act of treason. This would be the line that a friend to Essex's memory would therefore take.[48] And all knew, and some had seen with their own eyes, how the "purposes mistook" had "fall'n on the inventors' heads" (a grim pun, that!)—bringing death to Essex, Blount, Danvers, and other chief conspirators, bringing imprisonment and disgrace to Shakespeare's patron.

The other point to notice is, of course, the reiteration with which we are told that a tragical history is to be recounted. Again and again the point is made, and now Fortinbras says,

> Let us haste to hear it,
> And call the noblest to the audience.

The references to the theater become increasingly plain.
   The king-to-be continues,

> For me, with sorrow I embrace my fortune;
> I have some rights of memory in this kingdom,
> Which now to claim my vantage doth invite me.

What "rights" is Fortinbras remembering? We have heard
nothing of his rights, and they must remain forever a mystery
unless we look beyond the play, for within it there is no
explanation to be had; the commentators maintain a prudent
silence.[49] In one sense, this would be simply James Stuart's
statement that he is entitled to the throne "in this kingdom"
of England. "Rights of memory" are "unforgotten rights,"
going back to the descent of James from Henry VII, the first
of the Tudors. But it follows that Shakespeare also has in
mind another word, the word he uses ten lines further on:
"rites." In this sense, "some rites of memory" are those
which James (and Essex's friends generally, including Shakespeare) owe to the memory of the late earl. (Nor did James
prove ungrateful;[50] one of his first acts, even before he
crossed the border, was to order the release of
Southampton.) This second meaning thus links up with "Let
us haste to hear it,/And call the noblest to the audience."
   Horatio then says,

> Of that I shall have also cause to speak,
> And from his mouth whose voice will draw on more:

Hamlet's voice, yes,[51] but the voice of the popular earl, who
had done what he could to make James king. But finally the
persistent theatrical imagery hints at another voice, the Voice
of all these voices. Whose voice will "draw on more" than
that of the popular dramatist himself?

> But let this same be presently perform'd . . . .

Let this same *play* be presently perform'd—

> Even while men's minds are wild, lest more mischance
> On plots and errors happen.

There have been many futile debates over the word "wild," all of which would have been obviated if it had been understood that these lines were prompted by the Essex uprising and those months of anxiety and disillusion which followed upon it. Shakespeare was "of an age": before widening his claim Ben Jonson calls him "soul of the age." It is an assumption consistent to the smallest detail that the closing lines of *Hamlet* are "the abstracts and brief chronicles of the time" (II.ii.555).

Fortinbras now begins the final eulogy.

> Let four captains
> Bear Hamlet, like a soldier, to the stage.

That is to say (on the level of ambiguity being here considered), put Essex in a play! No one thinks of Hamlet as a soldier. He seems about as far as possible from that. There has been nothing to connect him with the military profession, except one word of Ophelia's in the line "The courtier's, soldier's, scholar's, eye, tongue, sword" (III.i.160). But "the general of our gracious empress," everybody knows and everybody knew, was a soldier par excellence. Even his jealous rival-in-command at Cadiz, Lord Howard, acknowledged him "a great soldier."[52] Moreover, to come back to Ophelia's line,

> The courtier's, soldier's, scholar's, eye, tongue, sword

—it fits Essex in a way that has not been hitherto suspected. As part of the Accession Day celebrations in 1595, Francis Bacon wrote an allegory concerning Essex which presented before the queen and many spectators.[53] Essex was met by "a melancholy, dreaming hermit, a mutinous, brain-sick soldier, and a busy, tedious secretary," representing the three divergent ambitions of that noble lord, and after supper each of the characters in turn delivered a pretty speech, the cloistered scholar calling him to the Muses, the courtier begging him to attend to matters of state, and the soldier urging him to seek his fortune in the field.

> For he was likely, had he been put on,
> To have prov'd most royally:

This is most daring, but protected of course by its ambiguity of reference. "All the world's a stage" now, and Essex, "had he been put on," would have proved a worthy king of England.

>   and, for his passage,
> The soldiers' music and the rites of war
> Speak loudly for him.

Ostensibly "passage" means departure, death, and "speak" is a word of command. But "passage" can also mean "conduct" (e.g., "passages of life," *1 Henry IV,* III.ii.8), and "speak" can be indicative, with "rites" being turned back to "rights":[54] the soldiers' music and the rights of war speak loudly for the good conduct of the Earl of Essex: he deserved a better death.

> Take up the bodies:

This is the reading of the Second Quarto. The folios as well as the First Quarto have the singular:

> Take up the body: such a sight as this
> Becomes the field, but here shows much amiss.

Essex should have died a soldier's death. Instead, his severed head was held up for the rude mob to gawk at, and the body left sprawled in the straw of a scaffold.

So concludes my *explication de texte* of the ending of *Hamlet* at a level which is of little more than historical interest today, but which puts the play in its time and tries to recapture the associations of the original audiences. I do not claim that two meanings are better than one; I claim only that there is reason to suspect that two meanings are there, and that the playgoers of 1601 and 1602 could be depended on to catch them. In the light of both the old and the new points here presented, it seems to me an hypothesis worthy of serious and unprejudiced consideration that the last seventy lines of *Hamlet,* besides winding up greatly a great tragedy, constitute under the surface Shakespeare's farewell to the man who inspired that tragedy, with an attendant prophecy, as well as a fairly plain and continuous declaration that he is putting Essex on the stage. It is here, at the ceremonious close, that the dramatist would have been most under the temptation to step out of his timeless creation into time, or rather, like the riddling Hamlet, to bestride timelessness and time at once. This hypothesis will serve to explain certain marked peculiarities of the ending (as well as of other parts) of *Hamlet,* for which no other single explanation has ever been offered—except that easy one, the commentator's last and all too habitual resort, that Shakespeare was writing carelessly. Far from having written this ending carelessly, he seems to have felt, with his chief character,

> O! 'tis most sweet,
> When in one line two crafts directly meet.
> [III.iv.209–10]

The conjecturing that there are two crafts here takes away that Olympian Shakespeare, that Shakespeare who never alludes to anything contemporary, of whom some critics have been blindly fond, but it leaves us a characteristically serene Shakespeare, who spoke out reassuringly at a time when men's minds were wild, paying his respects to a popular idol and prophesying an untroubled succession for James.

PART 2

It seems to me that there are four principal objections to
be urged against the theory: first (and this is beyond
dispute), that it has not been proved; secondly, that it
outrages our critical sensibilities by being in its comparison of
characters and circumstances too crude; third, that in other
ways it is too ingenious (where a simple and natural
explanation is at hand); and fourth, that even if Shakespeare
had had the sympathies postulated he would not have dared
to give even covert expression to them.

The burden of proof lies with the other side, and for many
skeptics the failure of the data and the arguments stemming
therefrom to add up to proof will be in itself a sufficient
objection. Such readers might be willing to entertain, perhaps
have entertained in the past, on much more slender evidence,
a theory about Lyly's *Endymion,* or indeed *Love's Labour's
Lost.* But *Hamlet,* if mysterious at all, is not mysterious in
the way that those plays are—it is sufficient unto itself as a
drama—and to weave a web of double meanings around it
seems idle, an effect without a proper cause. (A more
prudent question is how much one would grant in the way of
an occasional cobweb, a topical allusion here and there, with
perhaps a cluster of them at the end.)

What would impress us? Short of an unequivocal statement
of intention from Shakespeare himself, we should at least
require a contemporary reference that made the Hamlet-
Essex equation (though it could still be argued that an
innocent play was being taken topically). The nearest I have
been able to come to such evidence is in two references to
the late earl that connect him, in the most casual way, with
the plot of *Hamlet,* not necessarily Shakespeare's.[55] Indeed,
there are no certain allusions to Shakespeare's *Hamlet* before
1604 (the Gabriel Harvey note—see note 3—being of unde-
termined date). For all that may be said, ruefully, about the
accidental character of such survivals, the most that the other
side can postulate is that there was a sly understanding that
did not cause much of a flurry. If the play had been a cause

célèbre reaching the Privy Council, we should surely have heard.

In passing on to the second main objection, it is important to note what advantage the theory is taking of our special ignorances—our uncertainty in regard to the date of the play and our ignorance of its immediate source. Date the play a few months earlier than I date it, and my interpretation of the ending becomes impossible. As for the *Ur-Hamlet*, no one has taken kindly to the suggestion of the original propounder of the Essex theory[56] that Shakespeare himself wrote the *Ur-Hamlet* in 1589, capitalizing on the interest in things Danish resulting from the marriage of James in that year to Anne of Denmark, and that the 1603 Quarto represents an intermediate version that would yet again be revised. Rejecting this hypothesis, we are left with a textual mystery, and of course know nothing about Shakespeare's major source except that it contained a ghost that cried revenge. How close was it to the present plot? Did it contain a rebellion and other matters that are being laid to the ghost of Essex? One can always ask, too, why the Essex connections, if intended, are not closer. If the earl of Leicester's poisoning of the first earl of Essex is really being recalled, the elder Hamlet should have died from not poison in his ears but in his food. "But after all, Shakespeare had to consider dramatic effect, was primarily, let us never forget, writing a play," the other side will point out—thereby having it both ways. It may be so, but poisoning and other elements possibly introduced by Shakespeare into the plot are too commonplace, especially when one thinks of Italianate influences, for anyone to wonder much about a particular source for them.

Moreover, if Shakespeare was leaving us a "signature" in "Absent thee from felicity awhile," he had another opportunity that he very strangely passed by. Essex was thirty-three when he died. It would not have affected the dramatic structure one whit to make the gravedigger give the figure for Hamlet's age as "three-and-thirty" instead of "thirty." The dramatist's failure to give us a hint in this relatively safe yet pointed way counts, in my mind, heavily against the theory.

If ever there was an opportunity for a topical allusion, that was it, and a round number in the midst of what seems to be otherwise careful arithmetic in the Second Quarto and First Folio (Yorick's skull lying "i' the earth three-and-twenty years") can hardly be made to serve.

But here higher truths intervene, as they do with Hamlet's character. The figures for the hero's age belie our total impression, just as no one functioning as a critic is going to be content to call Hamlet "a woman-hater." It is always embarrassing to compare the transformed character in a play or story with its original, even when there is known to be that relationship. To premise such a relationship is doubly embarrassing, and perhaps, in the light of the procrustean crudities that will inevitably result, inexcusable. The lines are, at best, to be faintly drawn, and then they may fit others just as well. As a colleague remarks, if this is the game we are playing, a good case could be made out—so far as character goes—for John Donne as the original of Hamlet! (And here the ages fit!)

Third, let us approach the details of the ending more open-mindedly. In an actual performance—and that is the test—who finds anything odd in the line "I am dead, Horatio. Wretched queen, adieu!"? Did Shakespeare ever dream that we should dwell on Hamlet's switch from "mother" to "queen"? It could be chance, or ceremony, or, if we are bent on extracting something from it, a subtle indication that Hamlet's problem has finally been resolved—that he feels free at last. As for a dying character saying adieu to a dead one, the queen has just fallen, and events are crowding one upon another fast: we may separate them as readers, weighing intervals, but this we cannot do as spectators. Bradley in his study may be disturbed and offer an untenable explanation: "He remembers his wretched mother and bids her adieu, ignorant that she has preceded him."[57] This assumes that Hamlet is not in command of his faculties. All that he yet says and does nobly refutes any such notion. Say rather that the solution of this and other questions is to get the play out of the study and onto the stage, where such questions will not be raised.

Looking at it from this angle we shall not brood, either, over

> I cannot live to hear the news from England,
> But I do prophesy the election lights
> On Fortinbras.

The words are in response to Osric's explanation of the "war-like noise":

> Young Fortinbras, with conquest come from Poland,
> To the ambassadors of England gives
> This war-like volley.

Maybe, sub specie aeternitatis, Hamlet ought not to waste his last energies by showing interest in the fairly certain fate of Rosencrantz and Guildenstern (though that, too, can be argued and one can say that he takes a certain pride in the way he has outwitted his enemies). But from a playwright's point of view it is perfectly natural, when these separate arrivals have just been announced, for Hamlet to mention them both and, moreover, distinguish between them. For the "but" can be taken as putting "the news from England" in its proper subordinate place: "I cannot live to hear the news from England [and I do not care about that], but [to pass on to what really matters] I do prophesy, etc."

It is enough to indicate thus the direction a protest against "unfair" questions (the kind that gives lunatics and theorists their opportunities) may take: Shakespeare wrote *currente calamo* a play that was never meant to be pondered over minutely; matters puzzling the overattentive student (when the student *is* being overattentive, not simply inattentive) originated in dramaturgical convenience or dramaturgical carelessness. So it is with what is doubtless the biggest crux here, Fortinbras's accession to the Danish throne:[58] Shakespeare at the last minute assigns him "rights of memory in this kingdom" in order to justify the claim. We are in a theater, not a courtroom, and it is idle—though a characteristic scholarly error—to ask for documentation. It is like

asking what songs the sirens sang, or what happened to Lady
Macbeth's children, or to Cassio's wife.

Finally, even if we allow Shakespeare the personal or
political sympathies postulated, how could he have dared to
be understood as expressing them? Never at any time did the
queen permit the question of the succession to be discussed,
and of course to say of Essex, after his rebellion,

> For he was likely, had he been put on,
> To have prov'd most royally,

was to lay oneself open to the charge of treason. In two
popular, oft-reprinted poems Shakespeare had declared himself a follower of the now convicted and imprisoned
Southampton, and the dramatist had openly admired Essex.
Moreover, the traitorous use to which *Richard II* had been
put on the eve of the conspiracy had called for close
questioning of Shakespeare's company. For a man so suspect
to take further risks in those arbitrary times seems little less
than suicidal. Indeed, the need for craft and caution in public
utterances did not cease with the reign of James, as is shown
by the case of Samuel Daniel, who, when his drama *Philotas*
was published in 1605, had to answer charges before the
Privy Council that that play dealt sympathetically with the
Essex rebellion. He was fortunately able to show "that the
first three acts had been read by the master of the revels and
Lord Mountjoy" in 1600, before the rebellion.[59]

On the other hand, it was permissible and even customary
in those last two years of the queen's reign to refer to the late
popular earl (even in letters to the earl's traditional enemy Sir
Robert Cecil) with regretful respect. Eighteen months after
the execution a German visitor found "Essex' Last Good-
night" was still being sung—even at Court![60] To pass over this
and other anonymous eulogies, the second year of the new
monarch's reign, the year of the Second Quarto, saw the
publication of Robert Pricket's *Honors Fame in Triumph
Riding, or, The Life and Death of the Late Honorable Earle
of Essex*, which hints that the earl was the victim of the
machinations of his enemies and stoutly declares:

It's false to say, hee would a King have bin:
From faith & honor he made no such digression:
His heart was cleare from such so foule a sin,
He always stood for this approv'd Succession,
Which happily doeth now the Throne possesse:
Heavens mighty God protect his Mightinesse.
Dead Earle, amidst bright Angels wings,
Amen thy heavenly Spirit sings.[61]

It was evidently with reference to this poem that Francis Morice wrote to Sir B. Gawdy: "Well and feelingly written and I think will not hereafter to be had as they are already called in and the printer called in question."[62] Pricket went to prison for his poem, only to be released soon after by appealing to Lord Salisbury.[63]

Indeed, the picture of the censorship at this period is full of contradictions. In March of the year in which Daniel was charged and the three authors of *Eastward Hoe* imprisoned, it was recorded that the players do not "forbear to present upon their stage the whole course of the present Time, not sparing either King, State, or Religion, in so great Absurdity, and with such Liberty, that any would be afraid to hear them."[64]

If Shakespeare had been taken to task for *Hamlet,* he could have replied that he was just revising an old play, dating back to the 1580s; besides (the other side will continue), his ambiguity at the end is very clever and "unconvictable," as is shown by its failure to trouble modern scholars. Moreover, he had himself found censorship a whimsical thing and was evidently willing to take his chances with it. There is one conspicuous case where it was exceedingly vigilant with him, and one conspicuous case where it was exceedingly relaxed. The case of vigilance is the 1600 Quarto of *2 Henry IV,*[65] where such lines as IV.i.55–70, doubtless written in all innocence, were apparently taken by the censor months later as referring to Essex and struck out, and indeed the whole play was mutilated.

Yet in the 1598 Quarto of *1 Henry IV,* Shakespeare turned a compliment to the queen into a hit, and the censor let it pass. It was all right for Falstaff to say (I.ii.28ff.), "Let us be Diana's foresters, gentlemen of the shade, minions of the moon; and let men say, we be men of good government, being governed as the sea is, by our noble and chaste mistress the moon, under whose countenance we steal." This is a compliment followed by a harmless jest. But the prince's reply is something else again: "Thou sayest well, and it holds well too; for the fortune of us that are the moon's men doth ebb and flow like the sea, being governed as the sea is, by the moon." This is a glance at the well-known uncertainty of the queen's favor. As Dover Wilson remarks in his edition,[66] "Diana being a common title for Elizabeth, this talk about 'minions of the moon' seems pretty daring, esp. as it exactly describes the condition of her favorites."[67]

What then are we to conclude? On May 10, 1601, "the Privy Council wrote to certain Justices of the Peace in Middlesex, concerning the players at the Curtain, who, it was reported, were representing upon the stage in their interludes 'the persons of some gentlemen of good desert and quallity that are yet alive under obscure manner, but yet in such sorte as all the hearers may take notice both of the matter and the persons that are meant thereby.' "[68] Did this boldness of the players at the Curtain (about which we hear nothing further) give Shakespeare, about to compose his version of *Hamlet,* his cue to go and do likewise? Or did he, on the contrary, take warning from such scandalous examples and their usual high price in punishment?

On the whole, the odds are against his taking the calculated risk. He will capitalize on current events so far as to have a rebellion in his play, but he will be careful to put it down with

> There's such divinity doth hedge a king,
> That treason can but peep to what it would,
> Acts little of his will. [IV.v.123–25]

The lines are so grand that one can forget it is a villain who says them.

Two lesser alternatives may stem from my examination of the ending. Shakespeare may be thinking of James in giving a prince from another country the throne, without especially having Essex in mind as Hamlet (though the dual reference, as the stanza from Pricket further shows, would seem almost inevitable). Or, putting all politics aside, it may be granted that the author in his constant theatrical imagery and terminology is referring, as he concludes his play, to his own art. And that by itself would be a fact of no small interest.

A final possibility is that, even as his sonnets may be imagined as having had both a public and a private meaning, so Shakespeare here *was* making the dual reference, but privately, or for the initiated few, without intending to be—and without being—understood by "the general."

One can only end by reiterating that the burden of proof lies with the other side, whereas what we have from there consists of suspicions based on circumstantial evidence. Perhaps the overall moral is that we ought not to consider *Hamlet* too curiously. Once we start, we shall be led, link by link, to strange historical conclusions.

NOTES

1.   Dover Wilson's edition of *Hamlet* (Cambridge, 1936), introduction, p. lxvi. The main assembler of points in favor of the Essex theory has been Lilian Winstanley in *"Hamlet" and the Scottish Succession* (Cambridge, 1921; reprinted Freeport, N.Y., 1970) and *"Hamlet* and the Essex Conspiracy," *Aberystwyth Studies*, 6, 7 (1924-25). The earlier study contains interesting points connecting Essex with Hamlet not repeated in the later study, but it unfortunately pursues at the same time, and with much greater enthusiasm, a very different and as it seems to me incompatible theory, linking *Hamlet* to the Darnley murder of 1567 (very ancient history, that!), the marriage of Mary Queen of Scots to Bothwell the murderer, with James as the infant avenger. I do not see how Hamlet can be identified with both James *and* Essex (and a piece of Southampton), Claudius with Bothwell *and* Leicester, Polonius with Rizzio *and* Burleigh, etc. Such ingenuity recoils back upon itself, leaving the average reader in no mood to consider either theory; whereas one of them is well worth exploring. These two

publications largely summarize, or expand, or offer further background to, points in the brilliant pioneering article by James T. Foard, "The Genesis of Hamlet," *Manchester Quarterly*. 8 (1889), 1-31, 122-152, 220-247, who by virtue of this article and other publications going back to 1862 seems to have been the founder of the Essex theory. See, further, Ernest Jones, *Hamlet and Oedipus* (New York, 1955), pp. 125-28. *Reader's Encyclopedia of Shakespeare*, ed. O.J. Campbell and E.G. Quinn (New York, 1966), pp. 215, 886, reminds that, besides the certain reference in *Henry V*, Essex has been found in *Merchant of Venice, King John, Troilus and Cressida, Much Ado*, "The Phoenix and Turtle." See also below, n.40.

2.   For a warning on this "clinical" approach to Hamlet see Louise C. Turner Forest, "A Caveat for Critics against Invoking Elizabethan Psychology," *PMLA*, 61 (1946), 651-672.

3.   I agree with H. D. Gray ("The Date of *Hamlet*," JEGP, 31 (1932), 51-61) that "all the indications that we have seem to point to the summer or autumn of 1601 for the composition and first production of *Hamlet*," and I am here adding to those indications. This year for *Hamlet* is one matter on which Dover Wilson and Sir E.K. Chambers agree (see the latter's *Shakespearean Gleanings*, Oxford, 1944). As for Gabriel Harvey's marginal note, Gray argues that it refers to the *third* earl of Essex, not the second, while Kittredge—in, for instance, his edition of the *Complete Works* (Boston, 1936, p. 1145)—found its present tense "indecisive." Chambers (p. 68) wonders if 'commendes' is not "a scribal error for 'commended.' " For opposing surveys, see Leo Kirschbaum, "The Date of Shakespeare's *Hamlet*," *SP*, 34 (1937), 168-75; E.A.J. Honigmann, "The Date of *Hamlet*," *Shakespeare Survey* 9 (Cambridge, 1956), 24-34. G.B. Evans dates Harvey's reference "not later than July 21, 1603." *Riverside Shakespeare* (Boston, 1974), p. 53.

4.   Joseph Quincy Adams, *A Life of William Shakespeare* (Boston, 1923), p. 319. The deposition scene in *Richard II* was significantly omitted from the first three quartos (1597, and 1598—two), and, just as significantly, its inclusion in the Fourth Quarto of 1608 was featured on the title page.

5.   Ibid, pp. 317-18.

6.   He ought to have invaded Whitehall instead of the City, for the queen was not guarded. To quote the leading modern authority, G. B. Harrison, *The Life and Death of Robert Devereux Earl of Essex* (New York, 1937), Essex's last fight ended "in miserable failure. Had it been well planned and resolutely followed the rising might have succeeded. If he had attacked the Court at dawn his force would have been greatly superior to any that could be mustered at a moment's notice, and even if he had not immediately broken in, he would have cut off the Palace from the City" (p. 293).

7.   The scandal was aired in a publication of 1584 which caused a furor by its scurrilities, *The Copie of a Letter Wryten by a Master of Arte of Cambridge to his Friend in London*, etc. (S.T.C. 1939),

usually referred to as *Leicester's Commonwealth* (which title it bore when republished in London in 1641). It is possibly worth mentioning that a manuscript copy of this pamphlet as well as of that allegorical device of Bacon's which I cite below, along with other material relating to Essex, formed part of the mysterious Northumberland manuscript which some have, very dubiously, sought to connect with Shakespeare (see E. K. Chambers, *William Shakespeare,* Oxford, 1930, I, 506, and II, appendix B, no. xvi). Clara Longworth de Chambrun is one of those who contend that the dramatist once possessed and scribbled on this manuscript (*Shakespeare Rediscovered,* New York, 1938, pp. 267ff.), and she even finds a verbal parallel between *Leicester's Commonwealth* and *Hamlet* (unimpressive, involving the word "quietus," III.i.75), all the while being apparently unaware of the claims that may be advanced for *Leicester's Commonwealth* as one of the sources of *Hamlet.* I quote from the only modern reprint of the pamphlet, that in Frank J. Burgoyne (ed.) *Collotype Facsimile & Type Transcript of an Elizabethan Manuscript preserved at Alnwick Castle, Northumberland* (London, 1904), p. 90.

8. *Annals, or, the Historie of the Most Renowned and Victorious Princess Elizabeth, Late Queen of England,* 3rd ed. (London, 1635), pp. 190–91. (The original Latin edition was published in 1615.)

9. See the more extensive summary in Wilson's *The Essential Shakespeare* (Cambridge, 1932), pp. 92–107. But a word from Sir John Harington should be added on how mad Essex seemed in the last months of his life: "He shifteth from sorrow and repentance to rage and rebellion so suddenly, as well proveth him devoid of good reason as of right mind. In my last discourse he uttered strange words, bordering on such strange designs, that made me hasten forth and leave his presence." *Nugae Antiquae,* quoted by Walter Bourchier Devereux, *Lives and Letters of the Devereux, Earls of Essex* (London, 1853), II, 130.

10. Lytton Strachey, *Elizabeth and Essex* (New York, 1928), p. 162. It might be Hamlet speaking when Essex writes the queen, "When I remember that your Majesty hath, by the intolerable wrong you have done both me and yourself, not only broken all laws of affection, but done against the honour of your sex, I think all places better than that where I am. . . ." Ibid., pp. 176–177.

11. Ibid., p. 237.

12. See Ray Heffner, "Essex, the Ideal Courtier," *ELH,* 1 (April, 1934), 7–36.

13. Robert Lacey, *Robert, Earl of Essex* (New York, 1971), pp. 92, 201–02. The historian A.L. Rowse has said that Essex "was as temperamental and unbalanced, as hysterical and moody, as subject to melancholy, as Hamlet," and allows the possibility of "touches of Essex" in the play. *William Shakespeare* (New York, 1963), pp. 320–21, 322. The Essex-Southampton circle, for their part, were evidently (as was Queen Elizabeth I) taken with Falstaff. Ibid., p. 250.

14.   The first that led, in cheerful colours clad,
      In innocent white and fair carnation,
      Was he whose wisdom in his younger years
      And love to arms make him so far renown'd,
      The noble earl of Essex and of Ewe.

"Anglorum Feriae" in George Peele's *Works*, ed. A.H. Bullen (London, 1888), II, 349-50. This was on the occasion described above. p. 23. The preceding quotation, "Young Essex," etc. (cited by Foard, p. 125 and Winstanley), comes from "Polyhymnia," *Works,* II, 292.

15.   Harrison, p. 299.

16.   There were "divers knights and gentlemen to the number of about an hundred" within the Tower yard. Thomas Birch, *Memoirs of the Reign of Queen Elizabeth* (London, 1754), II, 482.

17.   Harrison, p. 322. To be very accurate, he was dressed in black up *to* the last moment. A contemporary pamphlet (which can be checked with half a dozen other accounts in prose or verse) quoted in *Shakespeare's England* (Oxford, 1916), II, 102, describes his "gowne of wrought velvet a blacke sattin sute a felt hatte blacke and a little ruffe about his necke. After his speech to the spectators he put off his gowne and on finishing his prayers opening and putting off his dublet he was in a scarlet wastecote, and then ready to lay downe."

18.   It is just possible that there was another point of outward resemblance:

      Who . . .
      Plucks off my beard and blows it in my face?

                                                  [II.ii.607–608]

With Kittredge (ed. *Hamlet,* Boston, 1939, p. 204) I see no reason for regarding this as a purely imaginary beard, although most modern actors appear without it. The insoluble question is, how full and therefore how unusual a beard is meant? If—I make the conjecture just in passing and nothing of moment depends upon it—if this is all that survives of Shakespeare's instructions to the original Hamlet to wear a full beard, we have another striking correspondence before Hamlet has said a word. What a later century would call a goatee was common, but a full beard was rare in Elizabethan times. However, the earl of Essex took to wearing a full beard after the Cadiz expedition: it got a certain fame as "the Cadiz beard," and set a fashion (which would make it safer for an actor to wear it in 1601, meaning and yet not meaning Essex). An engraving of Essex in 1600 (reproduced in Harrison, op. p. 240; a copy in *The Fugger News-Letters*, 2nd ser. ed. Victor von Klarwill, London, 1926, op. p. 228, is engraved 1601) that was hawked on the streets until the sale was forbidden, shows this beard very amply. What emboldens me to make (in the seclusion of a footnote) this conjecture is that Shakespeare apparently *did* refer to Essex's beard in *Henry V* ("a beard of the general's cut," III.vi.83). For details, including Guilpin's satirical references to the "Cadz-beard," see my "Shakspere, Guilpin, and Essex," *Shakespeare Association Bulletin,* January, 1948, pp. 17-19.

19. It is not at all strange that Essex, the chief male figure at Court, should have developed a persecution complex. As early as 1596 he wrote, "I live in a place, where I am hourly conspired against, and practised upon" (Harrison, p. 137). His own conspiracy he regarded as a counter-conspiracy.

20. *The Character of Hamlet and other Essays* (Chapel Hill, 1941), p. 113.

21. Essex traced his descent from Thomas of Woodstock, duke of Gloucester, "which remote alliance with the blood royal constituted his sole claim to the crown." Wilson (ed.), *Richard II* (Cambridge, 1939), p. xxxi; for details see Evelyn M. Albright, "Shakespeare's *Richard II* and the Essex Conspiracy," *PMLA*, 42 (1927), 695.

22. The common identification of Polonius with Lord Burleigh does accord with the theory, for Essex scorned that doddering and devious and moralistic chief councilor. (For a connection between the name "Polonius" and Burleigh, see I. Gollancz, *A Book of Homage to Shakespeare*, Oxford, 1916, pp. 173–77.)

I have often wondered why the hero of the play has a worse reputation as a fencer than Laertes. Early in his hybristic career Essex lost a duel to Charles Blount (interesting name!), whose rapier nicked him in the thigh (Lacey, p. 62).

May Ophelia—she who sings the refrain "For bonny sweet Robin is all my joy" (IV.v.186)—insofar as she seems betrayed, stand for Essex's neglected wife? Let me give some "documentation" (in which, however, I do not much believe). Lady Essex, she "of ladies most deject and wretched, / That suck'd the honey of his music vows" (III.i.164–65), must have seemed a pathetic figure even in the days before her husband's eclipse; and during it we have the observation of Rowland White under date of November 4, 1599: "My Lady of Essex is a most sorrowful creature for her husband's captivity; she wears all black of the meanest price, and receives no comfort in any thing," and in this suppliant's mourning she haunted the court (Devereux, II, 88). She referred to herself as "an afflicted and woful lady" in her appeal to Cecil (ibid., 174). To come back to Ophelia's fragment of a ballad about "bonny sweet Robin," we have the tune but not the words: it may have concerned Robin Hood, but this is not certain, "Robin" being the diminutive of (and the queen's name for) "Robert." A letter to Essex from his mother commences, "Sweet Robin" (Devereux, I, 494). J. Payne Collier printed a poem (let us hope it is genuine!) called "The Robin" which covertly deals with Essex (*Ancient Biographical Poems,* Camden Society, 1855, pp. 21–23), of which lines 5 to 8 may be taken as a pertinent sample:

> This Robyn is a pretye one,
> > Well formed at point devise,
> A mynnion birde to loke uppon,
> > And suer of worthye pryse.

Essex in one of his own poems alluded to himself as "robin" punningly (*Poetry of the English Renaissance,* ed. J. W. Hebel and H. H. Hudson,

New York, 1929, p. 132). And to top all this, the countess of Essex was actually accused of making a ballad about her husband after his death. Richard Bancroft, bishop of London, complained on February 27, 1600–01, "A fellow goeth about the street, selling the ballads whereof here is a copy enclosed. He giveth it out that the Countess of Essex hath made it, which procureth many to buy it." Historical MSS Commission, part 11, 88, *Cecil Manuscripts*. This, one of Winstanley's three identifications for Ophelia—she offers it just en passant—is the only one that can for a moment be entertained, it seems to me, and then only in the light of the facts just adduced. I admire, but cannot follow, the ingenious process by which Ophelia becomes (*Aberystwyth Studies*, 7, 42ff.) "a kind of Kathleen Ni' Houlihan, or symbol of the Irish nationality."

23. I find "innovation" used of this very event (*Cecil Manuscripts*, as above, p. 538), and Shakespeare elsewhere means a political upheaval by the word (see Wilson's *Hamlet*, p. 177), but there is still nothing to give it that meaning here.

24. P. 562.

25. Stow dates the arrival of the embassy "at the Tower-wharfe" "About the 5. of September" (*Annales* [London, 1615], p. 795).

26. Compare the different account by Jacque-Auguste de Thou: "Au milieu de la conversation qui se tenoit à une fenêtre du Palais, la Reine & l'Ambassadeur jettèrent les yeux sur la tour de Londres, où l'on avoit exposé un grand nombre de têtes de criminels d'État. A cette vûe, Elisabeth crut devoir prévenir le ministre Francois, & pour empêcher que cet affreux spectacle ne la fit soupçonner de cruaté, elle parla fort au long sur les règles de la justice, & de la clémence des Rois; elle ajoûta ensuite: 'Vous voyez la tête du Comte d'Essex. Je l'avois élevé aux plus grandes dignités & il avoit toute la faveur de la Reine; mais ce téméraire abusant de mes bontés a eu l'audace de croire que je ne pourrois jamais me paser de lui.' " *Histoire Universelle* (London, 1734), XIII, 611. Thus, the legend gained currency abroad, especially as earlier conspirators against the queen *had* had their heads "stuck up on poles" (see *Fugger Letters*, 2nd ser., p. 229).

27. Here, then, is an explanation for those critics who have gone so far as to wonder why the only relics in the gravedigger's scene are detached skulls. Hamlet's jibes at the painting of female faces, here and to Ophelia, "I have heard of your paintings too, well enough; God hath given you one face, and you make yourselves another;" (III.i.149–52), represent nothing very unusual in the literature of the time. Guilpin's "Satyra secunda" (*Skialetheia*, 1598), for instance, is devoted to cosmetic satire. It takes an extravagant form in *Der Bestrafte Brudermord* (Furness *Variorum Hamlet*, II, 128). See, for a pre-Shakespearean thrust at "payntinges," More's *Utopia*, ed. J. C. Collins (Oxford, 1904), p. 105, and cf. Collins' note, p. 225. At the same time, cne cannot help thinking of Queen Elizabeth's grotesque refusal to face old age. E.g., Ben Jonson told Drummond of Hawthornden: "Queen Elizabeth never saw herself after she became old in a true glass; they

painted her, and sometymes would vermilion her nose" (*Conversations*, ed. R.F. Patterson [London, 1923], p. 30).

28. Harrison, p. 35.

29. "Well, Juliet, I will lie with thee to-night" (V.i.34), and V.ii.106ff. In fact, there is the same thought in *Hamlet*, in the pun on "union: "Is thy union here? / Follow my mother."

30. The only approach to this significant switch before had been in the formal and bitter statement,

> You are the queen, your husband's brother's wife;
> And,—would it were not so!—you are my mother.
>
> [III.iv.15–16]

31. As J. Q. Adams (p. 320) remarks, Shakespeare "seems not to have forgiven Elizabeth for her heartless treatment of the unfortunate Essex, and her long imprisonment of Southampton. This may perhaps explain why he refused, in spite of several protests, to write, as did so many poets, an elegy on the great Queen who had taken such delight in his plays, or to express any grief at her death."

32. *Britannia's Pastorals* (1613) follows an allegory about Leicester and the queen with one on Leicester's stepson, recalling the famous intrusion into the queen's closet by Essex on his return from Ireland, when he took her by surprise "with her hair about her face," and when, like Gertrude, she feared at first for her life:

> And coming through a grove wherein his fair
> Lay with her breasts display'd to take the air,
> His rushing through the boughs made her arise,
> And dreading some wild beast's rude enterprise,
> Directs towards the noise a sharpen'd dart,
> That reach'd the life of his undaunted heart,
> Which when she knew, twice twenty moons nigh spent
> In tears for him, and died in languishment.

Book 1, song 4, 753–60. For various views as to why the queen "gave her selfe over wholly to melancholly," see Camden, pp. 584–85; cf. Devereux, II, 203ff.

33. Quoted by Winstanley, *"Hamlet" and the Scottish Succession*, p. 143.

34. Harrison, p. 261.

35. "Satyra prima," sig. C3v (Shakespeare Association Facsimiles, 1931; see G. B. Harrison's introduction, pp. vii-viii):

> For when great *Faelix* passing through the street,
> Vayleth his cap to each one he doth meet,
> And when no broome-man that will pray for him,
> Shall have lesse truage than his bonnets brim,
> Who would not thinke him perfect curtesie?
> Or the honny-suckle of humilitie?
> The devill he is as soone: he is the devill,
> Brightly accoustred to bemist his evill:
> Like a Swartrutters hose his puffe thoughts swell,

> With yeastie ambition: *Signior Machiavell*
> Taught him this mumming trick, with curtesie
> T'entrench himselfe in popularitie,
> And for a writhen face, and bodies move,
> Be Barricadode in the peoples love.

36.   *Complete Poetical Works*, ed. R. E. Neil Dodge (Boston, 1908), 152–54.

37.   James had actually come from Norway in 1589, bringing back Anne of Denmark, whom he had married in person at Oslo, November 23rd. The Fortinbras-James equation dates back to Foard's article (p. 242) of 1889, but neither this writer nor Winstanley gives it any detailed consideration (the latter being handicapped, of course, by her belief that Hamlet is James).

38.   For a description based on the official accounts, see G. B. Harrison, *A Last Elizabethan Journal* (London, 1933), pp. 105-09.

39.   Harrison, *Essex*, p. 260.

40.   Ibid., pp. 324-25. So much, on the historical side, for A. C. Bradley's question, "Why did Shakespeare here, so much against his custom, introduce this reference to another life?" (*Shakespearean Tragedy*, London, 1905, p. 147.) Essex's last speech is regularly considered to have influenced *Henry VIII*, II.i. Sonnet 124, 14, has produced the comment: "Allusion to specific malefactors who died repentant has been suspected in the line. Various suggestions have included the Earl of Essex and his followers. . . ." *Complete Works*, ed. Irving Ribner and G. L. Kittredge (Waltham, Mass., 1971), p. 1720.

41.   *"Hamlet" and the Scottish Succession*, p. 144. "Essex's Last Good-night" and "The Death of Robert Devereux Earl of Essex" are in *The Roxburghe Ballads*, ed. W. Chappell (London, the Ballad Society, 1871), I, 564-74. It may be noted, apropos of my discussion of "Wretched queen, adieu!", that the former has the line, "Farewell, Elizabeth, my gracious Queen!", beginning a stanza of farewells. "Good-night" in ballads is, one would gather, a farewell applied regularly to doomed men. See F. J. Child's note, *English and Scottish Popular Ballads* (Boston, 1892), IV, 36.

42.   The best the editors can do is to quote from Arthur Brooke's poem *Romeus and Juliet*, 2817–18:

> The prince did straight ordain, the corses that were found
> Should be set forth upon a stage high raiséd from the ground,

but the circumstances in the poem are entirely different, as the context makes clear, the bodies of the two lovers being the *corpora delicti* of a crime of which two living persons are accused:

> Right in the selfsame form, showed forth to all men's sight,
> That in the hollow vault they had been found that other night;
> And eke that Romeus' man and Friar Laurence should
> Be openly examinéd; for else the people would
> Have murmuréd or feigned there were some weighty cause
> Why openly they were not called, and so convict by laws.
>
> [2819–24]

43.   There is no hint that a funeral pyre is meant, such as Amlethus orders for Fengo in Saxo Grammaticus ("extruite rogum:" *Sources of Hamlet*, Israel Gollancz (ed.), London, 1926, p. 134). A funeral pyre would be Danish, but Shakespeare, as usual, is making no effort to be Danish.

44.   Thereby drawing attention to yet a third meaning for "stage": the "stage" of execution (though "scaffold" also may mean the stage of a theater, as it does in the comparable prologue to *Henry V*).

45.   Quoted by Adams, p. 285 (from *The Guls Hornbook*, 1609).

46.   F. G. Fleay, *A Chronicle History of the Life and Work of William Shakespeare* (London, 1886), p. 209: "The comparison of the world to a stage . . . suggests a date subsequent to the building of the Globe, with its motto of *Totus mundus agit historionem*." So Rosencrantz's "Ay, that they do, my lord; Hercules and his load too."

47.   "Carnal" is as flexible a word as any other here. While Dover Wilson glosses "fleshly, adulterous," J. Q. Adams takes it as "murderous" (as in *Richard III*, IV.iv.56), and comments: "And what would Horatio tell? The full guilt of Claudius from beginning to end, but not the secret shame of Gertrude. Hamlet never had revealed that. His mother's great sin died with her" (ed. *Hamlet* [Boston, 1929], p. 332). There were "casual slaughters" on the day of the uprising—the slaying of Essex's page and of several citizens and soldiers. The possibly topical bearing of these lines did not, I find, escape Foard, p. 124, though his passing suggestion has gone unheeded, even by Winstanley.

48.   Robert Pricket expressed himself freely in his publication of 1604, *Honors Fame in Triumph Riding, or, The Life and Death of the Late Honorable Earle of Essex*:

> He dyde for treason; yet no Traytor. Why?
> The treason done, he did it ignorantly.
>> Intent and purpose in the act.
>> Is that which makes a Traytors fact.

[Grosart's reprint (1881), p. 17]. Camden himself said: "This commotion which some call a fear and mistrust, others an oversight; others who censured it more hardly termed it an obstinate impatience, and seeking of revenge; and such as spoke worst of it called it an unadvised and indiscreet rashness, and to this day there are few that ever thought it a capital crime." *Annals* (ed. 1630), bk. 4, 178, quoted by Charlotte C. Stopes, *The Third Earl of Southampton* (Cambridge, 1922), p. 221. The view persists, e.g., "Robert Essex, den die grausame Herrin hinrichten liess um einiger unbesonnener Redensarten und eines dummen Streiches willen" (Hermann Conrad in *Preussische Jahrbücher,* 79 (1895) 189-90.)

49.   William Witherle Lawrence posed the question and admitted the difficulty of answering it, "Hamlet and Fortinbras," *PMLA*, 61 (1946), 685–86.

50. In the words of Lord Macaulay, "The new King had always felt kindly towards Lord Essex, and, as soon as he came to the throne, began to show favour to the House of Devereux, and to those who had stood by that house in its adversity" ("Lord Bacon," in *Critical and Historical Essays*, London, 1874, p. 367.)

51. In the last scene, and in the last scene only, stress is laid on "this kingdom" as an elective monarchy—for presumably a very special reason. The explanation lies latent in these words of Dover Wilson's: "After all, was not the monarchy of Elizabeth and James an 'elective' one? The latter like Claudius owed his throne to the deliberate choice of the Council, while the Council saw to it that he had the 'dying voice' of Elizabeth, as Fortinbras has that of Hamlet." (*Hamlet*, p. lv)

52. Strachey, p. 106.

53. See Bacon's *Works*, ed. Basil Montagu (Philadelphia, 1857), II, 533–36; see also Harrison, *Essex*, pp. 90–91. In "The Statesman's Speech" is the advice, "To conclude, let him be true to himself."

54. The quartos and folios very naturally confuse the homonyms, the quartos reading "right" (singular) here, while ten lines above, the folios have "rites."

55. There is this stanza in "Verses upon the report of the death of the right Honorable the Lord of Essex," a ballad which clumsily attains to 792 lines:

> I cannot sleepe one winke, thy troubled spirit
> Doth still pursue me wheresoere I goe.
> I cannot rest by day, nor sleepe by night,
> Thy Ghost still asks me what I meane to doe.
> Reuenge! Reuenge! nought but revenge I heare;
> Revenge! thy Ghost still soundeth in myne eare.

Quoted from *Ballads from Manuscripts*, ed. W. R. Morfill (Hertford, the Ballad Society), II, 224. *Sir Thomas Smithes Voiage and Entertainment in Rushia* (London, 1605) contains three references to Essex, in one of which his conspiracy is compared with a contemporary Russian conspiracy. The rebelling prince says (sig. K) "His fathers Empire and Government, was but as the *Poeticall Furie in a Stage–action,* compleat yet with horrid and wofull Tragedies: a first, but no second to any *Hamlet*; and that now *Revenge*, just *Revenge* was comming with his Sworde drawne against him, his royall Mother, and dearest Sister, to fill up those Murdering Sceanes," etc.

56. See Foard's article, as cited above, n. 1.

57. Bradley, p. 147. Harley Granville–Barker, ignoring all indications that the queen *is* dead, presents us at this juncture with a "still-agonizing mother." "Speechless, she can yet have heard all; at the end nothing has been spared her." *Prefaces to Shakespeare,* I (Princeton, 1946), 156.

58. Perhaps an explanation quite good enough is that furnished by Harrison in his edition of the *Complete Works* (New York, 1952), p. 934, that "with the disappearance of all the family of the original King Hamlet the situation reverts to what it was before the death of Fortinbras' father. See I.i.80–95."

59. *DNB*, XIV, 28.

60. J. E. Neale, *Queen Elizabeth* (London, 1934), p. 379.

61. Ed. Grosart, p. 20.

62. Historical MSS Commission, *Gawdy MSS* (1885), p. 92.

63. *DNB*, XLVI, 348.

64. Winwood's *Memorials*, II, 54, cited by Virginia C. Gildersleeve, *Government Regulation of the Elizabethan Drama* (New York, 1908), p. 101.

65. See Alfred Hart, *Shakespeare and the Homilies* (Melbourne, 1934), pp. 154–218.

66. Cambridge, 1946, p. 120.

67. On Elizabeth as Diana or Cynthia or "the Mortal moon" in the flattery or allusions of the time, see Elkin C. Wilson, *England's Eliza* (Cambridge, Mass., 1939), ch. 5, "Diana"; also the present writer, *Endymion in England* (New York, 1944), ch. 3, "Endymion in Court Intrigue." N. J. Halpin thought not only that the "fair vestal throned by the west" of *MND*, II.i.158ff., was Queen Elizabeth but that the "little western flower" was none other than the first Lady Essex (*Oberon's Vision in the Midsummer-Night's Dream*, London, 1843).

68. Gildersleeve, p. 100. See Appendix p. 183.

III

Jack Donne: From Rake to Husband

Women were the sine qua non of Jack Donne's poetry, and the doctor of divinity gave vivid attention to lust in his sermons, right up to the end. Sounding and looking like a skeleton, he transfixed the courtiers of Whitehall with a shocking comparison between the kiss of Judas and the kiss of a woman. "About midnight" Jesus "was *taken* and *bound with a kisse,* art thou not *too conformable* to him in that? Is not that *too literally,* too exactly *thy case? at midnight* to have *bene taken* and *bound with a kisse?*"[1] But the sensuality of the poems, the mea culpa of the sermons (above all, the Lincoln's Inn sermons on the sins of youth, to an audience that included some of Donne's boon companions) are by themselves easily discounted as conclusive evidence.[2] The *Songs and Sonets* and the *Elegies* could be flights of erotic fancy, or satires on various love poets of the past, or didactic pieces[3] that furnish no clue to the personal life or even to the personality of the poet. It was not an age given to autobiography,[4] and no genius needs to be as literal as Gosse, eager for missing facts, thought Donne was. As for the first-person beating of the breast in the sermons, preachers were supposed to elicit a feeling of shared sin. "Objective observers report that religious converts commonly exhibit a tendency to exaggerate the darkness of the deeds they did before they entered into light."[5] Donne, looking back, could have thought, like Justice Shallow, that he was carnally bolder than he was.[6] Nevertheless, the sixteenth-century poet does show a preoccupation with sensuality, and nonliterary evidence of this is not lacking. If he was not a rake, he gave a good imitation of one.[7]

Was it a pose or was it real? Cleanth Brooks[8] has warned us against our "either-or" way of thinking: maybe it was "both-and." Let us start with the pose of an earlier John Donne, who was contemporary with, though known not to be, the great-great grandfather (unidentified) of the poet and was of the same tribe of the Donnes of Kidwelly, Carmarthenshire, South Wales, whose coat–of–arms was adopted by the poet. The Donne triptych by Hans Memlinc, now in the National Gallery, London,[9] was painted in Bruges in 1468. This Donne, one of the first of the Donnes to migrate from Wales to London,[10] had come to Flanders for the marriage of Charles the Bold of Burgundy to Margaret of York, sister of Edward IV. Sir John (as he is proleptically called, since he was knighted in 1471 for his services at the battle of Tewkesbury) kneels to the left of the enthroned, baldachined Virgin and Child, gazing out past; his fair wife Elizabeth and their small daughter kneel on the right. The whole secular family exudes self-satisfaction and worldly success; the pious postures have been assumed not for worship, but for portraiture. Sir John, who is handsome in a determined sort of way, has suffered the loss of hair above his brow, but has compensated by a careful overlapping of strands from the back.

We skip to the last decade of the sixteenth century for pictures of the young poet. Until recently we had only one, the William Marshall engraving for the 1635 *Poems*. This image, coarsely at odds with portraits of Donne in later life and carved unskillfully by the same engraver who botched Milton ten years later (and whom Milton satirized),[11] has received a surprising amount of praise, perhaps in the spirit of making the most of all we had for this decade of the 1590s.

In any case, it features the warrior, though it is not, perhaps, without hints of the lover.[12]

In 1959 John Bryson uncovered the lost Lothian portrait that Helen Gardner hails as "the most striking portrait we have of any English poet."[13] The pose that it strikes is that of Donne the melancholy lover. It refutes at last and forever any skepticism as to whether the poet acted out his poems. Here are the folded arms, the broad-brimmed hat (ready to be pulled down in despondency), the Byronic open collar, the blasphemous change in the Latin collect from Lord to mistress, "Domine" to "Domina": "Illumina nostras tenebras, Domina." At the end of his life, Donne still had this hanging in his deanery. He could at least have had the decency to black out the inscription.[14] Still, one remembers that on the threshold of entering the ministry he was barely dissuaded from flaunting his "false mistresses" by publishing an edition of his secular poems.

Ambiguous words characterize what Walton called "his irregular youth."[15] Tobie Mathew put him among the "libertines."[16] But what did he mean by that? This may have been a criticism of such daring thought as went into *Biathanatos*,[17] without reference to behavior, in contrast to Walton's comment: "All which time was employed in study; though he took great liberty after it."[18]

There is the famous reminiscence from Sir Richard Baker.[19] "Mr. *John Donne*, who leaving Oxford, lived at the Inns of Court, not dissolute, but very neat; a great *Visiter* of Ladies, a great frequenter of Plays, a great writer of conceited Verses." At least we understand the last phrase. As for playgoing, I have shown that Donne evidently went to see *The Taming of the Shrew*.[20] But what is meant by "not dissolute, but very neat"? Professor Sprott welcomes this "direct denial of dissoluteness."[21] I take it in conjunction with "neat" as a comment, not on conduct, but on dress: Donne was not (*Oxford English Dictionary* obsolete definition 3) "loose, lax, slack, careless, negligent, remiss." The open collar was planned. (Professor Pierre Legouis has called attention, in a letter, to a similar Latin use, *de vestimentis*, of "dissolutus" [loosened] as recorded in *Thesaurus Linguae Latinae.*)

We are left with "a great *Visiter* of Ladies," about which Professor Sprott remarks: "Perhaps it is fanciful to see in the italics in which *Visiter* is printed an indication of emphasis on the limited meaning of that word."[22] But Sprott is quoting from an edition printed fifty-one years after Baker's death: the first edition (1643) does not have the italics. Even if they had been the author's, one could just as well see a euphemism, an irony, meant to be understood—*verbum sapientibus*—by the more knowing, who would also savor Walton's comparison of Donne to "a second St. *Austine*, for, I think, none was so like him before his Conversion."[23] Mrs. Evelyn Simpson, in volume 10 of the *Sermons*, quotes a description of Augustine as "obsessed with the ravages which unbridled sexuality produces in human beings."[24]

We come, finally, to what Walton called "the remarkable error of his life,"[25] Donne's secret marriage. What exactly were its circumstances? We do not even know its exact date. In 1601 the author of *The Progresse of the Soule* made a personal reference to "beauties nets,"[26] and that was the year he became "irremediably"[27] committed to Ann More, Francis Wolley's cousin and the favorite niece of his employer's second wife. They probably met as early as 1598, when she was fourteen, he twenty-six. The love had ample time to ripen throughout 1599, with the two of them under the same roof, for the girl was a more or less permanent guest at Sir Thomas Egerton's official residence at York House in the Strand. Her father could spare her: Sir George had had nine children by his wife who died in 1590. He himself found it convenient to visit York House when he was in town.

But things changed in 1600. On January 20 the girl's aunt, the lord keeper's wife, died. He remarried October 21. Sometime between these dates Sir George grew suspicious of Donne, "and knowing prevention to be a great part of wisdom, did therefore remove her with much haste from that to his own house"[28] thirty miles to the southwest at Loseley Park, near Guildford, in Surrey. "But too late," adds Walton,

for Jack and Ann exchanged "faithful promises" before a
parting that was to last more than a year.

The chance to meet in the city again finally came with the
convening of Elizabeth's last parliament on October 27,
1601. Sir George More sat in that parliament; so did Donne,
who in due course wrote to inform Sir George of a secret
reunion, which must have been full of what Walton calls
"passion"[29] after such long separation. "At her lyeing in
town this last Parliament, I found meanes to see her twice or
thrice."[30]

The next sentence of Donne's letter reads: "We both knew
the obligacions that lay upon us, and we adventured equally,
and about three weeks before Christmas we married." The
word "adventured" contains a romantic consciousness of
going against the law. In marrying a seventeen-year-old girl
(legally an infant) without her parent's or guardian's consent
Donne was violating both the canon and the civil law, and he
did not have to be the lawyer that he was to know this. He
also was committing another breach, clandestinity. He had
hoped all this would not have the consequences it in fact did
have; thus his letter was carefully phrased, if ultimately
rather tactless. He persuaded an intermediary, the earl of
Northumberland, to carry the missive to his unwitting
father-in-law who, having been rendered uneasy by rumors, at
last had to be told.

The most curious word in the letter is "about": "about
three weeks before Christmas we married." The new husband
is writing "From my lodginge by the Savoy, 2 Februa" 1602;
he has been married barely two months, if that, but he
cannot remember what day? Surely, it was a time for
precision, for being definite in announcing a fait accompli
that it was hoped all parties concerned would accept. We are
used to husbands forgetting their anniversaries after some
years, but the author of "The Anniversarie" is disappointing
with his "about," as if he were dealing with a matter of no
particular importance.

However, at that time, dates were often vague, even in
legal depositions. When in 1613 Frances Howard petitioned

for a nullification of her marriage to Robert, the third earl of Essex, the word "about" was used repeatedly: "That the aforesaid Robert, at the time of the pretended Marriage, was about 14, and is about 22 or 23 at this time."[31] When the earl "put in his answer" he sounded just as shaky with regard to the same primary facts: "He thinketh that at the time of his Marriage, he was full 14 years, and is now 22 and upwards."[32] Did he not *know*? From John Milton the elder, the scrivener, we have nineteen legal depositions made between 1604 and 1635 that indicate birthdates for him ranging anywhere from 1562 or 1563 to 1569. "In the five earliest depositions he is 'aged 40 years or thereabouts'; seven years later he is '45 years or thereabouts.' "[33] John Milton the poet, despite his scholarly bent, entered into his family Bible a tantalizing note regarding his brother Christopher's birth: "Christofer Milton was born on Friday about a month before Christmass at 5 in the morning 1615."[34] In dating his first wife's death, this poet also uses "about." If Milton and many others were so casual, there is no reason to cross-examine Donne.

But Donne, writing so soon after the event he is announcing, may have chosen his "about" with care. He may, for one conjecture, have wished to leave it open as to whether Advent had or had not come, since if it had, that would be another count against the marriage. The first Sunday of Advent (November 29 in 1601) ushered in a closed season for marriages (unless a special license was obtained) that lasted until the octave of the Epiphany (January 13), a restriction that William Shakespeare and another Ann had had to reckon with nineteen years before.[35]

For another conjecture, Donne's "about" may signal a strong hope that no one will press him too hard, under oath, as to the exact date of the ceremony. For a document has survived that gives no countenance whatsoever to Donne's December date. Yet he has been taken unswervingly at his word, even by the latest and most definitive biographer, R. C. Bald. And perhaps he should be, for the document, like everything else we have been dealing with, is somewhat ambiguous. In this case it seems that Donne was not only ambiguous himself, but the cause of ambiguity in others, for one, a judge of the Court of Audience of Canterbury.

What occurred first, however, was court action by Sir George More, the outraged father-in-law, who did not react to Donne's letter of February 2, 1601/2, in the way Donne had hoped. More intended to challenge the marriage and punish those who had taken part in it. In Bald's words, he "insisted that the culprits should be brought before the High Commission."[36] This is a fair inference, though the records of the Court of the High Commission were apparently destroyed by Parliament during the Civil War. Donne refers in subsequent letters to "the Commissioners,"[37] and a similar case had been brought before the Court in 1601.[38]

Punishment was not long in coming. Next time Donne writes to Sir George it is "From the Fleete, 11 Febr."[39] The two Brooke brothers were thrown into two other prisons, Christopher for having given the bride away, the Reverend Samuel for having officiated. These two friends and abettors of the poet remained confined longer than he, who was released after three or four days on grounds of health. Sir George remained far from pacified, and all that Donne could express in a letter to Goodyer of February 23 was "hopes." He offered a pretty paradox: "The Commissioners by imprisoning the witnesses and excommunicating all us, have implicitly justified our marriage."[40] In other words, if it were not a valid marriage, why would the authorities be taking such extreme steps to punish it? They must be upset about something, not nothing, a nullity, an empty ceremony. This is an ingenious hope, as compared to the ingenuous hope, in the same missive, of Sir George's "good nature."

The marriage of John Donne and Ann More was eventually validated, though nobody knows on what grounds. We have nothing from the Court of the High Commission. We do have a copy of a decree of another court, to which little or no attention has been paid. This document has had a checkered history. Sir George More kept it among his papers at Loseley House. A. J. Kempe neglected it when he printed a selection of *The Loseley Manuscripts* in 1836. It was cataloged, but inaccurately, in the appendix to the *Seventh Report of the Royal Commission on Historical Manuscripts*, 1879.[41] Donne scholars, as Lady Mary Clive remarked in her 1966 biography *Jack and the Doctor*, left this tome "apparently unopened."[42] Sir Edmund Gosse, in 1899, mentioned the document, but evidently did not read it.[43] This is understandable, for it is in a formidable secretary hand. It is now among the Donne papers at the Folger Shakespeare Library, Washington, D.C. Following the lead of Lady Mary's book, I requested a Xerox and published a preliminary note, drawing conclusions that Mr. W. Milgate[44] disagreed with in print. Through him I learned that Professor Bald, who died in 1965, had, as would be expected, examined the document. He gives it passing mention in his *John Donne: A Life*, edited by Mr. Milgate, which appeared in 1970. "It is not a very informative document," commented Professor Bald, "though its purport is clear."[45] I must beg to differ. At a major point its purport is *not* clear, and I find it *very* informative.

For one thing, it clears up a mysterious statement by Izaak Walton, who does not mention the High Commission or any suit by Sir George More. He does mention one by Donne, to win back his wife: "He . . . was forced to make good his title, and to get possession of her by a long and restless suit in Law."[46] When I was writing my life of Donne, published in 1965, I assumed Walton had become confused here, as he so often had. But he had not.[47] Donne did sue to have his marriage validated and to get back his wife. Richard Swale, who may also have sat in February on the Court of High Commission, sat for the case as the Court of Audience of the province of Canterbury. Dr. Swale rendered his judgment in favor of the plaintiff on April 27, 1602.

Sir George More is not mentioned, though he was the force that came between man and wife: Walton discreetly employs the passive—the "wife was (to her extream sorrow) detained from him."[48] Donne said in his letter of February 23 to Goodyer, "Sir George will, as I hear, keep her till I send for her: and let her remain there yet, his good nature and her sorrow will work something."[49] Days passed, but Ann remained sequestered. When further letters of petition failed,[50] Donne took the matter to court, the same court that had looked into the hasty and overprivate marriage of Sir Edward Coke and the Lady Hatton in 1598.[51] Donne's suit was promulgated or "promulged" on March 2. It dragged on for eight weeks.

"*IN DEI NOMINE AMEN: Auditis visis et intellectis ac plenarie et mature discussis per nos Richardum Swale legum doctorem Curie audientem Cantuariensis causarum et negotiorum auditorem legitime constitutum. . . .*"[52] This judge, this assessor, repetitiously and with the full panoply of legal jargon, recognizes that the parties have long been kept in suspense as to whether they were legally married. Having consulted with others, he renders his final decree ("hoc nostrum finale decretum"):

> . . . *Cum consilio Jurisperitorum cum quibus in hac parte communicavimus prenominatos Johannem Dunnum et Annam Moore alias Dunnum mense Januarij Anno domini 1601 in hac parte libellatos ab omni contractu matrimoniali et ab omnibus sponsalijs (exceptis inter eundem Johannem et Annam) liberos et immunes atque in huius libertate et immunitate notarie existentes matrimonium verum et purum inter sese contraxisse et solemnizari procurasse matrimoniumque verum et purum fuisse et esse inter dictos Annam Moore alias Dunnum et Johannem Dunnum rite initum necnon solemnizatum per presbiterum ad effectum predictum habilem et competentem et in praesentijs testium fidedignorum dictosque Johannem Dunnum et Annam Moore alias Dunnum fuisse et esse legitimum virum et uxorem et legitimo in matrimonio copulatos proque viribus et valore matrimonij predicti inter eos solemnizati pronunciamus.*

The only date in the body of the decree is January, 1602 (new style), not Donne's December, 1601. What is Swale saying? Is he saying what Bald interprets him as saying, "that in January 1601/2 John Donne and Anne Donne alias More were free from all marital contracts or obligations except those into which they had entered with one another, and that their marriage, duly celebrated by a priest, was good and sufficient, and that they were therefore lawful man and wife"?[53] Or is Swale saying what the cataloger of 1879 and Donne's biographer of 1966, Mary Clive, find him saying, that the Donnes married in the month named?

Mr. Milgate, Bald's editor, while granting that "Swale's judgment is . . . ambiguous in phrasing," supports Bald: "The document does not say that the marriage *took place* in January 1601/2, but that in that month Donne and Ann *were* free of any other marital obligations and *had* been properly married. . . . As far as the court was concerned, this was apparently as true of January 1st as of January 31st, and it seems reasonable to interpret the words to mean that by January 1601/2 the marriage *had* taken place."[54] If Swale meant to state that during that month the couple were free of any marital obligations except to each other, I should think he would have used, instead of the ablative of point of time, the accusative of duration, not "mense" but "mensem." In any case, any who favor the Bald-Milgate interpretation should explain why Swale plucks out of the air the month of January.[55] At the same time, one has to wonder why, if Swale was pointing to the time of marriage, he did not give the day, why he was even airier than Donne about that.

Possibly nothing should be made of the discrepancy. For one thing, court records of the time could be incredibly sloppy and careless. For a famous instance, it seems that the clerk, in preparing Shakespeare's marriage license, wrote "Whately" instead of "Hathaway."[56] Would one learn anything by finding a document parallel to Swale's decree, as in the case of John Kidder, weaver, who in a London allegation dated November 25, 1598 "allegeth that he hath commenced a suite in the Court of Audience against . . . Catherine Draycott upon a contract of marriadge and hath had a sentence deffinitive passed on his side in the said Court, wherein she is adjudged to be his lawfull wyfe"?[57] Perhaps there are students of antiquarian or ecclesiastical law who could clarify the "mense Januarij" as routine. It would be the beginning of a new year only in the popular, not the legal or ecclesiastical, reckoning (as witness the 1601 date). Would it be likely that Swale had no interest in dating except to antedate More's action of February? It seems perverse to be so casual at the finale of a long and what purports to be a most carefully considered case. Could it be a slip of the copyist, despite the attestation of deputy registrar Thomas Gibson that this is a true and faithful copy—a slip that More himself left uncorrected?

I cannot see the document as making sense except as dating the marriage of Donne and Ann. As Professor David Novarr comments in a letter: "If they were married in December, just what is proved about the legality of a *December* marriage (and I gather that this is what is at stake) by saying that in *January* they were free to marry?"

Pending a plausible alternative explanation, I am left with the conclusion that Donne did not tell the truth to his father-in-law, for a reason that has to be conjectured. Donne concealed many things from More; the letter in which he finally told him something not only has the word "about" in it but fails to recollect exactly how often Donne and the daughter had met ("twice or thrice")[58] the preceding fall. Within a sequence of three sentences Donne explains the situation and declines to name those present at the important ceremony. It can be said that this last was for the protection of friends. Any predating of the marriage would have been mainly for the protection of Ann More, a gallant gesture. "I humbly beg of you that she may not to her danger feele the terror of your sodaine anger."[59] Clement of Alexandria had remarked that a good man usually speaks the truth, but that, for one of a number of allowable exceptions, a physician may further the healing of his patient with a lie.[60] Donne obviously regarded the headstrong man with whom he was dealing as one who could not be asked to swallow too much truth at once.

As I see the sequence of events, Ann and John, after a separation of many months, found each other irresistible when at last they met again several times in the fall of 1601. They had made solemn promises to each other, and looked forward to marrying. Physical union was not an evasion of, but a way into, marriage: it strengthened their legal claims on each other.[61] So, with the dissolution of Parliament on December 19, Ann was taken back by her father to Loseley, neither a virgin nor a bride. In January, it probably was, the girl sent word to her lover in London that she had reason to believe she was pregnant. Thereupon, perhaps on the occasion or pretext of a visit to her former host, the avuncular Egerton, she escaped from her father long enough for a secret ceremony. Egerton's secretary, when at last he had to inform Sir George More, predated the marriage so that the couple's first child, Constance, would be born nine months afterwards, not seven or eight.[62] Constance's birth or baptismal date is, alas, unknown[63] because the Pyrford records were lost.

Perhaps the actual ceremony occurred in late January, but Swale, though of course he could not conspire to falsify the month, gave the couple as much leeway as possible by refraining from naming the day. He was, after all, pronouncing what amounted to a *sanatio in radice,* and in law the child, no matter how soon born, would be legitimate. By April 27 it would have been very apparent indeed that Ann was with child, a fait accompli bound to influence both the Court and her father.

Toward the end of his first letter[64] to his father-in-law, Donne uncomfortably anticipated the ill things that Sir George had heard about him. Specifically, as Donne's letter of February 13 brings out, there were the two accusations "of having deceived some gentlewomen before, and that of loving a corrupt religion."[65] I do not know whether the latter charge included embracing the doctrine of mental reservation, but I think I know what "deceived" means. Surely the charge was not that Donne had secretly married other women before, nor, like Mr. B with Pamela, plotted to lead them through a fraudulent ceremony. "Deceived" must mean seduced.

In contrast to the rhetoric[66] he used with Sir George, Donne was straightforward with Dean Morton in 1607, when that future bishop offered him a benefice if he would "enter into holy Orders": "I dare make so dear a friend as you are my Confessor; some irregularities of my life have been so visible to some men," that the "sacred calling," despite postmarital reform, might be brought into "a dishonour."[67]

Walton, as usual, is not to be pinned down. In the final version of his narrative of this period he moralizes over "a passion! that carries us to commit *Errors* with as much ease as whirlwinds remove feathers, and begets in us an unwearied industry to the attainment of what we desire. And such an Industry did, notwithstanding much watchfulness against it, bring them secretly together (I forbear to tell the manner how) and at last to a marriage too, without the allowance of those friends, whose approbation always was, and ever will be necessary, to make even a vertuous love become lawful."[68] Donne's secretiveness has been repeated.[69] What is meant by "even a vertuous love"? Does "at last" point to a considerable break in time between the unsanctified union and the sanctified (though unsanctioned) union, the clandestine meetings that led finally to the clandestine marriage? Does "at last" have any flavor of "high time"?

Whatever the details of the scandal, it was big enough for King James, who was in Scotland at the time, to recall it and use it as a reason for not advancing Donne seven years later. Donne's phrasing (in a letter to his would-be patron Lord Hay) about this blot in his past is piquant: "the worst part of my historie ... my disorderlie proceedings ... that intemperate and hastie act of mine."[70] The last sounds remarkably critical, as stern as the line in *Comus* (67) about "fond intemperate thirst," which in turn sends us back to Donne's own sonnet on his wife's death: "A holy thirsty dropsy melts mee yett." What began as "disorderlie" and "intemperate" ended as a longing for a saint in heaven.

The usual apology constructed for Will Shakespeare and Ann Hathaway, whose daughter Susanna was born six months after the wedding ceremony, is that they had plighted their troth before witnesses. This gave them something like marital rights.[71] But there is no evidence for such an engagement, and Walton is careful to deny it for our later couple: "These promises were only known to themselves."[72] The apology for Jack and Ann, if perchance their daughter Constance was born a little early (say, around September 1[73] in 1602), is love. I do not doubt it was mutual and true and lasting unto the grave and beyond. Ann, as well as God, was to be thanked for delivering Jack "from the Egypt of lust, by confining my affections."[74] Whatever "lover-like"[75] poems Donne addressed to Lucy, countess of Bedford, or Mrs. Magdalen Herbert, it just does not fit the total later picture to postulate, as Yeats did,[76] a Donne unfaithful to his wife or even her memory. This husband has been criticized, in a way that is historically unfair, for having worn out his wife with repeated pregnancies.[77] But this signifies that he continued to find her, or they each other, irresistible, even when he was forty-five, which in those days was the threshold of old age. As he wrote in a letter of 1614, "We had not one another at so cheap a rate, as that we should ever be weary of one another."[78]

I am even hesitant about calling the young man a rake, in any place more sober than a title, for there is the Aristotelian problem of definition: how many acts make a man such and such? As a character in a John O'Hara story[79] says, "I did some raking, but I don't think I was a rake." In gazing at the fascinating Lothian portrait, one agrees with a contemporary who said of Donne: "Neither was it possible that a vulgar Soul should dwell in such promising Features."[80] The works, by and large, bear that out.

NOTES

1. John Donne, "Death's Duel," *Sermons,* ed. George R. Potter and Evelyn M. Simpson, 10 vols., (Berkeley, 1953–62), 10:246.

2. See the early part of my *Grace to a Witty Sinner: A Life of Donne* (New York and London, 1965). The present essay is an addendum to that book and to my note (which contains some details not repeated here), "The Date of Donne's Marriage," *EA,* 21 (1968), 168–69.

3.   N. J. C. Andreasen, *John Donne: Conservative Revolutionary* (Princeton, 1967).

4.   But a change was coming, and it would be like Donne to be in the vanguard. See Joan Webber, *The Eloquent "I": Style and Self in Seventeenth-Century Prose* (Madison, 1968).

5.   S. Ernest Sprott, "The Legend of Jack Donne the Libertine," *UTQ,* 19 (1950), 343.

6.   This is T. S. Eliot's conclusion. "It is pleasant in youth to think that one is a gay dog, and it is pleasant in age to think that one *was* a gay dog." Theodore Spencer (ed.), *A Garland for John Donne* (Cambridge, Mass., 1931; rep. ed., Gloucester, Mass., 1958), p. 10.

7.   "Although to try to connect particular lyrics with particular ladies and write a *Vie Amoureuse de John Donne* out of the Elegies and 'Songs and Sonnets' seems to me to be to chase a will-of-the-wisp, I cannot believe that Donne's poetry had no relation to the development of his moral, intellectual, and emotional life, and that his readers in our century were wholly astray in finding in his poetry the revelation of a very powerful individuality." Helen Gardner (ed.), *John Donne: A Collection of Critical Essays* (Englewood Cliffs, N.J., 1962), pp. 11–12.

8.   *The Well Wrought Urn* (New York, 1947).

9.   R. C. Bald, *John Donne: A Life* (Oxford, 1970), p. 21, puts the painting "at Chatsworth," but it passed from the collection there of the Duke of Devonshire in 1956.

10. The first may have been John Don the elder, mercer, whose will, dated August 28, 1480, and proved in December, is summarized in the *Transactions* of the Carmarthenshire Antiquarian Society (vol. 25, part 60 [1935], 63). I owe this reference to Mr. W. H. Morris of Sunnymead, Kidwelly, Carmarthenshire, South Wales. Prosperous but childless, Don was called "the elder" because he had a younger brother also named John (just as, for another instance of a bygone practice, Martin Luther's father and one of his brothers were baptized respectively Gross-Hans and Klein-Hans).

11. In the four lines of Greek iambics "In Effigiei Eius Sculptorem." This frontispiece of the 1645 *Poems* was dropped in 1673. It was galling to the author of *Eikonoklastes* that Marshall did better by the martyred Charles I in *Eikon Basilike,* and his caricature of the sectaries drew a pun in *Tetrachordon:* "for which I do not commend his marshalling." *Works of John Milton,* ed. Frank Allen Patterson, 18 vols. (New York, 1931–38), IV, 69.

12. John Donne, *The Elegies and the Songs and Sonnets,* ed. Helen Gardner (Oxford, 1965), appendix E: "The Marshall Engraving and the Lothian Portrait" (p. 266), cites the "love locks" and the motto based on "the protestation of a fickle mistress."

13. Ibid., p. 269.

14. Cf. Mary Clive, *Jack and the Doctor* (London, 1966), p. 10.

15. Izaak Walton, *Lives* (London, 1936), p. 52.

16. Sprott, "Legend of Jack Donne," p. 339.

17. Ibid., pp. 339–41; George Williamson, "Libertine Donne: Comments on *Biathanatos*," *PQ*, 13 (1934), 276–91. The date of Mathew's reference is 1608, when Donne was already the father of four. If any activity other than conversation is meant, it may be the meetings of the "Sireniacal" drinking fraternity of which Donne was a member. But it does nothing for his reputation that Mathew pairs him with Richard Martin, described by Bald (p. 190) as "frivolous," "the acknowledged leader in all revels within the [Middle] Temple," who "never lost an opportunity for convivial gaiety" and was the putative father (p. 249) of an illegitimate child.

18. Walton, p. 67.

19. In *A Chronicle of the Kings of England*, quoted by Sprott, p. 341, from the "9th impression" of 1696. Bald, p. 72, quotes the first edition, 1643 (part 2, p. 156), which I have checked.

20. Le Comte, *Grace to a Witty Sinner*, p. 255.

21. Sprott, 341.

22. Ibid.

23. Walton, pp. 47–48.

24. See 10.348, from J. N. D. Kelly, *Early Christian Doctrines* (London, 1958), 365. Later Mrs. Simpson was to remark that Donne "found in Augustine's *Confessions* a striking parallel with his own stormy and licentious youth." *John Donne's Sermons on the Psalms and Gospels,* ed. Evelyn Simpson (Berkeley, 1963), p. 5.

25. Walton, p. 60.

26. Stanza 5, 6.

27. His own word in his first letter to Sir George More, p. 444 of John Hayward's edition of Donne's *Complete Poetry and Selected Prose* (New York, 1936).

28. Walton, p. 27.

29. Ibid.

30. Donne, *Complete Poetry,* ed. Hayward, p. 444.

31. T. B. Howell's *A Complete Collection of State Trials* (London, 1816), 2.785.

32. Ibid, 787. Donne was more precise when he testified for a case on June 17, 1618, that he was "aged 46. yeres or nere thereaboutes" (Bald, p. 335).

33. William Riley Parker, *Milton: A Biography* (Oxford, 1968), II, 684.

34. Ibid., 705. See the flyleaf of Milton's Bible reproduced as the frontispiece of that volume; also note the entry that the blind poet instructed Jeremy Picard to enter on the death of Mary Powell Milton. In the allegation concerning his third marriage, "Milton gave his age as 'about 50 years' [he was actually 54]" (1095).

35. See *The Reader's Encyclopedia of Shakespeare,* ed. Oscar James Campbell and Edward G. Quinn (New York, 1966), p. 503.

36. Bald, p. 135.

37. Roland G. Usher, *The Rise and Fall of the High Commission* (Oxford, 1913), pp. 36–37, gives examples of the late sixteenth-century usage and comments: "Such usage . . . makes it clear that contemporaries employed 'Commission' and 'Commissioners' as the equivalents of 'court' and 'judges,' and understood them to connote a permanent institution of so settled a character that it could properly be spoken of in the singular number. . . . The great bulk" of the resulting decrees were "issued in matrimonial and testamentary cases" (p. 102).

38. Bald, pp. 132–33.

39. Donne, *Complete Poetry,* ed. Hayward, p. 445–46.

40. Sir Edmund Gosse, *The Life and Letters of John Donne* (New York, 1899; repr. ed., Gloucester, Mass., 1959), I, 109.

41. Le Comte, "The Date of Donne's Marriage," 168.

42. Despite the fact that the volume is listed as a source in the English *Dictionary of National Biography* article on Donne (1138). This article, by Augustus Jessopp, unfortunately slips or misprints in giving the year of the marriage: "about Christmas 1600" (V, 1130), an error for 1601 that is still copied: e.g., Beatrice White, *Cast of Ravens: The Strange Case of Sir Thomas Overbury* (London, 1965), pp. 193, 203. Jessopp knew better. See his *John Donne, Sometime Dean of St. Paul's* (London, 1897), pp. 22–23.

43. Gosse, I, 117.

44. W. Milgate, "The Date of Donne's Marriage: A Reply," *EA,* 22 (1969), 66–67.

45. Bald, p. 139.

46. Walton, p. 29.

47. For some of his hits and misses see David Novarr, *The Making of Walton's Lives* (Ithaca, 1958); Bald, "Historical Doubts Respecting Walton's *Life of Donne,*" in Millar MacLure and F. W. Watt (eds.), *Essays in English Literature from the Renaissance to the Victorian Age Presented to A. S. P. Woodhouse* (Toronto, 1964), pp. 69–84.

48. Walton, p. 29.

49. Gosse, I, 109.

50. Those in Gosse, I, 112–15, the first day of March, to More and to Egerton.

51. See Catherine Drinker Bowen, *The Lion and the Throne* (Boston, 1957), pp. 123–24, 295. Mr. Milgate (of the Australian National University, Canberra) provided me by letter with a quotation from John Godolphin, *Repertorium Canonicum* (London, 1678), p. 106, citing Sir Edward Coke (I gathered from W. S. Holdsworth, *A History of English Law,* London, 1903, I, 371, that this is 4th Instit. 337) as saying that "this Court . . . meddleth not with any matter between

party and party of any contentious Jurisdiction, but dealeth with matters *pro forma* . . . and with matters of voluntary Jurisdiction, as the granting of the Guardianship of the Spiritualities *Sede vacante* of Bishops, . . . dispensing with Banns of Matrimony, and such like." Nevertheless, while omitting any reference to that "contentious" third party, Sir George More, Swale's decree is presented as the issue of an adversary proceeding between Donne, the plaintiff, *partem agen*tem *sive querelante*m, and Ann More, alias Donne, the defendant, *ream sive querelata*m, both with legal representatives or procurators—Price and Milberne respectively. The proceedings took place in London.

After our public disagreement of 1968-69, I started a correspondence with Mr. Milgate, who proceeded to share with me the pertinent contents of Professor Bald's book, then as yet unpublished. Mr. Milgate also provided me with his own knowledge and further reflections, thus helping me with the utmost generosity to develop an article at odds with (but, I trust, cautiously so) this well-known Donne specialist's own views.

How difficult fathers could be is seen in the 1599 case of a former lord mayor of London: "Our Sir John Spenser of London was the last week committed to the Fleet for a contempt, and hiding away his daughter, who they say is contracted to the Lord Compton, but now he is out again and by all meanes seekes to hinder the match, alledging a precontract to Sir Arthur Henninghams sonne: but upon his beating and misusing her, she was sequestered to one Barkers a proctor and from thence to Sir Henry Billingsleyes where she yet remains till the matter be tried." John Chamberlain, *Letters,* ed. N. E. McClure, 2 vols. (Philadelphia, 1939), I, 73. This case may be reflected in *The Shoemaker's Holiday. See* Novarr, "Dekker's Gentle Craft and the Lord Mayor of London," *MP,* 57 (1960), 233–39.

52.   Friends and colleagues came to my assistance in making out the handwriting. Professor Robert O. Fink, Latin paleographer at the State University of New York at Albany, made a transcription of most of the document. Mr. Milgate passed on to me, as a check, Professor Bald's transcription (not printed in his book). The unitalicized expansions are mine.

53.   Bald, *John Donne,* p. 139.

54.   Milgate, "The Date of Donne's Marriage: A Reply," 66.

55.   Mr. Milgate's next sentence read: "The specifying of this month rather than December 1601 might simply be due to Donne's having brought the suit late in January, or to his, or Swale's, wish to make clear that the suit antedated that brought by Sir George More before the High Commission after receiving his son-in-law's confession (in a letter dated February 2, 1601/2)." However, he has withdrawn this on noticing the pro*mulgata fuit* . . . *secundo Marci* appendage to Swale's final decree.

Professor David Novarr of Cornell, on reading a draft of the present essay, asks, "Would Swale have avoided December because of Advent?" But he adds, "Why, then, not use November?" In reply to my question concerning Swale's lack of interest in dating except to antedate More's action of February, my colleague Professor Francis Sypher suggests that if the Latin means that the couple was married *as of* January 1601/2, Swale was deliberately postdating to avoid placing the marriage in the forbidden season. He could not predate because they were not married in November. Furthermore, the litigation was brought to decide the validity of the marriage, not its date. Professor Sypher posits that "the judge avoids and *closes* the possibility of further objections on any ground connected with the date or circumstances of the marriage." I lack the knowledge of law to have an opinion on this.

56.   Campbell and Quinn, *Encyclopedia of Shakespeare*, p. 941, s.v. "Whately, Anne." Unless it was another William Shakespeare or another Anne. For similar errors, see Joseph William Gray, *Shakespeare's Marriage* (London, 1905), p. 26.

57.   Gray, *Shakespeare's Marriage*, p. 194. Irene J. Churchill, *Canterbury Administration: The Administrative Machinery of the Archbishopric of Canterbury Illustrated from Original Records* (London: S.P.C.K., 1933), I, 470–99 gives some Latin formulae used by the court in the Middle Ages, but Act Books of the Audience seem not to exist.

58.   He probably does not use "twice or thrice" as a literal statement, but rather as an idiom meaning "a few times" (see the *Oxford English Dictionary* [1961], s.v. "twice" 1d). Mr. Milgate points out this same usage in the opening of "Aire and Angels": "Twice or thrice had I loved thee. . . ."

59.   Donne, *Complete Poetry*, ed. Hayward, p. 444.

60.   This, from the *Stromata*, was entered by Milton in his Commonplace Book under "De Mendacio" (*Works of John Milton*, XVIII, 141). This poet, whose honor has not been questioned in our century except by obscure Continental scholars and Hilaire Belloc, went on to state in his *De Doctrina Christiana:* "No rational person will deny that there are certain individuals whom we are fully justified in deceiving. Who would scruple to dissemble with a child, with a madman, with a sick person, with one in a state of intoxication, with an enemy, with one who has himself a design of deceiving us, with a robber?" (XVII, 299). See Ruth Mohl, *John Milton and his Commonplace Book* (New York, 1969), pp. 71ff.

61.   "A valid but clandestine marriage might be made merely by sexual intercourse preceded by promises to marry; but all such unions were stigmatised by public and ecclesiastical opinion." C. L. Powell, *English Domestic Relations, 1487–1653* (New York, 1917), p. 6. Although his *Treatise of Spousals* was not printed until 1686, Henry Swinburne wrote around this time that "albeit there be no Witnesses of the Contract, yet the parties having verily (though secretly) Contracted Matrimony, they are very Man and Wife before God; neither can either of them with safe Conscience Marry elsewhere, so long as the other party liveth" (*Spousals,* p. 87, quoted by Powell, *Domestic Relations,*

p. 17). Thus, Donne may have used "married" in one sense while allowing it to be understood in another. His two crucial sentences require interpolation: "We both knew the obligacions that lay upon us, and we adventured equally, and about three weeks before Christmas we married [without benefit of clergy]. And as at the doinge, [which extended into the formal ceremony performed by the Reverend Samuel Brooke in January] there were not usd above fyve persons, of which I protest to you by my salvation, [this he is willing to swear to] there was not one that had any dependence or relation to you, so in all the passage of it [hint of an extensive period of time?] did I forbear to use any suche person, who by furtheringe of it might violate any trust or duty towards you." He could say, as Claudio did, "She is fast my wife, / Save that we do the denunciation lack / Of outward order," (*Measure for Measure*, I.2. 151–53). But, to repeat, the couple, however right they might seem to each other (Clay Hunt thought that the girl in bed in "The Good-morrow" was Ann More—see *Donne's Poetry: Essays in Literary Analysis* [New Haven, 1954] pp. 68, 232) risked opprobrium: "And when matrymony is thus laufully made / yet the man maye not possesse the woman as his wyfe / nor the woman the man as her husbonde ... afore suche tyme as that matrymony be approued and solempnysed by oure mother holy chyrche / and yf they do in dede they synne deedly." William Harrington, *Commendacions of Matrymony* (1528), quoted by Powell, p. 233. In very obvious cases the marriage register could bear the notation "by necessity," or pointedly substitute "singlewoman" for the word "maiden." Gray, p. 188, cites an instance where "maiden" was written, then cancelled. For percentages on prenuptial pregnancies, see Peter Laslett, *The World We Have Lost* (New York, 1965), p. 139.

The misogynist Joseph Swetnam was to recommend in 1615 that if a man was bent on marrying, a maid of seventeen (Ann's age) would be "flexible and bending, obedient and subject to doe anything." Quoted by Louis B. Wright, *Middle-Class Culture in Elizabethan England* (reprinted in Ithaca, 1958), p. 487. Shakespeare's child-brides are not typical: as Swetnam implies, even seventeen was exceptionally young for a bride—see Laslett, p. 82.

62. Mr. Milgate remarked ("A Reply," 67), "It is, moreover, difficult to see what difference the antedating of the wedding by a few weeks could have made to Ann's reputation." On reading this, I came to the conclusion that Mr. Milgate must be a bachelor, which he is. To my pressing argument, Mr. Milgate replied (in a letter): "In the circles in which Donne and the Mores and most of Donne's friends moved, 'reputation' doesn't seem to me (*pace* Legouis, [a reference to the *jugement de Salomon* pronounced on the controversy by editor Pierre Legouis as an appendage to "A Reply," p. 67]) to have been assessed in mid-Victorian terms (and so much of these as survive today); that the indiscretion of the marriage itself would have been the chief scandal." I agree that the elopement would have been the greater scandal, but because of this beginning, and what with contention and lawsuits, there would have been those in the social circles referred to—and Donne

would have feared there would be—who would have counted the months on their fingers. The country folk took "country matters," along with their "accidents," in stride; at the opposite extreme in drawing attention were the prominent courtiers and lords and the pregnant maids of honor, Raleigh-Throckmorton, Southampton-Vernon, Pembroke-Fitton. Still, one can imagine the passing comment a gossip like Chamberlain would have bestowed on the Donnes, if they had come to his attention; one can imagine it from his actual comment on a prominent case four years earlier: "Mistris Vernon is from the court, and lies in Essex House; some say she hath taken a venew [thrust] under the girdle and swells upon yt, yet she complaines not of fowle play but sayes the erle of Southampton will justifie yt: and yt is bruited underhand that he was latelie here fowre dayes in great secret of purpose to marry her and effected yt accordingly." Chamberlain, *Letters,* I, 43–44. It was still, even in 1602, the reign of the Virgin Queen. Under the Stuarts, Chamberlain deplored that Donne persisted in his youthful vice of writing poetry. "I send you here certain verses of our Deane of Paules upon the death of the Marquis Hamilton, which though they be reasonable wittie and well don yet I could wish a man of his yeares and place to geve over versifieng." *Letters,* II, 613.

The remainder of Mr. Milgate's objection ("A Reply," p. 67) was: "Such a lie would, however, have been particularly fatuous, since Donne knew that the circumstances of the marriage would be fully investigated, partly at his own instigation, by two important Courts; and it can hardly be supposed that the other persons present at the marriage could have been persuaded to lie also." I cannot see at all that "Donne knew" what was going to happen, though he knew what *could* happen. He hoped for the best, the acceptance of the marriage (and his word), fait accompli. He did not foresee that he would be thrown into gaol, that there would be lawsuits, his or anyone else's. When he learned that nothing was going to be glossed over, as he had hoped, he may promptly have expanded—or retracted—his own "gloss" on the date. But he had counted, as he says, on "good nature"; (he was blithe as late as February 23, even after these consequences descended upon those concerned: letter in Gosse, *Life and Letters,* I, 109).

63.   As Mr. Milgate wittily comments, "to the flourishing of scholarship"!

64.   "If any take advantage of your displeasure against me, and fill you with ill thoughts of me, my comfort is, that you know that fayth and thanks are due to them onely, that speak when theyr informacions might do good; which now it cannot work toward any party. For my excuse I can say nothing, except I knew what were sayd to you." Donne, *Complete Poetry,* ed. Hayward, pp. 444–45.

65.   Gosse, I, 106.

66.   Donne argues that the charges "are vanished and smoked away (as I assure myself, out of their weakness they are), and that as the devil in the article of our death takes the advantage of our weakness and fear,

to aggravate our sins to our conscience, so some uncharitable malice hath presented my debts double at least," Ibid. For references in Bald to Donne's equivocations, see my review in *JEGP*, 70 (1971), 155–56.

67. Walton, p. 34.

68. Ibid., pp. 27–28. His first version, *The Life and Death of Dr. Donne, Late Dean of St. Paul's* (London, 1640), read: "Their love (a passion which of all other Mankind is least able to command and wherein most errors are committed) was in them so powerful that they resolved and did marry without the approbation of those friends that might justly claim an interest in the advising and disposing of them." Mary R. Mahl (ed.), *Seventeenth-Century English Prose* (Philadelphia, 1968), p. 318. Had he received any new information in the interim, or was he stretching out his style with what he himself calls "some double expressions"? (Walton, "The Epistle to the Reader," *Lives*, p. 6). Novarr, p. 70, comments: "He did not have a single important fact to add to this account in 1658, but he would expand this section showing the secular Donne to preserve the relative equilibrium between it and the expanded later life. He therefore rewrote it in more leisurely fashion and added many wise saws which tend to justify the behavior of the principal actors." "Secretly," "the manner," and "at last" were not added until 1675.

69. To quote Grierson, "It was, one suspects from several circumstances, a little Donne's way in later years to disguise the footprints of his earlier indiscretions." Donne, *Poems*, ed. Grierson (Oxford, 1912), 2:xviii.

70. Bald, *John Donne*, p. 161.

71. Cf. the latter part of the third scene of the first act of Webster's *The Duchess of Malfi* and such statements from the heroine as "I have heard lawyers say, a contract in a chamber / *Per verba* [*de*] *presenti* is absolute marriage" and "How can the church build faster? / We now are man and wife, and 'tis the church / That must but echo this."

72. Walton, p. 27.

73. ". . . The christening, perhaps in August," says the Clive biography, slyly (p. 65), after stating on p. 56 that "the wedding ceremony took place in January." If I am casting wanton aspersions on Ann, I feel better for having been preceded by two ladies, of whom one, Lady Mary Clive, had looked at (though I gather from p. 61 not too carefully) the Swale decree, and the other, Evelyn Hardy (*Donne: A Spirit in Conflict* [London, 1943], p. 83), was making a guess based on her view of Donne. Then there are the modern critics: for a review, see Pierre Legouis, "Donne, L'Amour et Les Critiques," *EA*, 10 (1957) 115-22. Theodore Redpath, ed., *The Songs and Sonets* (London, 1959), p. xviii, uses the word "liaison." Judah Stampfer also opined, "in 1600, a virginal sixteen–year–old child–woman, his house companion for over a year, became his new mistress." *John Donne and the Metaphysical Gesture* (New York, 1970), p. 46.

74. Donne's *Essays in Divinity*, ed. Evelyn M. Simpson (Oxford, 1952), p. 75.

75. Donne, *Poems*, ed. Grierson, II, xxii.

76. *Letters of William Butler Yeats*, ed. Allan Wade (New York, 1955), pp. 571, 710, 902. Cf. Donaphan Louthan apropos of "Twicknam Garden," *The Poetry of John Donne* (New York, 1951), pp. 149–50.

77. See the quotations and discussion in my *Grace to a Witty Sinner*, pp. 171–73.

78. Gosse, II, 48.

79. "Mrs. Stratton of Oak Knoll," *The O'Hara Generation* (New York, 1969), p. 122.

80. John Hacket, *Scrinia Reserata* (Savoy, 1693), p. 63.

IV

The 'Haemony' Passage in *Comus*

In 1719 Francis Peck referred to Milton's Ludlow Castle masque by the title *Circe*.[1] The source of his confusion Peck himself made sufficiently clear twenty-one years later when he became the first of a long line of commentators to dwell on the obvious analogy between Homer's myth and Milton's.[2] The scholarly pastime of discovering literary influences on *Comus* soon achieved a complexity which Peck, no mean speculator himself, might have relished, but it is still possible and even convenient to view *Comus* as an allegory suggested by the Circe episode in Homer and Ovid.[3] The convenience lies in the fact that Milton's poem, thus viewed, becomes part of a history of interpretation which extends back to the time of Plato.[4] For reasons that will appear, a discussion of the most cryptic passage in *Comus* ought not to proceed without our glancing at this background, in its pagan and its Christian phases.

We need not go far afield, for both phases are to be seen in a little book which Milton bought and marked in 1637,[5] three years after *Comus* was produced but while the author was still revising[6] for its publication by Henry Lawes that year. Conrad Gesner, in his 1544 editing and translating into Latin of the *Allegoriae in Homeri Fabulas de Diis,* had mistakenly identified the Greek author as Heraclides Ponticus, a contemporary of Aristotle,[7] though he was another Heraclitus centuries later. His allegories are sometimes naturalistic, sometimes moral, and often based on extremely fanciful etymology.[8] According to this defender, Homer has been unjustly accused of impiety by Plato and others who do not look to the hidden meaning of his fables.

> Ile tell ye, 'tis not vain, or fabulous,
> (Though so esteem'd by shallow ignorance)
> What the sage Poets taught by th' heav'nly Muse,
> Storied of old in high immortal vers . . .[9]

There is a meaning beneath the surface. Let us search for it, beginning with the first book of the *Iliad.* It cannot be that Apollo is here a vengeful god slaying innocent men with his arrows because of Agamemnon's slight to Chryses— "tantaene animis caelestibus irae?" By Apollo, *ho Phoibos*— the shining one—Homer intends the sun, whose rays (arrows) are the causative agents of the plague, which at that season, in the crowded, swamp-ridden camp of the Greeks, was but too likely to break out. As is natural, the pestilence attacked the animals first, the mules and the dogs (*Iliad,* 1.50); the men caught it from them. Again, the incident of Athene coming down and restraining Achilles from assailing Agamemnon with his sword is certainly not to be taken literally. The deity was not present in person. The figure is Homer's way of telling us that prudence overmastered the rash concupiscent faculty in Achilles' triple Platonic soul. In such manner "Heraclides" moves cursorily through the *Iliad* and parts of the *Odyssey,* picking out points to interpret. For him Bacchus, stirrer of frenzy, is simply a personification of wine, even as Comus is Milton's dramatic embodiment of revelry or excess. The Elder Brother asks a question not dissimilar to those raised by Heraclides, and his answer carries on the same rational and didactic tradition, or one kindred to it:

> What was that snaky-headed *Gorgon* sheild
> That wise *Minerva* wore, unconquer'd Virgin,
> Wherwith she freez'd her foes to congeal'd stone?
> But rigid looks of Chast austerity . . .[10]

Heraclides discerned in the three heads of Cerberus the three divisions of philosophy, rational, natural, and moral. It was fitting for Hercules, who was endued with heavenly wisdom,[11] to drag forth that symbolic beast into the no less symbolic day.

Milton had before him a truncated text of the *Allegoriae* in which Circe receives only passing mention.[12] On turning, however, to the shorter pieces by other writers whom Gesner included in the same volume with Heraclides but did not put into Latin,[13] Milton would have found at the very end an "anagoge"[14] on the transformations of Circe. The last leaf of a book (as Professor John Livingston Lowes noted,[15] and Petrarch before him), is an irresistible pausing place for browsers, and it becomes tempting to wonder if Milton's purchase of 1637 signifies a reacquaintance with at least this much of Gesner's little anthology. For what the Byzantine schoolman and neoplatonic philosopher Michael Psellos wrote about the transformations of Circe has a surprising validity for the transformations of Comus, as a close rendering of the Greek will show.

Anagoge by Michael Psellos on Circe who would transform Ulysses:

> Circe wants to transform Ulysses and drive him into a pigsty, and she made a mixture of everything that might bring this change about. But her plot is frustrated, the hero drawing his sword on her. Yet he, being a prudent fellow and wonderfully shrewd, was not readily driven to the act of revenge. Needless to say, that wholly corrupt wanton nearly breathed her last in her terror of the weapon. She so changed that you could see the change—nor does his fury abate, and he looks at her with a dreadful gaze. As for his comrades, they are as yet no care of his, for he has been too busy thinking about himself. And there they stood—but, alas! their faces! Her art worked its pleasure on them. On one man she had already completed

the metamorphosis. Another was still undergoing it, and a third was about to. Thus, the first had had his nose finished off to a snout, and was the victim of a change perfect in its swinishness. The second had suffered a transformation of eyes, and was just now yielding to shortness of features: not yet had his nose turned up to a point. The face of the third had swollen, and the process was beginning.

Now what was this mixing bowl, and what did she mix in it? O friend, the poet has here veiled a philosophic meaning. Harken, and do not censure the guise of a fable, for there lurk poetically under this various form the secrets of deep wisdom. Know that Circe is downright pleasure-transformer of human souls—in which passionate direction all are moved. The potion is a blended drink, even the cup of utter forgetfulness. He who drinks of this cup estranges himself from his faculties, for it is a fact that souls forget their proper worth to drink the cup of sin. Wherefore, having disregarded innate reason, the soul takes on beastly form. Now, Circe has power over such souls as these: terrible she seems to them, fierce and awful in her beauty.

The spirits of the souls centered in the mortal body and nature undefiled are shaken, but by no means do they succumb to the onslaught of Circe. They did not change in their outward form, but, confronting more nobly her whom they fear, they escape the transformation which relates to the passions.[16] Such a miraculous thing is the love of wisdom, and not only from the rich swelling earth does it draw for itself fresh waters, but even from sharp crags is wont honey-sweet to flow.

It will be noticed that in two particulars Psellos is nearer to Milton than to Homer. His emphasis is exclusively on the changed countenances ("prosopa") of Circe's victims, and in his interpretation he not only gives a reason for this, but speaks of the transforming cup as a "cup of forgetfulness." Now, in Homer and Ovid—and this is a favorite point with the early editors of *Comus*—the brute change overtakes the entire body, and the victims remain conscious of their misfortune, pathetically aware that they had once been men. But Milton's Attendant Spirit says of Comus's crew:

> Soon as the Potion works, their human count'nance,
> Th' express resemblance of the gods, is chang'd . . .

All other parts remaining as they were,
And they, so perfect is their misery,
Not once perceive their foul disfigurement,
But boast themselves more comely than before
And all their friends, and native home forget
To roule with pleasure in a sensual stie.[17]

"Souls forget their proper worth to drink the cup of sin." The anagoge by Psellos forms, then, an interesting if quite gratuitous gloss on Milton's own allegory. There is, of course, no reason to suppose, in the face of external evidence to the contrary, that we have here a hint which was actually put to service in the composition of *Comus*. Had such hints been needed, they could have been found elsewhere. For example, the two departures from the Homeric myth just noticed in Milton are also in Ariosto.[18] What matters is that Psellos, like Milton and unlike "Heraclides," had his own Christian reasons for transfiguring classical story. How startlingly far these devout perversions could go is illustrated by what happened to Virgil in the Middle Ages ("virga" [magic wand]; "virgo" [Holy Virgin]), the Christianizing of Ovid (in lieu of Homer, not directly known), and Natalis Comes's handbook *Mythologiae sive Explicationis Fabularum Libri Decem* (Padua, 1616).[19] Nicetas of Byzantium, the teacher of Psellos, explained that the country that Circe's drugs caused Ulysses' men to forget was none other than the New Jerusalem.[20]

The New Jerusalem—it may not be an inappropriate thought to have in connection with the saved in *Comus*. But before coming to that we have Milton's adaptation of the Circe myth in Latin works written in his Cambridge days.[21] The one in the first elegy distinctly echoes the past briefly cited above. The poet expressed his intention "to keep far away from the infamous halls of treacherous Circe, with the aid of divine moly." The figure of speech used here in reference to the allurements of London life is precisely that used by Roger Ascham in warning young Englishmen who go into Italy. Let them be like Ulysses (*The Scholemaster* advises), who took care

... to feed dayly upon that swete herbe Moly with the blake roote
and white floore, given unto him by Mercurie, to avoide all the
inchantmentes of *Circes* .... [For] some, sometyme my deare
friendes, ... partying out of England feruent in the love of Christes
doctrine, and well furnished with the feare of God, returned out of
Italie worse transformed, then euer was any in *Circes* Court.[22]

The phrase "divini Molyos usus ope" looks forward to the
plant "of divine effect" in *Comus* and the passage in which
its characteristics are—at length, and with great apparent
earnestness—set forth. The situation does not need much review: the Attendant Spirit, disguised as Thyrsis, is explaining
that, in order to save their sister from the "hellish
charms" of Comus, the Brothers must have with them a
certain plant which Thyrsis received from a "Shepherd Lad"
skilled in simples:

> Amongst the rest a small unsightly root,
> But of divine effect, he cull'd me out;
> The leaf was darkish, and had prickles on it,
> But in another Countrey, as he said,
> Bore a bright golden flowre, but not in this soyl:
> Unknown, and like esteem'd, and the dull swayn
> Treads on it daily with his clouted shoon,
> And yet more med'cinal is it then that *Moly*
> That *Hermes* once to wise *Ulysses* gave;
> He call'd it *Haemony,* and gave it me,
> And bad me keep it as of sovran use
> 'Gainst all inchantments, mildew blast, or damp
> Or gastly furies apparition. [629–41]

In the midst of what Felix Schelling called "an obvious
and well sustained allegory"[23] the poet makes an elaborate
pause over a specially named plant, for reasons which, if
allegorical, have proved far from obvious to the generality of
commentators. The several interpretations that have been
offered do not agree, and they all suffer for lack of tangible
evidence as to Milton's meaning or even as to whether, at this
particular juncture, he had a meaning. That significance is
aimed for does seem likely in view of the author's ethical

seriousness, the background of allegory which had previously interested him, and the length and detail of the passage: are we really being presented here with thirteen lines of triviality? As Rosemond Tuve has said, "Upon the great hinge of the Circe-Comus myth Milton's whole invention moves."[24] Lines 629–41 are a most important juncture.

Two clues are the name "haemony," and the comparison of haemony with moly. A close translation of the tenth book of the *Odyssey,* lines 302–06, sets forth the parallel between Homer's plant and Milton's:

> Therewith the slayer of Argos gave me the plant that he had plucked from the ground, and he showed me the growth thereof. It was black at the root, but the flower was like to milk. Moly the gods call it, but it is hard for mortal men to dig; howbeit with the gods all things are possible.[56]

The inspiration here for the lines in *Comus* is obvious.[26] Milton was undoubtedly giving his impression of moly when he began by describing the protective plant as "a small unsightly root." If he shortly departed from this model, it continues to be felt as a general influence down to the specific references of lines 636-37. There is a correspondence —between the "darkish" leaf of haemony and the black root of moly, between the one's milk-white flower and the other's "bright golden." The Attendant Spirit parallels Hermes. Both descend from above to proffer charms which, though they grow in terrestrial soil, have an other-worldly aura about them.

Citing Homer or Ovid is as far as commentary went until 1939, when Professor George Whiting[27] quoted Pliny the Elder, who treated moly as an actual plant and stated it had not always been assigned a white flower. "Greek authors depicted it" as having a "florem luteum."[28] Whoever these Greek writers were, their description survives only in Pliny, that Pliny whose *Naturalis historia* Milton regarded so highly that he conducted his young nephews through "a great part" of it.[29] Since "a bright golden flowre" is as nice a rendering

as one could wish of "florem luteum," there is good reason
to add Pliny's words to Homer's as an element in the fusion
of memory out of which the passage in question sprang. Also,
the picture Pliny gives of moly as an onion-like plant easily
warrants the adjectives "small" and "unsightly."

Another tradition forges a link between the very name of
Milton's plant and moly. This is to find in "haemony" a
double entendre, for there already exists an explanation of
the word that is sound and convincing.

The etymology that has served well for a hundred years—
with Milton scholars rather than lexicographers—was first
proposed by Thomas Keightley in 1859.[30] Keightley guessed
that Milton derived the name of his plant "from Haemonia,
or Thessaly, the land of magic." The inference seems above
criticism. Not only do many references[31] show that
Haemonia, or Thessaly, was in repute among the ancients as a
place of magic and enchantment; we have testimony in
Milton's own writings before *Comus* that he was alive to
these associations.[32] And none other than Edmund Spenser
had set the precedent for "Haemony" as an English word. [33]

Yet there is a myth about moly that points to a different
etymology of "haemony." In this connection it is worth
noting that our modern dictionaries ignore Keightley's suggestion in favor of an unexplained surmise of their own. They
derive "haemony" from "haimonios" (blood-red). Neither
Webster's New International[34] nor *Funk and Wagnalls' New
Standard*[35] offers any alternative. The etymology as given in
the *Oxford English Dictionary*[36] reads: "f. [Gr. *haimon* skil-
ful or *haimonios* blood-red]." The alternative here explains
an obscurity by an obscurity, for no modern authority is
certain just what this "haimon" (which makes a single appearance in the *Iliad*[37]) means. In a context that is not in the
least suggestive, it seems to praise Scamander's ability in
hunting. Would Milton be making a reference to a word that
occurs only once in Greek literature, when he could have
picked a more standard word for "knowing" if that is what
he meant by "haemony," as John M. Steadman theorized-in
1962?[38] As for "blood-red," it attaches to nothing.

There is, however, a Greek adjective identical in form with "haimon" and derived, like "haimonios," from "haima" (blood) that Milton may well have had in mind if he knew the myth told of moly by Eustathius, the Homeric scholiast.

Eustathius[39] credits the myth to "Alexander the Paphian." One of the giants, Picoloos, having been routed by Zeus, fled to Circe's island and assaulted her. The Sun came to his daughter's rescue and slew the giant. From the blood that overflowed on the ground, a plant sprang up, to be named moly after the memorable struggle ("molos") that had taken place. "The blossom is milk-white because of the bright sun; and the root black because the giant's blood was black, or because of Circe's terror." That Milton had read this account in Eustathius is very likely. He frequently cites Eustathius in his Pindaric marginalia.[40] He used the 1560 Basle reprint of the 1542–50 Rome edition of the *Commentarii*,[41] to which the serious student of Homer refers as inevitably as the serious student of Virgil refers to the *Commentarii* of Servius Grammaticus.

With the introduction of this piece of evidence, the affinity between haemony and moly acquires its coping stone. Milton, it can be plausibly urged, was remembering the bloody[42] origin of haemony's prototype when he gave his plant its name. It would not be the first nor the last time he indulged a fondness for recondite allusion. The scholiast provided the cue by following his account of Picoloos with the remark, "The poet does not say what men call moly, since it is unknown to them." Here was an invitation to supply that deficiency, to appoint a mortal name for moly.[43] "He call'd it Haemony . . . . " At the same time the poet of *Comus* had set free the magical connotations of the ancient name for Thessaly.

Of course, haemony is still not moly, and a new name was required for that reason. In a final review of the passage, however, on a literal plane, one finds little that moly cannot be called on to elucidate. The phrase "but of divine effect" merely echoes the adjective "divinus" already applied to moly in the first elegy. Pliny apart, "a bright golden flowre" is a natural development from the story told by Eustathius. The "darkish" leaf with "prickles on it" elaborates, without impugning, the descriptions of moly in Homer and Pliny. As for the use to which haemony is put—" 'Gainst all inchantments, mildew blast, or damp / Or gastly furies apparition"— Todd[44] reminds us by a quotation from Wierus that moly was known in the Middle Ages as "fuga daemonum." Were we to isolate Milton's lines and forget who wrote them, we could even clear up the mystery of "another Countrey" by harking back to this same plant. The other country is Circe's island, the scene of Picoloos' fertile death. The words "in another Countrey Bore a bright golden flowre, but not in this soyl" could be a way of indicating that the plant *grows* in another country, not "here." There, in that other country, the dull swains do their treading.

No doubt, this is to be too literal, for there are signs that the passage holds what Coleridge called "an interior meaning." These signs are independent of any guess as to Milton's sources. At the same time one may conservatively find it probable that if the young poet at Horton was being influenced by the myth of moly's origin, the allegorical interpretation[45] which Eustathius gives first, wrought more deeply still. It may even be that the scholiast's emphasis on the *kakopatheia* which ensues from moly (*paideia*) occasioned the prickles of haemony.[46]

At all events, the moment when the Attendant Spirit offered his protection to the brothers was a fitting moment to veil symbolically some appropriate truth, an opportunity which the moral earnestness of the poet was not likely to let slip. He ventured therefore upon an allegory in little within the larger allegory of his masque. The venture is not completely graceful. That he had difficulties with it the Cambridge manuscript and the passage's still imperfect syntax show. When he next employed the figure of a plant, he would attempt less and make it plain that he was being figurative.[47]

What, then, do the thirteen verses signify? James Holly Hanford found in them the "Platonic doctrine of virtue."[48]

He took "another Countrey" as a strictly geographical
reference to southern Europe, the home of ancient and
modern culture, as contrasted with those northern climes
(notably England) where genius does not flourish. But these
suggestions, applied to what the Attendant Spirit actually
says, yield neither a clear nor a thoroughly consistent
allegory. There have been a number of similar proposals in
recent years, along secular or philosophical lines,[49] but the
Spirit commenced the poem with an unmistakably nonpagan
reference to those who "after this mortal change" attain "the
palace of Eternity" (10,14). Jon S. Lawry in 1968[50] made
the general comment, "Christian salvation is so heavily inti-
mated in the myth that it dissolves the impression of pure
abstractness or aestheticism." We are invited to consider that
at the present juncture an even stronger ethical influence
than Platonism is operating.

So Coleridge thought, and the interpretation he set forth
in a letter to a friend should be given serious attention.[51] It is
true that Coleridge's exposition is a little too rigid, and his
analysis of the word "haemony"[52] Professor Hanford[53]
justly laid aside as untenable. But the one poet set the other
poet's lines brilliantly aglow with meaning when he saw in
them a fable of Christian redemption. "This soil" becomes
(to quote "Lycidas") this "mortal soil"—man's life here on
earth, and the plant the favor from on high which only a
virtuous few are willing and able to maintain amid trial and
suffering until "haemony" blossoms for them in heaven.

Everything fits lucently into place. The notion of life as a
hard pilgrimage ending for the righteous in the fruit of
heaven goes back to Hebrews.[54] It has even been claimed that
there is a connection between the imperiled Lady and a verse
in Revelation (12:6): "And the woman fled into the
wilderness, where she hath a place prepared of God."[55] The
poet of *Comus* was affirming anew such sentiments as these
of Richard Hooker:

> If they that labour in this harvest should respect but the present
> fruit of their painful travel, a poor encouragement it were unto them

to continue therein all the days of their life. But their reward is great in heaven; the crown of righteousness which shall be given them in that day is honourable. The fruit of their industry then shall they reap with full contentment and satisfaction, but not till then.[56]

The allegory is not only appropriate to the dramatic situation; it harmonizes beautifully with the first part of the prologue and the concluding couplets of the epilogue. Milton, while dedicating his poem to two virtues in particular,[57] was hymning virtue at large. To quote the prologue more amply, the Attendant Spirit speaks of

> .... the crown that Vertue gives
> After this mortal change, to her true Servants
> Amongst the enthron'd gods on Sainted seats.
> Yet som there be that by due steps aspire
> To lay their just hands on that Golden Key
> That opes the Palace of Eternity. [9–14]

When the same heaven-sent emissary comes to tell of haemony, he has changed his metaphors, but not his theme. This humble, unsightly plant does not itself signify virtue, but has some connection[58] with the grace given those who are virtuous.

> Com Lady while Heaven lends us grace,
> Let us fly this cursed place. [938–39]

It involves those who accept of it in trial and hardship "in this soil," but it bears (the phrase is George Herbert's) "the next world's bud" ("Sunday," l. 2).

While Milton here, as everywhere in the masque, casts the veil of his art over his religious faith, the ultimate implication must be that haemony would never bloom for men, were it not for the Savior's blood. Thus, again "haimon" puts forward its etymological claim, and the phrase "but of divine effect" takes on a new significance. One last conjecture, founded on circumstantial evidence, remains to be developed. Did Milton have, besides moly, a further model for haemony which links it definitely with the saving blood of Christ?

One of the recognized "sources" of *Comus* is the Spenserian pastoral drama by John Fletcher, *The Faithful Shepherdess.* [59] One part of this play which must have drawn Milton's particular attention was the scene in which Clorin the shepherdess is introduced "sorting of herbs and telling the natures of them." It cannot be urged too strenuously that Clorin was the prototype of the "certain Shepherd Lad" and his "simples of a thousand names," as this sorting of herbs was something of a literary convention [60] —Milton may even have been recalling an incident in his own life [61] —but in any case the parallel scene from a drama which contributed so much to *Comus* would inevitably have hovered prominently in the mind which composed the haemony passage.

The "superstitious imagery" of the herbs runs on for thirty-five lines. Clorin apostrophizes:

> You,. . .
>   . . . give me your names, and, next, your hidden power.
> This is the clote, bearing a yellow flower;
> And this, black horehound; both are very good
> For sheep or shepherd bitten by a wood
> Dog's venomed teeth: these rhamnus' branches are,
> Which, stuck in entries, or about the bar
> That holds the door fast, kill all enchantments, charms —
> Were they Medea's verses — that do harms
> To men or cattle: these for frenzy be
> A speedy and a sovereign remedy,
> The bitter wormwood, sage, and marigold,
> Such sympathy with man's good they do hold:
> This tormentil, whose virtue is to part
> All deadly killing poison from the heart:
> And, here, narcissus root, for swellings best:
> Yellow lysimachus, to give sweet rest
> To the faint shepherd, killing, where it comes,
> All busy gnats, and every fly that hums:
> For leprosy, darnel and celandine,
> With calamint, whose virtues do refine
> The blood of man, making it free and fair
> As the first hour it breathed, or the best air:
> Here, other two; but your rebellious use

Is not for me, whose goodness is abuse;
Therefore, foul standergrass, from me and mine
I banish thee, with lustful turpentine;
You that entice the veins and stir the heat
To civil mutiny, scaling the seat
Our reason moves in, and deluding it
With dreams and wanton fancies, till the fit
Of burning lust be quench'd, by appetite
Robbing the soul of blessedness and light:
And thou, light varvin, too, thou must go after,
Provoking easy souls to mirth and laughter.[62]

And so the long enumeration came to an end, surely not
without having proved suggestive to the poet of *Comus*. One
could begin to align certain drifting similitudes, but there is
little profit in this. What *can* be important is that in
Fletcher's list of fifteen virtuous plants only one is described
as having the special virtue for which the brothers require
haemony, the power to protect from enchantments: "These
rhamnus' branches are, / Which . . . kill all enchantments,
charms . . . . " But I have been quoting from a modern text.
In the only editions of *The Faithful Shepherdess* available to
Milton, there was a further, fortuitous reason for him to
pause over this plant rhamnus (or "ramnus," for the older
spelling sometimes omitted the breathing).[63] The word had
been misprinted. Milton faced the necessity of making sense
out of either: "These ramuus branches are," [64] or "These
ramuns branches are."[65] The eighteenth-century editors of
Beaumont and Fletcher, aware that something was wrong,
proved superior to the small correction called for by
substituting ingenious but tangential readings of their own.[66]
By Warton's day the branches had become "ramson's
branches,"[67] and as ramson was undeniably a plant,[68] the
editorial duty of getting an intelligible text seemed fulfilled.
It was not until 1843 that Alexander Dyce restored the
proper reading.

Whichever misprint the poet who was to write *Comus*
encountered, he did not need to be one of the most learned
young classicists in England to realize what had happened,

that a letter had been reversed or transposed. The nature of
the misprint is such that the most unscholarly reader with
common sense and the curiosity to investigate could soon
evolve the required adjustment. But, being what he was,
Milton had met with the Greek word "rhamnos," perhaps
even remembered that the inexhaustible Pliny had devoted a
chapter to this rhamnus, "inter genera ruborum."[69]

It is even possible that Milton's acquaintance with plants
and plant lore enabled him to recognize Fletcher's allusion at
once. But this is an idle speculation, worth bringing forward
only in connection with the discovery that made Warton call
Milton "a student of Botany."[70] Warton noted an extraordinary correspondence, extending to verbal detail, between
the description of the marvelous fig tree in the ninth book of
Paradise Lost (1099–113)—the tree from which Adam and
Eve took leaves "to gird their waste"—and the account of
this tree to be found in Gerard's *Herball.*[71] It looks on the
whole like a demonstrable fact that, on this occasion at least,
Milton drew material from the most famous of English
herbals.

At the time the poet was engaged on *Comus,* the second
edition of John Gerard's *Herball, or Generall Historie of
Plantes* was yet fresh from the press. The first edition, "the
folio volume which has made Gerard's name a household
word,"[72] had appeared in December, 1597, to be recognized
as "what was in English the greatest botanical work of the
sixteenth century."[73] When Michael Drayton, writing about
his own Warwickshire, wished to indicate the infinite variety
of that country's flora, he listed some specimens, and said:

Of these most helpful hearbs yet tell we but a few,
To those unnumbred sorts of Simples here that grew.
Which justly to set downe, even *Dodon* short doth fall;
Nor skillful Gerard, yet, shall ever find them all.[74]

The great Dutch botanist Rembert Dodoens had furnished
"skillful Gerard" with the basis for his *Herball.* Gerard died
in 1612. In October, 1633,[75] his celebrated herbal was

offered to the public in a new edition, "very much enlarged and emended by Thomas Johnson."

The phytographically curious contemporary who referred to this lately published work could have read about several sorts of rhamnus. Chapter 28 of book III gives an account "Of Ramme or Harts Thorne," while "Buck-Thorne or laxative Ram" is treated in chapter 30.[76] But it is the intervening chapter which has the best chance of catching the eye: "Of Christes Thorne." Rhamnus "kills all enchantments," Fletcher said, and Christ's-thorn is a rhamn, though it went under a third name, too. Gerard proceeds, according to his formula:

Of Christes Thorne. Chap. 29

*The description

Christs Thorn or Ram of Lybia is a very tough and hard shrubby bush, growing up sometimes unto the height of a little tree,[77] having very long and sharpe pricklie branches: but the thornes that grow about the leaves are lesser, and not so prickly as the former. The leaves are small, broad, and almost round, somewhat sharpe pointed; first of a darke greene colour, and then somewhat reddish. The floures grow in clusters at the top of the stalks of a yellow colour: the husks wherein the seeds be contained, are flat and broad, very like unto small bucklers as hard as wood, wherein are contained three or foure thin and flat seeds, like the seed of Line or Flaxe.

*The place

This Thorne groweth in Lybia; it is better esteemed of in the countery of Cyrene than is their Lote tree, as *Pliny* affirmeth. Of this shrub *Diphilus Siphnius* in *Athenaeus* in his 14 booke maketh mention, saying, that hee did verie often eat of the same in Alexandria that beautiful citie.

Petrus Bellonius[78] who travelled over the Holy Land, saith, that this shrubbie thorne *Paliuros* was the thorne wherewith they crowned our Saviour Christ: his reason for the proofe hereof is this, that in Iudaea there was not any thorne so common, so pliant, or so full of cruell sharpe prickles. It groweth throughout the whole countrey in such abundance, that it is their common feull to burne; yea so common with them there, as our Gorsse, Brakes, and broome is here with us. *Iosephus* in his first booke of Antiquities, and 11 chap. saith,[79] that this Thorne hath the most sharpe prickles of any other; and therfore that Christ might be the more tormented, the Iewes rather tooke this than any other. Of which I have a small tree growing in my garden, that I have brought foorth by sowing of the seede.[80]

The inference readily presents itself that here in Gerard is the further model for haemony, and with it a linking of elements tending in the allegorical direction pointed by Coleridge. In this account of Christ's-thorn Milton could have found both a physical and a spiritual model for his own plant.

> The leaf was darkish, and had prickles on it,
> But in another Countrey, as he said,
> Bore a bright golden flowre, but not in this soyl.....[631–33]

We may fancy for the moment that "he" is Gerard.[81] Of course, the prickles on the leaf and the golden flower come too directly to reveal anything about the protean workings of a poet's mind, but the case of "darkish" is different: Milton has compressed into one word Gerard's ten—"first of a darke greene colour, and then somewhat reddish." To go still further on the literal plane, this counterpart to haemony bears a golden flower "in another Countrey" (namely, Libya), "but not in this soyl" (England), as the rhamnus native to England is a different plant, and bears no flower that can be called "bright golden." This straining of the parallel, however, serves a purpose only as a reminder that, as regards the present investigation, it is the name, with what has been written around the name, that counts, not the plant back of the name. The cluster of potential associations surrounding "rhamnus" was not likely to be impaired by the fact (often very obvious) that one writer meant by "rhamnus" something totally outside the consciousness of another writer who used the same word.

This point can be put to immediate use toward accounting for:

> . . . the dull swayn
> Treads on it daily with his clouted shoon. [634–35]

Milton undoubtedly had his allegorical reasons for saying
this, but he may at the same time have been recollecting an
incident in one of the idylls of Theocritus. As has been
suggested, the poet in his reading of the classics would have
met with the Greek word "rhamnos." It is, moreover, a
common experience for students of foreign languages to
recall precisely where an unusual word has occurred.
Theocritus mentions "rhamnos" but once. In the Fourth
Idyll, the goatherd Battus steps on a thorn, whereupon his
fellow goatherd Corydon tells him: "When you go off to the
mountain, go not shoeless, Battus, for in the mountains
rhamnus and prickly shrubs abound."[82] Was Milton uncon-
sciously responding to this passage when he wrote about the
dull swain treading with his clouted shoon? His intimacy with
Theocritus lives in all the poems composed at Hammersmith
or Horton.[83]

We are concerned, then, with rhamnus, alias Christ's-thorn,
alias paliuros. Three names, each with a literary past peculiar
to itself, are connected in Gerard. And there is reason to
suppose Milton's interest in one of these names led him to
Gerard, where, in the manifest fact that Christ's-thorn was
deemed a species of rhamnus, new and sacrosanct associations gathered round the mere magic of Fletcher's plant
(and the something more than mere magic of Homer's). Here
was inspiration of a quite literal sort, but—and this is a more
momentous point—here also was the germ of allegory. It
developed along conventional Christian lines, exquisite in its
simplicity once the reader has recognized its presence.[84]

As regards the bush's supernatural powers, "The Vertues"
credited to it in Gerard are strictly "med'cinal."[85] Fletcher's
source would have been another herbal, Henry Lyte's, which
states: "Some hold, that the branches or bowes of Rhamnus
stickt at men's dores and windowes, do drive away sorcerie,
and inchantments that Witches and Sorcerers do use against
men."[86] It seems that rhamnus was already a magical plant

before it acquired the sanctity of being associated with the Savior. The impetus given its believed power by this association may easily be imagined. While other plants have at various times been proposed for the crown of thorns,[87] this bush under one or another of its names held the ascendancy in Milton's day.[88] The skeptical might, like Sir Thomas Browne, consider such inquiries vain,[89] but they thought so in the face of a venerable and widespread legend. And the legend, in superimposing a new name on rhamnus, or paliuros, inevitably hallowed and enlarged the plant's classic virtue every time it was mentioned.[90]

Thus, this last hypothesis explains anew why haemony was said to be "of divine effect" and points to the connection between haemony and Christ's blood. By way of summing up one cannot do better than to quote from the *Travels of Sir John Mandeville,* which tells of no less than four crowns scornfully bestowed on Jesus the night of His trial. This is what is related of the first of these crowns:

> . . . And ye shall understande that our Lord in that night that he was taken, he was led into a garden, and there he was examined sharply, & there the Jewes crowned him with a crown of abbespine braunches that grew in the same garden & set it on his head so fast, that the blood came downe by many places of his visage, necke, and shoulders, and therefore hath the abbespine many vertues, for he that beareth a braunche of it about him, no thunder, nor any maner of tempest may hurt him, nor the house that it is in may no evill ghost come, nor in no place where it is.[91]

It is a fascinating assumption, at least, that the Homeric plant was subtly exalted in Milton's mind or (rather) fused with the conception of another and more glorious plant. The very word "haemony" can be viewed as ingeniously exemplifying this blend of two worlds, classical and Christian.

It is not claimed that the conjectures presented here, however well documented, are all true. It is claimed only that each has its appropriateness. As for their disconcerting plurality, we have the lesson of all past study and research that there is no such thing in John Milton as a single influence.

One can easily become impatient with such complications and reject them all. Robert M. Adams has done so. He wishes to simplify. First he simplifies the plant. "All Thyrsis has of the plant is the root."[92] This is not true, as shown by the reference to leaves. "Root" once meant, by extension, the whole plant, as the *OED* and the Columbia *Variorum Commentary* explain.[93] The latter adds, "Homer (*Od.* 10.302-06) mentions the root of moly but also says that the gift of Hermes was the whole plant."

Next Professor Adams gives a simple but illogical explanation of haemony: "temperance." But the brothers presumably already have temperance—it would be an insult to indicate that they did not, and of course it is manifested at great length that their sister does not lack it. Moly often stood for temperance, as Adams shows, but Milton has gone out of his way to put us on notice that haemony is different and better, "more med'cinal."

Finally, Adams refutes himself by quoting the popular and influential "Natale Conti, who speaks of the 'divina clementia . . . quod per munus Ulyssi a Mercurio datum intelligitur.' "[94] Divine mercy—*that* will do very well as the meaning of haemony.

The following is strong only rhetorically:

> The notion that he gave it the name 'haemony' as a way of referring not only to Pikolous' blood but to Christ's seems ingeniously esoteric; could Milton really have expected the Earl of Bridgewater and his guests to make on their own the not-even-suggested connection with Eustathius' *Commentaries*, and, supposing they made it, could he have doubted that the equating of Christ with a monster caught in the act of rape would have caused them anything but disquiet? Scarcely less extravagant is the assumption that they would all have read Fletcher's masque and Gerard's *Herbal* and would remember that the rhamnus misprinted in Fletcher was the same as the Christ's Thorn described in Gerard and that Christ's Thorn bore a vague resemblance to haemony.[95]

All this is beside the point of making a necessary separation between what Milton from his reading associated and what he could reasonably expect others to understand from the deliberately suggestive words that he used. Also, there must be a separation between hearers and the leisurely reader ("Where more is meant than meets the ear"–"Il Penseroso," 120). If Adams had studied the Bridgewater manuscript, he would have discovered that six of the thirteen lines–632–37–were not presented at all on that festive night of September 29, 1634. Either they were cut, presumably by Lawes, or they had not yet been written. Thus, there was no mention of "another Countrey," of "a bright golden flowre," of the dull swain treading, or even of moly. (And eighteenth-century stage adaptations gradually eliminated the rest of the passage.[96]) Yet Adams asserts (probably from examination of the Trinity manuscript only), "Not one of [the textual alterations in *Comus*] is aimed at deepening or elaborating the allegory or symbolism" ![97]

The reader, with the full passage before him, *can* get its thinly disguised Christian message–and without browsing in herbals or Homeric commentaries or *The Faithful Shepherdess*. Coleridge got it in 1802. John A. Himes, independently of Coleridge,[98] got it in 1921. All that is required to take the hint is acquaintance with the Greek word for "blood," as rooted in many English words. Milton never asked less in the way of learning, whatever he himself brought to the passage. He does expect a bit of contextual thoughtfulness. He mixes magic and meaning.[99] On the whole, his plant metaphor is as evident as Spenser's:

> Revele to me the sacred noursery
> Of Vertue, which with you doth there remaine,
> Where it in silver bowre does hidden ly
> From view of men, and wicked worlds disdaine;
> Since it at first was by the gods with paine
> Planted in earth, being deriv'd at furst
> From heavenly seedes of bounty soveraine,
> And by them long with carefull labour nurst,
> Till it to ripenesse grew, and forth to honour burst.[100]

NOTES

1. *Sighs upon the Death of Queen Anne,* p. xlv. Quoted by Raymond D. Havens, *The Influence of Milton on English Poetry* (Cambridge, Mass., 1922), p. 422. I seem to have been the first, in my *Milton Dictionary* (New York and London, 1961), p. 71, to trace the title *Comus* back to John Toland, 1698, and Elijah Fenton, 1725.

2. *New Memoirs of the Life and Poetical Works of Mr. John Milton* (London, 1740), p. 15. Dr. Johnson's statement is the most succinct: "The fiction is derived from Homer's Circe . . . " (*Lives of the English Poets,* ed. G.B. Hill, Oxford, 1905, I, 92).

3. *Odyssey,* 10.135ff.; *Metamorphoses,* 14.241-307.

4. Milton's indebtedness to Plato and Spenser in his treatment of the chastity theme was analyzed nearly half a century ago by James H. Hanford, "The Youth of Milton," *Studies in Shakespeare, Milton and Donne,* by Members of the English Department of the University of Michigan (New York, 1925), pp. 137-43. As Herbert Agar (*Milton and Plato,* Princeton, 1928, p. 30) conveniently summarized, "The whole of *Comus* is permeated with . . . Spenserian Platonism." See, further, B.A. Wright's edition of the *Shorter Poems* (London, 1938); Irene Samuel, *Plato and Milton* (Ithaca, 1947); John Arthos, *On a Mask Presented at Ludlow-Castle* (Ann Arbor, 1954), pp. 27-50, and "Milton, Ficino and the *Charmides,*" *S. Ren,* 6 (1959), 261-74; Sears Jayne, "The Subject of Milton's Ludlow Mask," originally *PMLA,* 74 (1959), 533-43, revised in *A Maske at Ludlow: Essays on Milton's "Comus,"* ed. John S. Diekhoff (Cleveland, 1968), pp. 165-87; J.B. Leishman, *Milton's Minor Poems* (Pittsburgh, 1969), pp. 174-246; A.S.P. Woodhouse, *The Heavenly Muse: A Preface to Milton* (Toronto, 1972), pp. 56-83.

5. Harris F. Fletcher, "Milton's Copy of Gesner's Heraclides, 1544," *JEGP,* 47 (1948), 182-87.

6. According to the analysis of John T. Shawcross, "Certain Relationships of the Manuscripts of *Comus,*" *Papers of the Bibliographical Society of America,* 54 (1960), 38-56; "The Manuscript of *Comus:* An Addendum," ibid., 293-94.

7. The book was issued from Basle, Oporini, with some pieces by others added but not translated into Latin: "una cum aliis, lectu dignissimis." There is no point in following Gesner's faulty reasoning in his Epistola Nuncupatoria about the authorship of the *Allegoriae.* I retain the name "Heraclides" for convenience. See Georg Wissowa, William Kroll, *Paulys Real-Encyclopädie der Classischen Altertumswissenschaft,* Neue Bearbeitung (Stuttgart, 1912), VIII^1, s.v. "Herakleides," the 45th of the name, p. 482: "Falschlich gab man dem H[erakleiden] früher, nach einem Irrtum Conr. Gesners, die *Allegoriai Homerikai* des Herakleitos." Information about the latter Heraclitus (ibid., 508) is wholly deductive; but his citation of Alexander of Ephesos advances him into the first century A.D.

8. E.g., to show that Diomedes, with Athene or Wisdom as his ally,

was wounding Folly when he wounded Aphrodite (*Iliad*, 5: 330ff.), Heraclides does not hesitate to connect "aphrodite" with "aphrosune." Any Greek lexicon will be eloquent on the difference between "aphros" and "aphron."

9. *Comus*, 513–16. My quotations from *Comus* are based on the 1645 text, as given in the *Poetical Works*, ed. H.C. Beeching (London, 1900), which results in a difference of one in line numbering as compared to 1673 (line 167, "Whom thrift keeps up about his Country gear," having been dropped in 1673), which not every scholar realizes—e.g., T. P. Harrison, Jr., in *PQ*, 22 (1943), 251.

10. *Comus*, 447–50. The thorough classicism of the first three of these lines is more than a matter of feeling. Emmanuel Des Essarts, *De Veterum Poetarum tum Graeciae, tum Romae apud Miltonem Imitatione* (Paris, 1871), p. 22, pointed out that "unconquer'd Virgin" translates literally Aeschylus's "admetas admeta," verse 149, *Supplices*. In my *Yet Once More: Verbal and Psychological Pattern in Milton* (New York, 1953), p. 12, I pointed to the link with "Palladis invicta virtus" of Prolusio I, Milton's *Works*, ed. Frank A. Patterson et al. (New York, 1931–38), XII, 124.

11. "sophias ouraniou mustes gegonos."

12. Gesner's text depends on the *editio princeps* of Aldus, Venice, 1505, which stops short with the word "pneousai" at the end of cap. 71, p. 94, of the modern B. G. Teubner edition, Heracliti *Quaestiones Homericae* (Leipzig, 1910). The one other printed text then available to Milton, that issued in Geneva, 1586, as an appendix to the *Odyssey*, had the same deficiency. (See Francis Oelmann's Prolegomena to the Teubner *Quaestiones Homericae*.) So the poet of *Comus* missed the explanation, which immediately follows in the fuller text, of the plant moly as the symbol of prudence ("phronesis"), a gift, like haemony, reserved for the elect few. But Eustathius had a similar message. See below.

Hanford, not having examined Milton's purchase, made a mistake in calling "Heraclitus Ponticus" to witness the statement: "The myth of Circe had long been established as a Platonic symbol of the degradation of the soul through sensuality" ("The Youth of Milton," p. 139). Michael Psellos ought to have been cited, instead. See just below.

13. Contrary to the assertion in [Louis G.] Michaud's *Biographie universelle ancienne et moderne*, 2nd ed. (Paris, [1880]), XXXIV, 446.

14. Strictly speaking, "This occurs when a writing is spiritually expounded, which even in the literal sense by the things signified likewise gives intimation of higher matters belonging to the eternal glory;" Dante's *Convivio*, trans. William Walrond Jackson (Oxford, 1909), Tractate 2, 1.74.

15. *The Road to Xanadu* (Boston, 1927), p. 39.

16. See a parallel lesson in George Sandys' *Ovid's Metamorphosis English'd, Mythologiz'd, and Represented in Figures* (London, 1632), pp. 480–81, quoted in Merritt Y. Hughes, general editor, *A Variorum*

Commentary on the Poems of John Milton, II, *The Minor English Poems*, ed. A.S.P. Woodhouse and Douglas Bush, (New York, 1972), 932. In 1566 William Adlington similarly interpreted *The Golden Ass*: "Verily under the wrap of this transformation is taxed the life of mortal men, when as we suffer our minds so to be drowned in the sensual lusts of the flesh and the beastly pleasure thereof (which aptly may be called the violent confection of witches) that we lose wholly the use of reason and virtue, which properly should be in a man, and play the parts of brute and savage beasts." Lucius Apuleius, *The Golden Ass*, with Adlington's English translation revised by S. Gaselee (London, 1915, Loeb Library), p. xvi.

17.   *Comus*, 68–69, 72–77. Cf. Spenser's *Faerie Queene*, 2.12.86–87.

18.   Edward G. Ainsworth, "Reminiscences of the *Orlando Furioso* in *Comus*," *MLN*, 46 (1931), 91. Milton had classical precedent for the transformation into several kinds of beasts: Virgil's *Aeneid*, 7.15–20. Readers of *The Scholemaster* (1570) were misinformed: " . . . Homer, like a learned Poete, doth feyne, that *Circes*, by pleasant inchantmentes, did turne men into beastes, some into Swine, some into Asses, some into Foxes, some into Wolues etc . . . " (Roger Ascham, *English Works*, ed. W. A. Wright [Cambridge, 1904], p. 226.) Newton guessed the change was confined to the head or countenance for the convenience of the stage ("like Bottom," remarks David Masson, in his edition of the *Poetical Works* [London, 1874], III, 399); the crucial line, "All other parts remaining as they were," does have the prosiness of a practical afterthought. Still, as Milton was probably aware, William Browne's *Inner Temple Masque*, likewise based on the Circe myth, called for completely metamorphosed antimaskers. Cf. however the *Argonautica* of Apollonius Rhodius, IV, 672ff. A good literary source for these non-Homeric variations would be Spenser's description of Maleger's troop of the sins of the five senses (*Faerie Queene*, 2.11.8.10ff.) that attack Alma's citadel of Temperance. As Milton appears to have been influenced by a picture elsewhere (Henry John Todd's variorum edition of the *Poetical Works*, London, 1801, V, ver. 561; also III, 38), it is worth noting that the Greeks, in illustrations of the Circe myth on amphorae, portrayed Odysseus' men, Egyptian fashion, with only the heads of beasts. (For plates and commentary consult ch. 3 of J. E. Harrison's *Myths of the Odyssey in Art and Literature* [London, 1882]; cf. Sir Edwin Landseer's painting *Comus with His Crew*.) Five years before, the Nativity Ode mentioned, among other Egyptian deities, "the Dog *Anubis*" (212), meaning the dog-headed Anubis. In George Sandys' *Relation of a Journey begun An. Dom. 1610* (2nd ed., London, 1621), a book which there is reason to believe the poet of *Comus* had read (see D. Bush, "Notes on Milton's Classical Mythology," *SP*, 28, [1931], 262–63), occurs this statement of Mahometan belief (p. 58): "Then shall another blast restore beauty to the world, and life unto all that ever lived. The good shall have shining and glorified faces; but the bad, the countenances of dogs and swine, and such like uncleane creatures." There is a suggestive passage

in the *Comus, sive Phagesiposia Cimmeria: Somnium* of Erycius Puteanus (Oxford, 1634) which led Alfred Stern, *Milton und seine Zeit* (Leipzig, 1877), part 1, p. 230, to declare: "Ganz von selbst führte eine Stelle in Puteanus Arbeit (p. 26) dazu, den Mythus von Circe mit der Gestalt des Comus in Verbindung zu setzen." Circe herself is nowhere mentioned in Puteanus's narrative, albeit (for no evident reason) a character in one of the interludes further on (pp. 157–74) bears that name; but the passage to which Stern alludes does portray Comus, the pleasure God, as surrounded by masked figures. A character explains, " . . . his vinclis oris dentiumque feritas coercetur. Quos homines putas, lupi sunt, et e Daunia, Getuliave monstra morsu infesta" (pp. 25–26). Finally, the Lady of *Comus*, Alice Egerton, having danced in the Circean masque by Aurelian Townshend, *Tempe Restored* (1632), the "beast-headed costumes designed by Inigo Jones" for it "may have been borrowed from the Revels storeroom for the antimasque of Circe's son in *Comus*": see the plate following p. 96 in John G. Demaray, *Milton and the Masque Tradition* (Cambridge, Mass., 1968).

19.   King James I of Aragon at a formal assembly "rose and began a text of Scripture" (Edward K. Rand, *Ovid and His Influence* [New York, 1925], p. 136)–only it turned out to be a line from the *Ars Amatoria*, the same work which two centuries afterwards, in 1467, a monk of Paris copied "ad laudem et gloriam Virginis Mariae" (Clyde B. Cooper, *Some Elizabethan Opinions of the Poetry and Character of Ovid* [Menasha, Wisconsin], 1914, p. 11). Outstanding studies include Domenico Comparetti, *Vergil in the Middle Ages*, trans. E.F.M. Benecke (London, 1895); Douglas Bush, *Mythology and the Renaissance Tradition in English Poetry* (rev. ed., New York, 1963); Davis P. Harding, *Milton and the Renaissance Ovid* (Urbana, 1946); Jean Seznec, *The Survival of the Pagan Gods* (New York, 1953); Dewitt T. Starnes and Ernest W. Talbert, *Classical Myth and Legend in Renaissance Dictionaries* (Chapel Hill, 1955); Edgar Wind, *Pagan Mysteries of the Renaissance* (New Haven, 1959); Hugo Rahner, *Greek Myths and Christian Mystery* (London, 1963).

20.   Ch. Zervos, *Michael Psellos* (Paris, 1919), p. 92.

21.   Elegia I, 87–88; Prolusio VII (*Works*, XII, 280). Cf. Elegia VI, 73.

22.   Ascham, *English Works*, pp. 225–26.

23.   *Elizabethan Drama 1558-1642* (Boston, 1908). II. 134.

24.   "Image, Form, and Theme in *A Mask*," in Diekhoff, p. 129. (A chapter from *Images and Themes in Five Poems by Milton*, Cambridge, Mass., 1957.)

25.   Butcher and Lang.

26.   Charles Lamb, when he wrote *The Adventures of Ulysses* for children, confused the two plants. See W. Bell's edition of *Comus* (London, 1890), p. xix; or Lamb's *Works*, ed. E. V. Lucas (London, 1903), III, 218.

27.   *Milton's Literary Milieu* (Chapel Hill, 1939), pp. 86–87.

28.   Pliny, *Naturalis historia*, XXV, 4(8).

29. Edward Phillips, "The Life of John Milton," (1694) in Helen Darbishire (ed.), *The Early Lives of Milton* (London, 1932), p. 60.

30. (Ed.), *The Poems of John Milton* (London, 1859), I, 108. Keightley was followed immediately by Immanuel Schmidt, *Milton's Comus, übersetzt und mit einer erläuternden Abhandlung* (Berlin, 1860), p. 21.

31. For an extensive list, see Eugene Tavenner, *Studies in Magic from Latin Literature* (New York, 1916), p. 20, n. 98. The *locus classicus* perhaps for the tradition is the opening of book II of *The Golden Ass* of Apuleius.

32. Viz., his apostrophe to the university beadle (Elegia II, 7–8): "O dignus tamen Haemonio juvenescere succo, Dignus in Aesonios vivere posse dies," and the rhetorical query in the Sixth Prolusion: "Ecqua me *Thessala* saga magico perfudit unguento?" (*Works*, XII, 240). The allusion to the story of Medea who (according to Ovid, *Met.*, 7.219ff.) mounted a chariot and toured Thessaly nine days and nights collecting the simples that, compounded, would restore Aeson his youth is a reminder that Haemonia was the land of magic because it was the land of *magic plants*. "On peut même dire que toute la sorcellerie se fonde essentiellement sur la science de ces propriétés des herbes," writes Angelo de Gubernatis, *La Mythologie des plantes* (Paris), I (1878), 172; again, ibid., 218: "La science des magiciens est essentiellement une science botanique." Under the circumstances, nothing could be more logical than the name "haemony" for a magic plant.

33. "About the grassie bancks of Haemony . . . " ("Astrophel," l. 3). An effort has been made by S. R. Watson, *N&Q*, 178 (1940), 260–61, to relate the two poems and even their flowers, but these latter are alike only in that both are mysterious.

34. 2nd ed. Springfield, Mass., 1934. The 3rd edition, the 1961 vulgarization, lacks (of course!) the word, as do *The Random House Dictionary* (New York, 1966) and *The American Heritage Dictionary* (New York, 1969).

35. New York, 1937. I have been wrongly described as "favouring" this derivation: John Carey and Alastair Fowler, eds., *The Poems of John Milton* (London, 1968), p. 207.

36. Oxford, 1933.

37. V, 49. The grammarians associate the word with "daemon." Henry Stuart Jones's revision of *Liddell and Scott's Greek-English Lexicon* (Oxford, 1925), conjectures, s.v.: "dub. sens., perh. eager." Georg Autenrieth, *A Homeric Dictionary*, ed. and trans. Robert P. Keep (New York, 1877), wonders if it is cognate with "amans." For Renaissance definitions, see Steadman's article (n.38 below).

38. "Milton's *Haemony*: Etymology and Allegory," *PMLA*, 77 (1962), 200–07. Another objection is that this obscure "haimon" was bound to get mixed up with the much more recognizable "haimon" cited in my next paragraph. In a Greek context, it is not likely that Milton is wandering off into Hebrew "aman," as Sacvan Bercovitch

proposes, "Milton's 'Haemony': Knowledge and Belief," *HLQ*, 33 (1970), 351-59.

39. (Archiepiscopus Thessalonicensis), *Commentarii ad Homeri Odysseam* (Leipzig, 1825), I, 381.

40. See the Patterson-Fogle index to the Columbia *Works* for these references to vol. XVIII.

41. See Harris F. Fletcher, "Milton's Homer," *JEGP*, 38 (1939), 229-32.

42. Milton knew Euripides with the thoroughness of the textual critic, and the word "haimon" makes a significant appearance early in the *Hecuba* (90). Hecuba has had a strange prophetic dream, ill-omened, "For I saw a dappled hind in the bloody claw of a wolf." The use of the dative, giving what, transcribed, is "haemony," has a chance interest all its own.

43. Following the pattern of Homer in the case of Briareos and Aigaion (*Iliad*, 1.403-04), "chalkis" and "kumindis." (ibid., 14.291).

44. H. J. Todd (ed.), *Comus* (Canterbury, 1798), p. 91.

45. Hermes, as usual, represents logos; moly, *paideia*. Education, beginning with the black root of ignorance, culminates after many trials in the milk-white flower of radiant knowledge.

46. Or perhaps the association with "molos."

47. "*Fame* is no plant that grows on mortal soil," etc. ("Lycidas," ll.78ff.) See William G. Riggs, "The Plant of Fame in 'Lycidas,' " *Milton Studies*, IV (1972), 151-61.

48. "Haemony," *TLS*, Nov. 3, 1932, p. 815. Cf. *A Milton Handbook*, 3rd ed. (New York, 1939), pp. 159-60.

49. See the useful summaries in Demaray, 169-70; *Variorum Commentary*, II, 932-38.

50. *The Shadow of Heaven: Matter and Stance in Milton's Poetry* (Ithaca, N.Y.), p. 71.

51. Letter to William Sotheby, Sept. 10, 1802. I quote from Joseph A. Wittreich, Jr. (ed.), *The Romantics on Milton* (Cleveland, 1970), p. 166:

> They [the commentators] thought little of Milton's platonizing Spirit—who wrote nothing without an interior meaning. 'Where more is meant, than meets the ear' [*Il Penseroso*, l.120] is true of himself beyond all writers. He was so great a Man, that he seems to have considered Fiction as profane, unless where it is consecrated by being emblematic of some Truth / What an unthinking & ignorant man we must have supposed Milton to be, if without any hidden meaning, he had described [it] as growing in such abundance that the dull Swain treads on it daily—& yet as never *flowering*—Such blunders Milton, of all others, was least likely to commit—Do look at the passage—apply it as an Allegory of Christianity, or to speak more precisely of the Redemption by the Cross—every syllable is full of Light!—['] a *small unsightly* Root[']—to the Greeks Folly, to the Jews a stumbling Block—['] The leaf was darkish & had prickles on it[']—If in this Life only we have hope, we are of all men the most

miserable / & [a] score of other Texts–['] But in another country, as he said,
Bore a bright golden Flower'–the exceeding weight of Glory prepared for us
hereafter /–[']but [not] in this soil, unknown, & like esteem'd & the dull
Swain treads on it daily with his clouted shoon['] / The Promises of Redemption offered daily & hourly & to all, but accepted scarcely by any–['] He called
it Haemony [']–Now what is Haemony? *Haima-oinos* Blood-wine. –And he
took the wine & blessed it, & said–This is my Blood– / the great Symbol of the
Death on the Cross.

cf. ibid., p. 283, n. 27. Coleridge's biblical quotations are, in order,
1 Cor. 1:23; 1 Cor. 15:19 (also cited by Milton, *Works*, XV, 224);
2 Cor. 4:17.

52.   We would expect "haemoiny," the diphthong not being one to
vanish.

53.   *TLS*, as above, n. 48.

54.   12:11, and 11:13. See, further, Samuel C. Chew, *The Pilgrimage
of Life* (New Haven, 1962), ch. 7, "Strangers and Pilgrims,"
pp. 174–225.

55.   Alice Lyle Scoufos, "Stock Characters in *Comus*" a paper read at
the MLA Convention in New York, December, 1972, as abstracted in
SCN, 31 (1973), 24.

56.   *Of the Laws of Ecclesiastical Polity*, Everyman's Library, I,
345–46.

57.   According to his own classification (*De Doctrina Christiana*, II.ix,
in *Works*, XVII, 212ff.), *Sobrietas* and *Castitas, Temperantia* being the
larger heading under which these are grouped.

58.   I believe that Milton, when he wrote the passage, fully intended
haemony to signify grace, but at the end of his masque he decided to
have Sabrina play a (mainly lyrical) part and thereby he undercut his
magic plant and appears to have—with her baptism-like drops—one
grace too many. Logically, the magic plant should have been potent
enough to free the Lady from her seat. It is, in the fairy tale of Jorinda
and Joringel to which John Arthos has called attention (*On a Mask
Presented at Ludlow-Castle* p. 48). I quote from *Grimm's Fairy Tales*
(New York, 1944), pp. 339–41. "If anyone came within one hundred
paces of the castle he was obliged to stand still, and could not stir from
the place until she [the witch] bade him be free. But whenever an
innocent maiden came within this circle, she changed her into a bird.
. . . . At last he [Joringel] dreamt one night that he found a blood-red
flower, in the middle of which was a beautiful large pearl; that he
picked the flower and went with it to the castle, and that everything he
touched with the flower was freed from enchantment; he also dreamt
that by means of it he recovered his Jorinda." The dream is fulfilled.
"Swiftly he sprang towards her, touched the cage with the flower, and
also the old woman. She could now no longer bewitch anyone." A.S.P.
Woodhouse tried to solve the problem of Milton's two magics with a
distinction between "actual grace" and "habitual" or "saving grace"
(*Variorum Commentary*, II, 936–37), but this is, needless to say,

difficult territory, not to be trodden too heavily with clouted shoon. I should say that ll. 629-41 constitute an allegory-of-the-moment, sufficient unto itself. At the end Milton returns to the same subject. As long ago as 1899 W. V. Moody was saying, "Yet there can be little doubt that the plant symbolizes Christian grace." *Variorum Commentary*, II, 790.

59.   First Quarto, c. 1610; Second Quarto, 1629; Third Quarto, 1634.

60.   Thomas Warton (in Todd, l. 636) cited Michael Drayton's *Muses' Elysium*, the fifth nymphal, where Clarinax, a hermit, is introduced "his sundry simples sorting," among them, moly, vervaine, and dill (ll. 201-02, 209-10).

61.   His close friend Charles Diodati, being a medical student, may have exhibited to him various healing herbs. See *Epitaphium Damonis*, 150-52:

> Tu mihi percurres medicos, tua gramina, succos
> Helleborumque, humilesque crocos, foliumque hyacinthi,
> Quasque habet ista palus herbas, artesque medentum.

This may be poetic truth only. The literal-minded have inferred that "a certain Shepherd Lad" is Diodati himself.

62.   II.ii.10-44 (in *The Works of Francis Beaumont and John Fletcher*, variorum ed., gen. ed. A. H. Bullen [London, 1908], III, 43-45).

63.   "Rhamnos." "Ram" and "ramme" were common spellings: see the *OED* and below.

64.   First Quarto, Dyce and Bodleian copies (W. W. Greg's textual note, ed. cit., III.44.15).

65.   Later editions (Rev. Alexander Dyce's textual note, in his edition of Beaumont and Fletcher's *Works*, London, II, [1843] 46), and First Quarto, British Museum copy (Greg). See Greg's comment on this Quarto (III, 4): "The only difficulty arises through different copies presenting a number of variant readings, but it will soon be perceived that this is only due to certain copies containing one or more uncorrected sheets."

66.   "Mr. Theobald would read *Raymund's*, and has left us a long Note relating to the History of *Raymund Lilli*, [Lully] the great Philosopher and Chymist, from whom he supposes some Alexipharmick to have taken its Name." Beaumont and Fletcher, *Works*, 1750, III ("printed under the inspection of Mr. Seward"), 127.

67.   Warton quotes the passage in his edition of the *Minor Poems*, (London, 1791), p. 212. His page and volume references show that he used Seward's edition of 1750. Seward, after noting that Theobald "was certainly in a wrong Track," went on to explain: "The true Word, as Mr. Sympson discovered, is *Ramson's*, the *Allium Silvestre* or *Wild Garlick*." The word reappears in *Select Plays of Beaumont and Fletcher* (Glasgow, 1768), II, 20. The notes in Todd at l. 633 of *Comus* are adequate proof of the scant respect given to puzzling texts by

eighteenth-century editors. Seward, for example, would have read, "Bore a bright golden flower, but in this soil / Unknown and light esteem'd." Hurd found "the passage before us . . . certainly corrupt, or, at least, inaccurate." Richard Bentley was not alone.

68.   Though incapable, alas! of sprouting branches, as Sympson and Seward, after identifying the plant as a garlic, might have suspected.

69.   *Naturalis historia*, XXIV, 14.76.

70.   Warton's ed., p. 155.

71.   1st ed., 1597, London, but Warton quotes from the revised *Herball* of 1633 (reprinted, 1636) which Milton probably used. See the aptly italicized excerpts in Warton, pp. 155-56, or Todd, III, 226-27. There were other descriptions of the Indian fig tree available (see Kester Svendsen, *Milton and Science*, Cambridge, Mass., 1956, pp. 31–32), but Gerard's is the verbally closest.

72.   *DNB*, VII, 1100.

73.   J. Reynolds Green, *A History of Botany in the United Kingdom from the Earliest Times to the End of the Nineteenth Century* (London, 1914), p. 34.

74.   *Poly-Olbion*, song 13, ll.231-34.

75.   Johnson's notice "To the Reader" is dated, "From my house on Snow-Hill, Octob. 22, 1633."

76.   *Herball* (1633), pp. 1334 & 1337.

77.   The *Herball* of 1597 read: " . . . hard shrubbie tree, growing up sometimes into the height of a tal tree . . . . "

78.   Pierre Belon (du Mans), *Les Observations de plusieurs singularitez et choses memorables, trouvées en Grece, Asie, Iudëe, Egypte, Arabie, et autres Pays Estranges* (Paris, 1553), p. 147v.

79.   An utterly false reference, the famous unique passage in which Josephus (or an interpolator) mentions Jesus Christ occurring in the third chapter of the eighteenth book and containing no allusion to the crown of thorns. In his preface ("To the Reader"), Johnson spoke of Gerard's "want of sufficient learning," since he was "very little conversant in the writings of the Antients."

80.   Gerard, *Herball* (1633), pp. 1335–36.

81.   Let me take occasion here to express my doubt that the "certain Shepherd Lad" can be—or need be—identified. None of the identifications that have been proposed for him—Diodati, Nathaniel Weld, the Apostle Paul, Jesus Christ, Milton—is especially convincing. (See the Woodhouse–Bush *Variorum Commentary*, II, 929.) He is a nonce device to fit the Attendant Spirit's role of Thyrsis, the devoted servant whose possession of such a wondrous plant must somehow be accounted for. The one distinguishing phrase, "Of small regard to see to," (620) can be explained as part of Milton's—of the Attendant Spirit's—stress on the humbleness and superficial unattractiveness of haemony.

John Arthos, "Milton's Haemony and Virgil's Amellus," *NQ*,

8 (1961), 172, briefly proposed a connection with Georgic 4, 271–8, but where are the "prickles"?

82. Theocritus, Fourth Idyll, 57–58.

83. He borrowed from the First Idyll the name of the skilled singer, Thyrsis. *Comus* has even been called an idyll adapted to the stage ("Ab initio hujus eclogae in scenam inductae," Des Essarts, p. 17).

84. Compare, also, l. 47 of *Comus*, "Bacchus that first from out the purple Grape, / Crush't *the sweet poyson of mis-used Wine*," with the following summary conspicuous at the very end of Gerard's digression on wine (p. 884): "Almighty God for the comfort of mankinde ordained Wine; but decreed withall, That it should be *moderately taken*, for so it is wholesome and comfortable: *but when measure is turned into excesse, it becommeth unwholesome, and a poyson most venomous . . .* [italics added]." This "vinum-venom" line, the "plures crapula quam gladius" theme, was not, needless to say, uncommon. Sir Richard Hawkins on a voyage to hostile South Sea islands found "the enemy less dangerous then the wine," which "overthrew many of my people." "To confirme which my beliefe, I have heard one of our learnedst physitians affirme, that he thought there died more persons in England of drinking wine and using hot spices in their meates and drinkes, then of all other diseases." *The Observations of Sir Richard Hawkins, Knt, in his Voyage into the South Sea in the year 1593*, reprinted from the edition of 1622, ed. C. R. Drinkwater Bethune (London, Hakluyt Society, 1847), pp. 153, 154. Cf. *Paradise Lost*, 11.472ff.

The combination "sweet poyson" has, as one would surmise, a previous history, though even those editors who, by Keightley's complaint, seek to turn Milton into a centoist, do not trace it. "Sweet poison" is to be found in Shakespeare (*King John*, I. i. 213; cf. *Coriolanus*, III.i.157) and, before Shakespeare, in Sidney (*Astrophel and Stella*, 5th song, 2nd stanza, 1. 2). Sir Tophas, in Lyly's *Endymion* (V.ii.19–20) found "love to be, as it was said of in old years, *Dulce venenum*." Burton (*Anatomy of Melancholy*, Everyman's Library, III, 205) Englishes the identical expression from Aeneas Silvius. Giles Fletcher the Elder has "poison sweet" (*Poetry of the English Renaissance*, ed. J. W. Hebel and H. H. Hudson, New York, 1929, p. 210). Bush, *Variorum Commentary*, II, 864, adds Thomas Campion, *Maske in honour of the Lord Hayes* (*Works*, ed. P. Vivian [Oxford, 1909], p. 67, 1.30).

85. "A remedy against poisons" (p. 1336) could be a mistranslation of "contra veneficia" but hardly of "contra venena," which is what Gerard's source (Remberti Dodonaei *Stirpium Historiae Pemptades Sex*, Antwerp, 1583, p. 744) has. Dodonaeus does not mention Christ.

86. *A New Herball*, 1619 (there had been three earlier editions: 1578, 1586, 1595), bk. 6, ch. 29, p. 500, quoted by Thomas P. Harrison, Jr., "The 'Haemony' Passage in *Comus* Again," *PQ*, 22 (1943), 252. Joannes Wierus, *De Praestigiis Daemonum et Incantationibus ac veneficiis Libri Sex* (Basle, 1583), p. 582, following the old division of

rhamnus into three kinds, declared the same: "Rhamni tertii ramum valvis fenestrisve impositum, veneficia omnia depellere, tradit Dioscorides." In the margin reference is made to Pliny and Dioscorides; Pliny does not allude to this virtue, but the Greek physician has been accurately cited. See *Medicorum Graecorum Opera quae exstant*, ed. C. G. Kühn (Leipzig, 1829), XXV, Pedanii Dioscoridis Anazarbei "Peri Iatrikes," I, cap. cxix.

87.   See T. F. Thiselton Dyer, *The Folk-Lore of Plants* (New York, 1889), p. 256.

88.   See the commentators of the time on Matt. 27:29: e.g., Franciscus Lucas Brugensis (Luc de Bruges), *In Sacrosancta Quatuor Iesu Christi Evangelia Commentarius* (Antwerp, 1605), p. 518; Cornelius Jansenius, *Tetrateuchus, sive Commentarius in quatuor Evangelia* (Louvain, 1639), p. 379. It was not until many years later that it became recognized that the Libyan rhamnus could not have been the plant used. Cf. Henry Alford (ed.), *The Greek Testament*(London, 1849), I, 211.

89.   *Pseudodoxia Epidemica*, bk 7, ch. 1: "But surely in vain we enquire . . . whether the Crown of thorns was made of Paliuros . . ." (Browne, *Works*, ed. Geoffrey Keynes [London, 1928], III, 262–63).

90.   As when George Sandys wrote: "[Circe] . . . could not prevaile over the person of Ulysses, secured by the hearbe Moly, which was given him by Mercury (a more cunning Magician, and inventor of that art) who forced her to restore their former shapes to his servants. For as the earth produceth malignant simples, so doth it Antidotes to resist their virulency; among those of this kinde they reckon on the Sarr-fish, the Iasper-stone, Christs-thorne, Agnus castus, and Fleawort . . ." (*Ovids Metamorphosis Englished, Mythologizd, and Represented in Figures*, London, 1640—previously issued in 1632—p. 264). Milton may well have read this very passage conjoining moly and Christ's-thorn. See Bush, *Mythology and the Renaissance Tradition in English Poetry* (Minneapolis, 1932), pp. 267–68.

91.   *The Travels of Sir John Mandeville* (1568), ed. Jules Bramont, Everyman's Library, p. 22.

92.   "Reading *Comus*," in Diekhoff's *A Maske*, p. 86. (Originally in *MP*, 51, 1953, 18–32; then in *Ikon: John Milton and the Modern Critics*, Ithaca, 1955, pp. 1–34.)

93.   II, 930.

94.   Diekhoff, p. 88.

95.   Ibid., p. 86.

96.   The Bridgewater text is conveniently available in Diekhoff, pp. 207–40. "*Comus, a Masque*, now adapted to the Stage, as alter'd [by John Dalton] from Milton's Masque at Ludlow-Castle" (London, 1760), p. 39, includes only ll. 629–30, 639–41. When at last the adaptation by George Colman the Elder, as shorter, superseded Dalton's, not a vestige remained of the magic plant: *Comus: A Masque, altered from Milton, as performed at the Theatre-Royal in the Hay-*

Market, "the Musick composed by Dr. Arne" (London, 1780). The "Advertisement" commences: "Pure Poetry unmixt with passion, how-ever admired in the closet, has scarce ever been able to sustain itself on the Stage. In this Abridgement of Milton's *Comus*, no circumstance of the Drama contained in the Original Masque is omitted. The divine arguments on temperance and chastity, together with many descriptive passages, are indeed expunged or contracted: But, divine as they are, the most accomplished declaimers have been embarrassed in the recitation of them. The speaker vainly laboured to prevent a coldness and languor in the audience . . . . "

97.   Diekhoff, p. 80.

98.   *Miltonic Enigmas* (privately printed, 1921), pp. 12, 16. Himes, "before I knew of S. T. Coleridge's nearly identical interpretation," had "haimon" allude to "the blood-stained cross of Christ." The early editions of E. Cobham Brewer's *The Reader's Handbook* (Philadelphia) were friendly to Coleridge's interpretation.

99.   They are not incompatible, as Arthos, pp. 44–45, contended. See Steadman, pp. 200–01.

100.   *The Faerie Queene*, 6, introduction, 3. With line 5 cf. Thomas Carlyle, "Like other plants, Virtue will not grow unless its root be hidden, buried from the eye of the sun." *Sartor Resartus*, Book Third, ch. 3, third paragraph.

V

"That Two-Handed Engine" and Savonarola and the Blackfriars Fatal Vespers

Scores of ingenious commentators on "Lycidas," 130–31, have done all they could to lead us away from one fact and one principle. The fact is that the verse paragraph which ends with these lines is based on the parable in John 10. And the principle is to ask ourselves what the contemporary reader could have been expected to make of the lines when he came upon them in this context. Assuming that Milton meant to be somewhat dark, but not hopelessly dark, when he foretold "the ruin of our corrupted Clergy, then in their height," these two criteria are our only bulwark against the frivolous modern pastime of treating the couplet as a secret to be penetrated by some private fantasy of one's own. Of the forty-five explanations of the "two-handed engine" listed in the 1972 Columbia *Variorum Commentary*,[1] all but one are too out of the way on this basis to be reasonable. Moreover, there are points to be made that will freshly confirm and also expand this one.

Of the fact above referred to we had better make as much as possible, for it is the only fact we have. Milton has carefully steered the reader to a recollection of Christ's parable of the good shepherd, with its animadversion on the hireling: "But he that is an hireling, and not the shepherd, whose own the sheep are not, seeth the wolf coming, and leaveth the sheep, and fleeth: and the wolf catcheth them, and scattereth the sheep" (John 10:12). When St. Peter speaks his third line about those who, "for their bellies' sake," "creep, and intrude, and climb into the fold!" we recognize, and are meant to recognize, this as a development of the subordinate clause in "He that entereth not by the door into the sheep–fold, but climbeth up some other way, the same is a thief and a robber" (John 10:1). The very presence of St. Peter with his keys is sufficiently inspired by "To him the porter openeth" (John 10:3). In short, all the main elements of the parable appear in the poem, including the good shepherd, the hirelings, who neglect their flocks and, in Milton, even rob them, thus becoming equated with the thieves, the sheepfold, the preying wolf. And it is necessary to add, since some modern readers get confused about it, that "the door" reappears, too: "But that two-handed engine at the door / Stands ready to smite once, and smite no more." So good an editor as A. W. Verity[2] takes "at the door" as an expression meaning "ready at hand." But if the primary meaning of "at the door" is "ready at hand," why is Milton so repetitious as to follow this phrase with "stands ready"? The door is the door of the sheepfold, which is the door of the Church (which is in turn the way to Heaven: thus, we are back in thought to the beginning of the passage, the keys of St. Peter–"The golden opes, the iron shuts amain"). The bad clergy have, by unhallowed roundabout ways, got into the Church, but for them a dreadful fate is at the door.

How much further can the parable take us? If the parable contained a clear threat against the bad shepherds, there would be no mystery about Milton's "two-handed engine." But the parable comes no nearer than this: "My sheep hear my voice, and I know them, and they follow me: And I give unto them eternal life; and they shall never perish, neither shall any pluck them out of my hand. My Father, which gave them me, is greater than all; and none is able to pluck them out of my Father's hand" (John 10:27–29). In other words,

the emphasis in the parable is on the saved; the emphasis in
Milton is on the doomed. But at least there is enough here to
settle readily who the wielder of the two-handed engine is.

For, be it observed that the last parallel between Milton
and his source is the idea of a Protector. God takes care of
His own, and if it is a question of vengeance, "Vengeance is
mine; I will repay, saith the Lord" (Romans 12:19). There
should be no doubt—it is surprising there has ever been
doubt—that St. Peter is making the ultimate reference. Christ
is in the foreground of the parable; a necessary decorum
prevents His appearing in the poem (not forgetting, however,
"the dear might of Him that walked the waves," [173] and
"might" rhymes with "smite"). St. Peter is substituted as
speaker, St. Peter, the archetype, as Ruskin notes,[3] of the
good bishop. But behind St. Peter stands Christ or God. The
Wielder of the engine can only be the first or second Person
of the Trinity—which, it is perhaps not important to decide.
"I and my Father are one" (John 10:30). All other interpretations are oblique and must be discarded. This is the one
interpretation that the contemporary reader, or, for that
matter, any reader brought up in the Christian tradition,
could be expected to arrive at. St. Peter would not be
speaking of himself, judging from his demonstrative "that."
And the popular suggestion that the avenger is the militant
archangel Michael is close,[4] but not close enough. (One might
almost as well say it is St. Paul, whose symbol is a sword.) It
is only toward the end of the next verse paragraph that there
enters in "the great Vision of the guarded mount." There is
absolutely no reason for thinking of Michael at the present
stage of the poem. Those who leap forward to *Paradise Lost*
and stress his role there would do well to take note that when
Michael makes his last appearance to escort Adam and Eve
from Paradise, it is not *his* sword which is prominent, but
"High in front advanced, the brandished sword of God before
them blazed."[5] On the other hand, "the sword of Justice" is
too secular to be thought of, not to mention that in *The
Tenure of Kings and Magistrates* Milton calls justice "the
Sword of God."[6] Other suggestions are private to the point

of absurdity: Spenser's Talus, for instance, or Janus, or the
two-handed sword of Huanebango in Peele's *The Old Wives'
Tale*, or "the Club of Hercules, the engine that slays the
Hydra of Sin on the walls of the Catacombs"! Was Milton
only talking to himself?

Now, what could the reader in 1637 or 1638 be expected
to think of as the instrument? He would certainly not think
of the ax that beheaded Laud in 1645, and the various
allegories which have been suggested are easily objected to:
the two houses of Parliament,[7] the two nations of England
and Scotland which were to unite in opposition to the
"corrupt Clergy,"[8] "spiritual power and civil."[9] On various
grounds one must discard the scythe of Time, the scythe of
Death, "the abhorred shears" of the blind Fury, a sheephook,
the keys of St. Peter. The last three have the advantage of
prior reference in the poem, but there are grave objections.
"The abhorred shears" (75) go very far back; wielded blindly,
they have nothing to do with just retribution, and are they
two-handed? does it take a two-handed instrument to "slit
the thin-spun life"? That sounds like overkill. There can be
no denying that in an emergency a sheephook *can* be used as
a weapon. (See *The Faerie Queene*, 6.10.36.) But so can a
book, or an inkwell. It is important to distinguish between a
possibility and a probability. The ordinary interpretation of a
passage in *Of Reformation* that we shall see Tillyard
quoting[10] is that Milton mentioned Christ's "Sheep-hooke"
and "the iron *Scepter* of his anger" in the same sentence only
to show what very different instruments they were. St.
Peter's keys are an important clue to meaning—we shall
return to them—but the ordinary rules of denotation are not
suspended because this is a poem: if St. Peter were referring
to something he was himself carrying he would say, not "that
two-handed engine," but "this two handed engine."[11] Moreover, the repeated "smite" seems to call for an instrument
that smites literally as well as figuratively.

If it is inescapable that the Lord is the agent, it is almost as
inescapable, to a student of the Bible, that His weapon is a
sword, a sword that, for its weight and power, and perhaps

for another reason, Milton has thought of as a two-handed sword.

Sword as *engine*? "Engine" makes the modern reader think only of a battery engine or a machine with moving parts. I have known students to be enchanted with my wife's suggestion that Milton was referring to a clock striking the hour of doom. Unfortunately, at the time clocks did not have two hands.[12] It is a by–gone time that we must think of, when the word "engine" was less restricted. Donne called human hands "engines."[13] Herbert used "engine" of prayer ("Prayer" [1], 5). Defoe, in *Robinson Crusoe*, wrote, "twenty Canoes full of Savages, arm'd with Bows and Arrows, great Clubs, wooden Swords, and such like Engines of War".[14] Of more immediate bearing on "Lycidas" is a quotation from Bunyan: one of the "Engines" Christian is shown at the Palace Beautiful is "the Sword . . . with which their Lord will kill the man of Sin in the day that he shall rise up to the Prey."[15] Milton's use comes under definition 5a of the *Oxford English Dictionary*: "A machine or instrument used in warfare. Formerly sometimes applied to all offensive weapons"; and also under definition 10, figurative: "Of a thing: An instrument, means, organ," this sword being the engine of "Gods just anger" (Columbia *Works*, III, 281). As late as 1883 definition 2 of *Worcester's Dictionary* was, "Any instrument, implement, or weapon," and it quoted Raleigh, "the sword, the arrow, the gun, with many terrible engines of death."

The sword is, as Grotius remarked, the regular symbol of *ultio* in the Bible.[16] "The sword of the Lord" is a common expression in the Old Testament, and "smite" is a common verb, either with "sword" or with God as the agent, and sometimes with both (Deuteronomy 28:22; Zechariah 13:7 even adds the pastoral imagery: "Awake, O sword, against my Shepherd, and against the man that is my fellow, saith the Lord of hosts: smite the Shepherd, and the sheep shall be scattered; and I will turn mine hand upon the little ones"). All this is evident from a glance at a concordance[17] to the King James version. On the other hand, despite interpretations of Jeremiah 51:20 and Matthew 3:10-Luke 3:9, the ax is not clearly the Lord's weapon, and is never used with "smite." In fact, total mention of the ax in the Bible (nineteen times) is as nothing compared to the number of times—approximately 440—the sword is mentioned, the sword being *the* weapon par excellence. Furthermore, particular passages in the New Testament support this obvious conclusion. Christ holds no weapon in the gospels, except the "scourge of small cords" with which He drives the money-changers out of the temple in John 2:15 (and a scourge is not an instrument with which to smite once). But the quotation "I came not to send peace, but a sword" (Matthew 10:34) is significant. Others cite the "sharp-edged sword" (*distomos*) that issues from the mouth of the Son of man in the vision in Revelation 1:16; cf. 2:12 and especially 16: "Repent; or else I will come unto thee quickly, and will fight against them with the sword of my mouth." (This in turn has led to the potentially ludicrous conjecture that the bad bishops are to be smitten with the Old and the New Testaments!) A final quotation to show the thoroughly aggressive imagery is Revelation 19:15: "And out of his mouth goeth a sharp sword, that with it he should smite the nations: and he shall rule them with a rod of iron: and he treadeth the wine-press of the fierceness and wrath of Almighty God."

In fine, one must think of the Lord as the agent of "that two-handed engine" because no other thought comes obviously and naturally in context, and one must think of the sword as the instrument, for the same logical reason.

The adherents of the ax, when they are not seeking to make Milton a prophet in the superstitious sense, cling to it probably because they regard an ax as something that obviously calls for two hands to wield. But this is not less true of the great two-handed sword—its overall length could be 7 feet—that was familiar to men of the sixteenth and early seventeenth centuries.[18] "The Christian Knight" Guy of Warwick uses it, one might say at length, in Drayton's *Poly-Olbion*,[19] Shakespeare mentions it,[20] the young Gargantua was taught to handle it,[21] but it is so rare to Milton's modern commentators that whenever they encounter an allusion to one in classical, medieval, or Renaissance literature, they conjecture that *this* is Milton's inspiration. Thus, the classical scholar Keightley compares the "amphidexion sideron" of Euripides (*Hippolytus*, 780) as if there were some connection.

Those who contend that the "engine" is a battery engine will have to (and do not) explain "two-handed." They do have a point, however. Milton's language is designedly ambiguous, his imagery mixed. The situation is not only one of personal smiting, but also of a siege. The wicked clergy are besieged within the Church where they have no right to be. The two paths of thought become one when we realize that the sword of God can smite a building as easily as it can smite a man. Besides wishing to be somewhat dark and therefore all the more ominous, as befits a prophet of wrath to come, Milton as a poet is capitalizing on the ambiguity of "engine." The word is masterfully chosen, or hit upon: no other could have done its double work.

In this connection, it is worth calling attention to a phrase in that document of Milton's which is closest in time to "Lycidas," his letter to Diodati dated September 23, 1637 (taken by the Yale editors as a mistake for November), the letter in which he says he is growing his wings and meditating poetic flight. He refers to his friend's "arcem . . . illud *epiteichisma* quod cervicibus nostris videris imposuisse. . . ." [22] In Masson's and the Yale translation, [23] the Greek word "epiteichisma" becomes a "battery": it is, rather, a fort fronting enemy territory. The Latin is good, but sufficiently Milton's to be interesting, for here, within weeks of his writing about the smiting of the two-handed engine, he has spoken of a fort in a personal way, as if it were an instrument (compare with the passage his reference in *Eikonoklastes* to the king's militia: "to hold a violent and incommunicable Sword over us, as readie to be let fall upon our own necks, as upon our Enemies" [*Works*, V, 173]), even as he was to surround a sword with the connotations of a siege. And, for either engine, "terribile" is the right word.

Let us return, for the last time, to our imagined contemporary reader and press him further as to the meaning of "two-handed." That the instrument is two-handed to emphasize its weight and power has already been granted. Whether the reader pursues his inquiry further will depend on how thoughtful he is and whether he realizes that he has to do with a poet who, especially at this critical, compressed juncture of the poem (the same was true of haemony), is not likely to employ an epithet for only one reason. Such a reader will wonder what dual yet simultaneous fate hangs over the false shepherds.

For a Christian there can be, again, only one answer: death and damnation. God will smite the unregenerate with sudden death ("Deceitful men shall not live out half their days," Psalm 55:23) and the iron key will shut amain—this at one stroke, in accordance with orthodox belief, St. Peter's keys being "the keys of hell and of death" (Revelation 1:18) and Hell being the "second death" (Revelation 2:11; 20:14; 21:8). The plague had been raging in Horton in 1637,[24] had carried away a number of people, and the theme of sudden death, natural on more than one account, pervades the poem. Here it covers the wicked and *their* fate. The poem is mainly about the problem of salvation—with reference to Lycidas, to Milton, to poets, to Christians—but here it turns off to deal, with terrible brevity, with *damnation*, with the iron key instead of the golden. As Don Cameron Allen summed up in 1954 (after my article of 1950), "The two-handed engine which carries the double death of body and soul, the *gladius Dei* of iron and gold that twice damns the atheist priest, will avenge St. Peter's wrongs."[25]

Having settled, on an orthodox and common-sense basis, the meaning and ramifications of the couplet, we may now turn to Milton's other writings for whatever parallels there may be. This provides an interesting check on conclusions already arrived at, but to start with his other writings and try to work backwards is fatal, as the multitude of conjectures reached in this way has shown. *Of Reformation in England*, for instance, is well worth turning to as Milton's first work in

prose against the bishops. It contains provocative passages—
indeed too many. E. H. Visiak[26] and many predecessors going
back to the eighteenth century, searching it for a "key" to
the two–handed engine, find it in the phrase about "the Axe
of Gods reformation hewing at the old and hollow trunk of
Papacie" (*Works*, III, 47). But Tillyard's[27] solution, derived
from the same pamphlet, is no less plausible: "the Pastorly
Rod, and Sheep–hooke of Christ, . . . the iron *Scepter* of his
anger that will dash him to peeces like a Potsherd" (III, 69).
Or perhaps we are interested in the conjecture of Professors
Stauffer[28] and Mutschmann[29] that the two–handed engine
stands for the future allies, England and Scotland. Then we
quote the paragraph which begins, "Goe on both hand in
hand O NATIONS never to be disunited," and ends, "joyn
your invincible might to doe worthy and Godlike deeds, and
then he that seeks to break your union, a cleaving curse be
his inheritance to all generations" (III, 61). E. L. Marilla[30]
sees Milton as a millenarian looking to "the Eternall and
shortly-expected King" (III, 78). Alas! here and elsewhere in
Milton's voluminous and often heated writing there are too
many threats, all vaguely relevant, and the only escape from
confusion is to be, at the start, like the original readers of
"Lycidas," free of all these works.

In due order, however, it is reassuring to be able to record
that the only time Milton ever used "two-handed" again was
in reference to a sword: "The sword of Michael smote, and
felled / Squadrons at once: with huge two-handed sway /
Brandished aloft, the horrid edge came down / Wide-
wasting" (*Paradise Lost*, 6:250–53). And the only time the
verb form "smite" occurs after "Lycidas" in Milton's poetry
is with reference to a sword: "The sword / Of Michael . . . /
met / The sword of Satan, with steep force to smite / De-
scending" (*P.L.*, 6:320–25). Finally, for a parallel to "Stands
ready to smite once, and smite no more" (Newton called
attention to 1 Samuel 26:8), there is this reference to
the duel between Michael and Satan: "one stroke they
aimed / That might determine, and not need repeat" (*P.L.*,
6:317–18). These passages have duly been cited by the

enthusiasts for Michael and a sword, but the last is not exclusively of Michael, and in the end, if preceding arguments have been valid, we shall do better to take them as a bit of supplementary evidence for the sword alone. It is evidence that means more in this author than in many authors, for Milton has, as two books of mine[31] have set forth at length, a "remarkable consistency." What interests him he comes back to, often in the same words. For instance, "the golden opes" ("Lycidas," 111) echoes "that golden key / That opes the palace of Eternity" of three years before (*Comus*, 13–14). It has lately been shown[32] that *Areopagitica* contains a punning reference to a two-handed sword, the cutting out from Knox's *History of the Reformation in Scotland* of "one sentence of a ventrous edge" (*Works*, IV, 326) about the "twa handed sweard" exchanged between Knox and the martyr George Wishart. But it does *not* follow that in 1637 "for Milton, Knox's two-handed sword was a symbol of the just vengeance of the Scottish reformers."[33] If we are going to bandy about Milton quotations retrospectively, I will parry with his language in *Defensio Prima* on the removal of the bishops: "Mirifica Dei manus . . . liberavit" (VII, 462).

To leave the instrument and return to the explanation given above of the dual fate that awaits the corrupt clergy, this explanation, so obvious that it is surprising it was not promulgated before, is confirmed by the unforgettable last paragraph, last sentence, of *Of Reformation*:

> But they contrary that by the impairing and diminution of the true *Faith*, the distresses and servitude of their *Countrey* aspire to high *Dignity, Rule* and *Promotion* here, after a shamefull end in this *Life* (which *God* grant them) shall be thrown downe eternally into the *darkest* and *deepest Gulfe* of Hell, where under the *despightfull controule*, the trample and spurne of all the other *Damned*, that in the anguish of their *Torture* shall have no other ease then to exercise a *Raving* and *Bestiall Tyranny* over them as their *Slaves* and *Negro's*, they shall remaine in that plight for ever, the *basest*, the *lowermost*, the *most dejected*, most *underfoot* and *downe–trodden Vassals* of *Perdition*.[34]

Milton is expressing here, in the plentitude of a thunderous oratory, exactly the curse he hurled, more cryptically, in "Lycidas," 130–31. The aspiring victims, their twofold fate, and the agent of their fate—are the same. Any difference is entirely a matter of imagery and the difference between the directness and fullness of periodic prose and the apocalyptic lightning of verse. Whether thunder or lightning, it means, in either case, death and damnation to the bishops and their followers.

Coming now to the third and last test, source, one must stress again that Milton needed no source outside the Bible.[35] But this is a different question from whether he did not in fact have one, whether he was not thinking of the famous and often uttered prophecy of that pre-Reformation reformer and inveigher against a worldly clergy Girolamo Savonarola: "Ecce gladius Domini super terram cito et velociter."

The above words constitute Savonarola's best-known utterance, and are inevitably quoted in the slightest sketches of his career. It is not supposing much to suppose that Milton knew them at the time he wrote "Lycidas." Actually, we are dealing with a prodigy of learning who was then in the midst of his studies of Italian history.[36] He was soon to be citing Savonarola. Probably the slightly earlier[37] of the two specific citations is that in the Commonplace Book, the first entry (it is in Italian) under "Leges":

> Savonarola, after a writ of excommunication had been sent him from Rome, did not submit to it, telling in his defense a fine parable, by which he shows 'that one should obey the spirit rather than the letter of the laws.' l.I. p. 48. 49 rinovation. della chiesa.[38]

Hanford in his pioneering study of the Commonplace Book failed to identify this title.[39] The pagination fits only the third, Venice, 1560, edition of a Savonarola anthology edited by Frate Luca Bettini, *Oracolo della rinovatione della chiesa*. In this excerpt from his sermon on Amos of February 17, 1496, when the Dominican had been forbidden by Alexander

VI to preach and was threatened with—though he had not yet received—excommunication, he says: "Oportet magis obedire Deo quam hominibus. Io te lo dimostro, per una parabola." [40] The parable that Milton thought "bella" concerns a citizen whose fine vineyard, well kept by his son, becomes an object of desire to some young thieves. In order to be free to pillage it, they write the father that the son is a wastrel and a lecher, and they send him—the father being too distant to get acquainted with the matter at first hand—letters to this effect purporting to come from respectable persons. The citizen, believing these scandals, sends for his son, who, seeing through the conspiracy, refuses to come. The son, writing to his father that the latter has been deceived, stays to look after the vineyard. Was he not right? asks Savonarola of his audience. "Sappendo"—and here Milton was quoting except for pluralizing "laws"—"che e'più tosto da ubbidire all' intentione della legge, che alle parole."

The other reference belongs to 1641. In *Animadversions upon the Remonstrant's Defence against Smectymnuus* Milton says in exasperation to Bishop Hall: "I would you would either mingle, or part, most true it is what *Savanarola* complaines, that while hee endeavour'd to reforme the Church, his greatest enemies were still these Lukewarm ones?" (*Works*, III, 125). Savonarola's denunciations in his sermons against "i tiepidi" are so numerous[41] that it is impossible to trace this to any one source. But some pages further on in his tract the English author launched a parable comparable to the above. "A certaine man of large possessions had a faire Garden," which a "strange Gardener" tries to take over (III, 158–59[42]).

To get back to "Ecce gladius Domini super terram cito et velociter," I think that is echoed in Milton's prose of this period too, in *The Reason of Church-Government*: "a very sword and fire both in house and City over the whole earth" (*Works*, III, 230). The Latin is not, as Savonarola was careful to point out to his audiences, a quotation from the Bible. It goes back to a vision he had in 1492, the night before his last Advent sermon. As depicted in medals and engravings of the

time and as described in the *Compendium revelationum*, first
published (in both a Latin and an Italian edition) in 1495,
the threatening sword of God was a one-handed sword. [43]
But that fact is not apparent in the many references to this
omen in the sermons,[44] and indeed in one of the two
sermons worth examining closely here the engine of retribution is explicitly two-handed.

It was the friar's message through all the famous years of
his preaching that "The church shall be renovated, but must
first be scourged, and that speedily."[45] He was constantly
warning of the "gran flagello" that impended, and regularly
seeing this as the "gladius Domini." His sermon of May 3,
1495, on John 10, *Ego sum pastor bonus*, is no exception.
But in containing a threat, the missing element in the parable,
it stands apart from other sermons and discourses on this
text, such as those cited by George R. Coffman[46] and those
to be found in Migne's *Patrologiae.* [47] The similarity in spirit
between Savonarola and Milton can be shown by a few
excerpts from this sermon:

> ... El pastore va vestito male e non di broccato, ma semplicemente,
> la casa del pastore non è molto differente alla casa delle pecorelle: lui
> dorme alla rugiada come loro, se tu menassi le percorelle ne' belli
> palazzi non vi vorriano stare. . . . Ma che dirai tu di quelli che sono
> lupi e hanno indosso la veste del pastore cioè vestiti da frati o da
> preti o padri di famiglia o altri simili? e'sono poi lupi. . . . *Audite
> verbum Domini: Veh pastoribus illis qui pascunt semet ipsos!*[48]

At the end Savonarola asks his audience if they think him
mad for prophesying, "Ecce gladius Domini super terram cito
et velociter." He assures them they will blanch when his
words come true.[49]

But of even greater interest—though it does not contain
the usual quotation about the sword—is the twenty-third of
the *Prediche sopra il Salmo Quam Bonus*, published at Venice
in 1528, 1539, and 1544. This sermon, unlike the others in
the series, is on Psalm 73, *Ut quid Deus repulisti in finem.* [50]
Specifically a daring denunciation of the corrupt clergy, the
"cattivi prelati," it gives a highly original picture of the

Church under siege that will remind English readers of Bunyan's *The Holy War.* The pristine Church, Savonarola says, was a magnificent temple built of fine marble and true gold, with columns of porphyry and doors of precious pearls. But in time it was besieged by the devil's party.

> La notte dipoi che seguitò mi parea vedere che di notte segretamente molti venissino con diverse macchine e strumenti per distruggere questo tempio. Alcuni portavano il fuoco per abbruciarlo, altri le scure e ascie per spezzare le porte, e chi avea uno strumento e chi un altro, e tanto feciono che lo distrussono, e vedevo che se ne gloriavano, e posonvi di poi le arme loro e rizzoronvi le loro bandiere e le loro insegne, acciò che ognuno vedesse che gli avevano ottenuto quello che desideravano.[51]

The new decorations, of course, were all false.

> Poi che gli ebbono fatto quello che volsono, vidi che in poco tempo lo riedificorno e assettorno a loro modo; ma era di legno ogni casa, quasi tutto dipinto a uso di marmo e di porfido: una parte v'era inorpellata, che parea oro fine; gli altari erano ornati con bellissimi paliotti e candellieri d'oro e d'argento, con molti lumi. Vedevo venire i sacerdoti con piviali di broccato indosso, [again that Puritan complaint!] con certi ornamenti in capo di gemme preziose; in mano portavano baculi d'argento; innanzi a loro andavano i cantatori con diversi strumenti musici, e cantavano e sonavano tanto dolcemente, che parea che s'aprisse il Paradiso.[52]

But it is a Paradise of Fools. Suddenly disaster strikes.

> Ora, stando così ognuno in festa e in tripudio, subito rovinò il tetto di quel tempio, che avea più peso che non si conveniva, e ammazzò ognuno che v'era dentro.[53]

"Satan, smitten with amazement, fell." (*Paradise Regained*, 4.562).

Savonarola proceeds to work out an elaborate allegory in accordance with a situation that he sums up in an epigram: "Nella primitiva Chiesa erano i calici di legno e i prelati d'oro; oggi la Chiesa ha i prelati di legno e i calici d'oro."[54] This saying, by the way, Milton quotes in *Of Reformation.*[55] But it is Savonarola's basic pattern of the besieged Church that is of present interest, this and the threats of heaven-sent vengeance at the beginning and at the end of the long sermon. For though in the quotation given in the preceding paragraph the roof of the false Church is represented as falling in of its own accord, this purifying event has not actually taken place, and both reformers, Savonarola and Milton, are looking for a heaven-sent stroke.

Quando tu vedi gli uomini buoni desiderare che venga il coltello e la peste e la fame e gli altri flagelli di Dio, non te ne scandalizzare, perchè lo fanno per zelo della Chiesa di Dio.[56]

This is near the beginning. Toward the end one seems to hear the hoarse voice getting more and more vehement.

Che fai tu adunque, Signore? Perchè dormi tu? *Quare obdormis Domine? Exsurge, et ne repellas in finem.* Levati su Signore, vienia liberare la Chiesa tua dalle mani de' diavoli, dalle mani de' tiranni, dalle mani de' cattivi prelati. Non vedi tu che l'è piena d'animali, piena di bestie, leoni, orsi e lupi, che l'hanno tutta guasta? *Quare obliviscéris tribulationem nostram?* Non vedi tu, Signore, la nostra tribolazione? Ti se' tu dimenticato della Chiesa tua? Non l'ami tu? Non l'hai tu cara? Ell'è pure la sposa tua! Non la conosci tu? L'è quella medesima, per la quale tu discendesti nel ventre di Maria, per la quale tu pigliasti carne umana, per la quale tu patisti tanti obbrobri, per la quale tu volesti versare il sangue tuo in croce! Adunque la t'è costata assai, Signore, a però noi ti preghiamo che tu venga, e presto, a liberala! Vieni, dico, e punisci questi cattivi, confondili, umiliali, acciocchè noi più quietamente ti possiamo servire![57] ... *Effunde iram tuam in gentes, quae te non noverunt, et in regna quae nomen tuum non invocaverunt.* Non ti maravigliare adunque se li santi uomini desiderano il flagello, perchè lo desiderano per escludere il male, e acciocchè il Regno di Cristo Gesù bendetto prosperi nel mondo.[58]

We see, then, amply the siege connotations of "engine at the door" and the divine source of the expected stroke. The favorite instrument, though not explicit in this sermon, is sufficiently conspicuous elsewhere. But what about "two-handed"? Savonarola has accounted for that, too, in discoursing, near the beginning of his sermon, on the psalmist's words "Leva manus tuas in superbias eorum":

Eleva, signore, la potenza tua contra questi iniqui distruttori della tua Chiesa, contra la superbia de' prelati, contra la superbia dei Re e dei Principi, che hanno dissipato il popolo tuo. Estendi loro la mano destra e la sinistra contro di loro: la mano sinistra dando loro punizione temporale, acciocchè e'si convertino o almanco e'si umilino e confondino, e non possino più nuocere agli eletti tuoi; e, quanto a quelli che non si vogliono umiliare nè confondere salubremente, leva la destra tua, cioè puniscigli eternalmente nell' Inferno.[59]

Raise, O Lord, Thy power against these iniquitous destroyers of Thy Church, against the pride of the prelates, against the pride of kings and princes, who have led astray Thy people. Stretch out Thy right hand and Thy left against them: the left hand giving them punishment in this world in order that they might be converted, or at least humiliated and confounded and rendered powerless to harm any more Thy chosen. And, as for those who prove resistant to a salutary humbling or punishment, lift up Thy right hand—that is, punish them eternally in Hell.

This is the meaning of Milton's epithet that has already been arrived at by another route. Since Milton regards the "corrupted Clergy" as too far gone to be recalled, their temporal punishment—"a shamefull end in this Life"—comes at one stroke with their eternal punishment.

Thus, we are helped to understand that when Milton foretold "the ruin of our corrupted Clergy, then in their height" (1645 headnote), he was thinking of "ruin" in more than one sense:[60] first, in the sense of undoing, second, in the Latin sense of a fall from a height, a fall, indeed, from earth to Hell—"with hideous *ruin* and combustion down,"[61] and third, in the sense of architectural collapse, when the engine at the door smites.

Moreover, so outstanding a sermon, once read, is not readily forgotten. It seems to have registered again with Milton when he was writing the first of his antiprelatical

tracts in 1641, the key word "ruin"—"ruining"—introducing a
similar train of imagery:

> But what greater debasement can there be to Royall Dignity, whose
> towring, and stedfast heighth rests upon the unmovable foundations
> of Justice, and Heroick vertue, then to chaine it in a dependance of
> subsisting, or ruining to the painted Battlements, and gaudy rot-
> tennesse of Prelatrie, which want but one puffe of the Kings to blow
> them down like a past-bord House built of *Court-Cards*. [62]

If Milton did read the sermon (a conjecture on which it must
be emphasized that my explanation of 130–31 does not
depend), we can understand how it would have impressed
one who so strongly felt that the decorated was the false and
who had himself so eloquently much to say against "embez-
zling the treasury of the Church on painted and gilded walls
of temples wherein God hath testified to have no delight"
(*Works*, III, 74). In 1641 the author was still a constitutional
monarchist. But in *Eikonoklastes* he turns similar imagery
against the king: "Yet here, like a rotten building newly
trimmed over, he represents it speciously and fraudulently to
impose upon the simple reader" (V, 98); and his sardonic
answer to the charge of the author of *Eikon Basilike* that
the Puritans "think all is gold of piety that doth but
glister with a show of zeal" is: "We know his meaning,
and apprehend how little hope there could be of him from
such language as this, but are sure that the piety of his
prelatic model glistered more upon the posts and pillars
which their zeal and fervency gilded over, than in the true
works of spiritual edification" (V, 147). Savonarola and
Milton alike distrusted the fair, especially the artificially fair,
exterior, including painted women, painted churches, and
brocaded bishops.

Savonarola loomed larger then, of course, than now. His
martyrdom had occurred less than 140 years before
"Lycidas" was written, and the many printings of his works
in the sixteenth century made him a living presence. It is
possible, seeing that Milton demanded elsewhere much of his

readers in the way of learned recall, that the poet's use of "that" for his engine is similar to Latin "ille," "that famous or well-known," "ille gladius." But more famous than Savonarola's, obviously, is the biblical sword of the Lord first heard of in Genesis 3:24, "a flaming sword which turned every way, to keep the way of the tree of life," and which connects with St. Peter's excluding key.

The recent author of a chapter entitled "The Decorum of St. Peter's Speech"[63] feels it would be a breach of decorum for a sword to be hovering in the neighborhood of St. Peter. He forgets the Gospels: "Then Simon Peter having a sword drew it, and smote the high priest's servant, and cut off his right ear" (John 18:10; cf. Matt. 26:51; Mark 14:47; Luke 22:50). He shows no knowledge of the iconography of the Last Judgment, as depicted in stained glass all round Milton. This is set forth in two very recent articles that would have the "engine" to be St. Michael's scales in which he weighs souls.[64] I shall continue to prefer an interpretation of "two-handed" and "smite" that is both literal and figurative to one that is only figurative, but the suggestion is good for meaning and brings us vivid pictures: of St. Michael beside St. Peter at the door of Heaven, the former with the scales in one hand and the sword of the Lord in the other. I think something Milton saw may turn out to be the final illumination. I turn, for example, to *The Hours of Catherine of Cleves*,[65] and there, "Last Judgement," is a mighty sword literally hovering by the mouth of Christ (following Revelation 1:16).

Finally, to return to such suggestive phrases as "a rotten building newly trimmed over" (*Eikonoklastes*) and "gaudy rottennesse of Prelatrie" (*Of Reformation*) and the idea of smitten idolatry latent in 130–31, life itself furnished a timely inspiration. Shortly before Milton's fifteenth birthday and only a few blocks from his home and his school occurred a mishap known as the Blackfriars Fatal Vespers, the collapse of a popish place of worship next to the French ambassador's residence on October 26 (which was noted to be November 5 by Continental reckoning—the anniversary of the Gunpowder Plot), 1623, fatal to almost one hundred persons. Milton's

schoolmaster Alexander Gill the Younger, the Puritan Samuel
Clarke, and others attributed the disaster to the hand of God.
"The preacher was one [Robert] Drury, a converted
Protestant. He inveighed bitterly against Luther, Calvin, and
Doctor [Thomas] Sutton, a reverent preacher sometime of
St. Mary Overy's, in London, who, travelling beyond the seas,
was drowned. This preacher said that the sea swallowed him,
because he was not worthy the earth should receive him. At
which words the house sank."[66] The analogy between
Edward King and Thomas Sutton is as plain as was, to a
Puritan, the analogy between the Laudian party and the
papists. In connection with my interpretation of "two-
handed," the closing words of a poem "In ruinam Camerae
Papisticae," Milton certainly read are provocative. They were
published by Gill in 1632,[67] who by then was Milton's friend
and correspondent. Gill warned the surviving English papists:

> Vos imminentem vindicis Dei manum
> (Nam vestra poena vigilat) extimescite.
> Etenim, futura praesagire si licet,
> Aut fallor, aut vos gravius exspectat malum.

> You had better fear the imminent hand of an avenging
> God, for your punishment is on the way. If I may
> prophesy, a still heavier evil awaits you.

What is this evil heavier than death? Gill was one of Milton's
contemporaries who would not have been particularly
puzzled by the "engine at the door." His former pupil
decided to follow in his path of prophecy.

I do not want to multiply sources unduly, any more than
with haemony, but can the striking resemblance between
these historical circumstances and those in "Lycidas" be only
a coincidence? Not only are Sutton and King equal in fate,
but so too are Drury and *his* kind. The two immediately
preceding lines about "the grim wolf with privy paw" refer
particularly to the Jesuits: "privy paw" describes their clandestine proselytizing activity in England, and as for "wolf,"

the commentators ought to note that the family arms of St. Ignatius Loyola were "argent, a pot and chain sable between two gray wolves, rampant." So John Webster in his character of "a Jesuite" says, "hee's a gray Woolfe."[68] A sixteenth-century balladeer praised Sidney and Essex for having "served and watched and waited late, / To keep the grim wolf from Eliza's gate."[69] The "Lycidas" lines fit Drury in a double way, since he had been notorious both as a Jesuit and as an apostate. Gill's explanatory note reads: "*Drurius* Iesuita, qui primo Papista, mox Evangelicam fidem amplexus est, postea ad *Romanam* haeresin relapsus." It was very much a literary tradition to take the Blackfriars Fatal Vespers as a divine warning to the papists and especially the Jesuits, and to augur from it the fall of the Roman Church. Edward Benlowes ended *his* poem on the subject: "Haec, Romista cave, domus una ut corruit hora, / Una sic hora Roma, caveto ruet."[70] ("Fear, Papist, that as this house collapsed in an hour, so thou must be afraid in one hour Rome will fall.") The Puritan minister William Crashaw (father of Richard) reported in a pamphlet, "For some gave out that it was the just punishment and vengence of God inflicted upon them for their Idolatrie."[71]

Having quoted Milton's prose in connection with Savonarola, I venture the same in this other connection: " ... settle the *pure worship* of God in his Church, and *justice* in the State. Then shall the hardest difficulties smooth out themselves before ye; *envie* shall sink to hell, *craft* and *malice* be confounded, whether it be home-bred mischeif, or outlandish cunning" (*Of Reformation, Works*, III, 61). "Envy shall sink to hell"–"sink" is a word that occurs in the diary I quoted: "At which words the house sank." Drury was showing "envy" at the moment he sank, and "outlandish cunning" seems to be an allusion to the Jesuits, as Charles Symmons[72] long ago observed: "This alludes to those popish intrigues, which certainly contributed to the calamities of our author's times. The court of Rome by its agents, the Jesuits, endeavoured in the first instance to gain the king and his party, and by their means to crush the Puritans. When the steadiness of the king to the Church of England disappointed them of this object, they turned against him, and were accomplices of his ruin."

"Ruin" in the Latin sense, the fall of a rotten, idolatrous structure—it is astounding how much there is of this in Milton (as I have noted elsewhere[73]), from *Comus*,[74]

> Till all thy magic structures, reared so high,
> Were shattered into heaps o'er thy false head, [798–99]

to *Samson Agonistes*,

> . . . Those two massy pillars
> With horrible convulsion to and fro
> He tugged, he shook, till down they came, and drew
> The whole roof after them with burst of thunder
> Upon the heads of all who sat beneath,
> Lords, ladies, captains, counselors, or priests . . . [1648-53]

itself reminiscent of a prose warning against the Restoration: "which will undoubtedly pull down the heavy judgment of God among us" (*Works*, VI, 103). Whether "Lords, ladies, captains, counselors, or priests," those who "aspire to high *Dignity, Rule* and *Promotion*" (III, 79) he spent a lifetime as a writer hurling to their ruin.

Whatever the "disconcerting plurality"[75] of possible influences, which honest reporting or research must not scant, it is hoped that a triple harmony—first, in what the reader at the time Milton wrote could have been expected to make of the crux, second, in the light that Milton's other writings throw on this interpretation, and third, in the consistency of source (Bible) or sources—makes a persuasive chord or composition, in competition with (but not always at odds with) the bibliography of one hundred items in the *Variorum Commentary*.

NOTES

1. Gen. ed. Merritt Y. Hughes, *The Minor English Poems*, ed. A.S.P. Woodhouse and Douglas Bush (New York), II, 686–706; articles by Rollinson and Felsen too recent to be in the comprehensive Bibliographical Index, pp. 1103–05, I refer to below. For an interpretation from Japan see *MQ*, 6 (1972), 21.

2. *Ode on the Morning of Christ's Nativity, L'Allegro, Il Penseroso, and Lycidas* (Cambridge, 1891), p. 148. He and others cite Matthew 24:33.

3. *Sesame and Lilies* (Everyman's Library), p. 16.

4. Edward C. Baldwin pointed out that "Michael" means "Who is like God," and that Milton tells us his sword comes "from the armoury of God" (*Paradise Lost*, 6.321) ("Milton and *Ezekiel*," *MLN*, 33 (1918), 212).

5. *P.L.*, 12.632–33. Cf. Genesis 3:24.

6. *Works*, Columbia ed. V, 3. Cf. V, 276 (*Eikonoklastes*): "would wrest the Sword of Justice out of Gods hand. . . . "

7. This suggestion, which has Milton striking a blow for constitutional government years before he entered the arena in prose, had its period of understandable popularity. There are difficulties. Any impending Parliament would include "the lords spiritual." Years were to pass before a Root-and-Branch party was to be organized, and more years and fighting before the bishops were ousted. It is well to keep in mind that Milton's own date for "Lycidas" is November, 1637. Besides, the nobles too

> . . . were standing in the main for the established Church and State. . . . In his prose writings, moreover, Milton the republican consciously or unconsciously addresses his hopes and his arguments to the House of Commons. The republican government concentrated in a single representative body, which he sketches in his *Ready and Easy Way to Establish a Free Commonwealth*, is implicit in his earlier writings. To accept the *two* Houses of Parliament as the two-handed engine is to make Milton's mental concept inadequate and his prophecy inaccurate. . . . In Scottish affairs, Charles in 1633 had persuaded Parliament (that two-handed engine!) to pass an act which compelled the clergy to wear white surplices rather than the Genevan black gown. [Donald A. Stauffer, "Milton's Two-Handed Engine," *MLR*, 31 (1936), 58]

In any case, if we are going to have Milton anticipate events of the 1640s, we may as well have him foresee the ax that beheaded Laud. Even if Milton did have an uncanny intuition of the future, there is always the problem of how the reader of the time could have been expected to follow him. Of course, it is possible to hold that he did not mean to communicate, or that he did not himself know what he meant: I proceed, however, on a less desperate assumption than either of these.

8. Were to unite, yes, but far from united in November, 1637. The only pertinent event, so far, in Scotland had been the riots over the Prayer Book. The Covenant belongs to the next year.

9. This is a step in the right direction, but vague, lacking a frame of reference. Whose power? It is the solution proposed by Mark Pattison (ed., *The Sonnets of John Milton*, New York, 1896, p. 196) quoting the Sonnet to Vane, 9–12. (See also H. Van Tromp, *TLS*, April 25, 1929, p. 338.) One should also quote *Observations on the Articles of Peace*: "The Covnant enjoyns us to endeavor the extirpation first of Popery and Prelacy, then of Heresy, Schism, and prophaness, and whatsoever shall be found contrary to sound Doctrin and the power of godliness. And this we ceas not to do by all effectuall and proper means: But these Divines might know, that to extirpat all these things can be no work of the Civil sword, but of the spirituall which is the Word of God" (*Works*, VI, 262).

We need not pause long over those interpretations which take Milton's "but" as adversative only to the preceding words, "and nothing said," rendering the engine "a further item in the list of evils under prelacy, not a sign of punishment to the wrongdoers" (see D. H. Stevens, *Reference Guide to Milton*, Chicago, 1930, p. 62). This reversal of meaning has led to such fancies as that the engine is Spain and France as the "double threat" of Catholicism against England, or the ecclesiastical and temporal powers of the Court of High Commission. The headnote of 1645 and 1673 disposes of this heterodoxy: "In this Monody the Author ... by occasion, foretells the ruin of our corrupted Clergy, then in their height." These words must refer to this couplet, since there is nothing else in the poem to which they *can* refer. For further objections, see the *Variorum Commentary*, II, 704–05.

10. Above, p. 108.

11. Much print has been wasted by ignoring this elementary point. Although Milton's printings and manuscript do not have quotation marks, "The Pilot of the Galilean lake" does not cease speaking at l. 129, but continues through 131, as 132 makes clear. Therefore, St. Peter cannot be referring to himself or anything he is or may be carrying, such as the keys, the sheephook, a crosier.

12. But Claud A. Thompson went on to do an article, complete with pictures, on the engine as a Jack o'th'Clock! " 'That Two-Handed Engine' Will Smite: Time Will Have a Stop," *SP*, 59 (1962), 184–200. Mr. Thompson was trained in theology; his remarks and quotations on the end of time and the final judgment are interesting, pp. 194–200.

13. In a passage Dr. Johnson quoted in his essay on Cowley:

> In none but us, are such mixt engines found,
>   As hands of double office: For, the ground
> We till with them; and them to heav'n wee raise;
>   Who prayer-lesse labours, or, without this, prayes,
> Doth but one-halfe, that's none .... [*Complete Poetry and Selected Prose*, ed.
> John Hayward (London, 1936), p. 165 ("To the Countess of Bedford")]

Accordingly, an attempt has been made to connect this with the crux: "Milton might well refer simply to Man, who, in his dual capacity of labour and prayer, stands ready ('at the door') to terminate the clerical abuses to which the poet has given attention in the preceding lines." E. S. Fussell, *NQ*, 193 (1948), 338.

14. Ed. Henry Kingsley (London, 1867), p. 398. The *OED* (citing another edition) quotes part of this, but cuts out "wooden Swords." The usage continues into the nineteenth century. Henry Wilkinson, *Engines of War* (London, 1841), has a section on swords (pp. 184–217), to say nothing of part 10, "On the Boomerang of Australia" (pp. 250–54).

15. *The Pilgrim's Progress*, ed. with *Grace Abounding*, by John Brown (Cambridge, 1907), p. 183.

16. *Criticorum Sacrorum*, VII (London, 1660), 4715.

17. Not confident that I would think of all possible key words to check in a concordance, I read the King James Bible from cover to cover in case there were lurking a suggestive passage not hitherto brought forward. I remembered how Milton scorned "the Ferrets and Moushunts of an Index" (*Works*, III, 35).

18. For illustrations and comments see pp. 754–56 of August Demmin, *Die Kriegswaffen in ihren Geschichtlichen Entwickelungen von den Ältesten Zeiten bis auf die Gegenwart* (Leipzig, 1891). The armory collection of the Metropolitan Museum, New York, abounds in specimens.

19. Song 12, 272ff. (*Works*, ed. J. W. Hebel, Oxford, 1933, p. 260).

20. *2 Henry VI*, II.i.46. For three early English references, see A. F. Pollard, *TLS*, Aug. 29, 1936, p. 697. See also Thomas Deloney, *Works*, ed. F. O. Mann (Oxford, 1912), pp. 203, 206–07, 209.

21. L. 1, ch. 23: "Puis ... saquoit de l'espée à deux mains ..." (*Oeuvres de Francois Rabelais*, ed. Louis Barré [Paris, 1856] p. 46).

22. *Works*, XII, 24.

23. Ibid., 25; *Complete Prose Works*, gen. ed. Don M. Wolfe (New Haven, 1953), I, 326.

24. See E.M.W. Tillyard, *Milton* (New York, 1930), p. 80.

25. *The Harmonious Vision: Studies in Milton's Poetry* (Baltimore, 1954), p. 68.

26. See Milton's *English Poems* (Oxford World's Classics, 1946), p. 505.

27. *Milton*, p. 387.

28. Pp. 57–60.

29. *TLS*, April 25, 1936, p. 356.

30. "That 'Two-Handed Engine' Finally?" in *Milton and Modern Man* (University, Alabama, 1968), pp. 114–17.

31. *Yet Once More: Verbal and Psychological Pattern in Milton* (New York, 1953; reprint edition, 1969); *Milton's Unchanging Mind: Three*

Essays (Port Washington, N.Y., 1973).

32.   Daniel Stempel, "John Knox and Milton's Two-Handed Engine," *ELN*, 3 (1966), 259–63.

33.   Ibid. 261.

34.   *Works*, III, 79. Italics in the original.

35.   There is one striking Old Testament parallel to the parable in John, Ezekiel 34, which has the characteristic Old Testament difference of containing the threat of punishment: "Woe be to the shepherds of Israel that do feed themselves! should not the shepherds feed the flocks? . . . Thus saith the Lord God; Behold, I am against the shepherds" (verses 2 & 10).

36.   As he told Diodati in the letter already mentioned: *Works*, XII, 28.

37.   Ruth Mohl dates it "in 1639 or 1640": *John Milton and His Commonplace Book* (New York, 1969), p. 224.

38.   Yale *Complete Prose* (New Haven, 1953), I, 423. I have corrected Mohl's translation from "law" to "laws": see Milton's Italian, *Works*, XVIII, 165.

39.   James H. Hanford, "The Chronology of Milton's Private Studies," *PMLA*, 36 (1921), 266 (and as reprinted in his *John Milton: Poet and Humanist*, Cleveland, 1966, p. 88) imagined the book was *Tratto [sic] delle revelatione della reformatione della chiesa*.

40.   *Oracolo della rinovatione della chiesa*, p. 48v. The parable may be found on pp. 187–89 of the anthology edited by P. Villari and E. Casanova, *Scelta di prediche e scritti di Fra Girolamo Savonarola* (Florence, 1898).

41.   See, for instance, the modern edition of the sermons of 1496, *Prediche Italiane ai Fiorentini* (Venice, 1930), ed. Roberto Palmarocchi, III, part 1, pp. 145, 306–07, 381, 384–85, 502–03; part 2, pp. 20, 156–57, 306–07, 346, 569–70.

42.   See, further, Mohl, pp. 224–25, who misprints "stranger Gardener."

43.   "Vidi . . . una mano in cielo, con una spada," etc. (Villari & Casanova, p. 357).

44.   Occurring (to take the sermons from 1494 to 1496 available in a modern edition) in *Prediche Italiane ai Fiorentini*, I, 10, 285; II, 33, 52–53, 54, 93, 147, 181, 203, 351; III, part 1, 177, 454; part 2, 114, 115, 567. See also Pasquale Villari, *Life and Times of Girolamo Savonarola* (New York, 1888), pp. 126, 450–51, 518, 602–03, 604, 638.

45.   Villari, *Life and Times*, p. 311.

46.   "The Parable of the Good Shepherd, 'De Contemptu Mundi,' and 'Lycidas,' " *ELH*, 3 (1936), 101–13.

47.   E.g., St. Augustine, *Patrologiae Latinae*, XXXV, 1727–30;

XXXVIII, 754–57. See the Index Parabolarum, *Patrologiae Latinae*, CCXIX, 268. The *Patrologiae Graecae* has as yet no equivalent index, but as an example see St. John Chrysostom, *Patrologiae Graecae*, LIX, 327ff.

48. *Prediche Italiane ai Fiorentini*, II, 141, 142, 144. The quotation from Ezekiel 34:2 illustrates how easy it is to go from John 10 to this Old Testament parallel. See above, n. 35.

49. Ibid., pp. 146–47.

50. Psalm 74 in the King James version, and there are crucial differences in translation. "Leva manus tuas in superbias eorum in finem" in the Vulgate (73:3) has become "Lift up thy feet unto the perpetual desolations" in the Anglican version (74:3). The equally suggestive "Exciderunt januas ejus in idipsum" (6) has been reduced to "But now they break down the carved work thereof." The modern opinion is that "the reference to 'doors' is more probable than that to 'carved work.'" *International Critical Commentary*, Charles A. and Emilie G. Briggs, *A Critical and Exegetical Commentary on the Book of Psalms* (New York, 1907), II, 153.

51. Large excerpts from the sermon are conveniently available in the Villari–Casanova *Scelta di Prediche*, pp. 35–52, and I quote where possible this (modernized) text, giving also page numbers for the complete text in *Sermoni e Prediche di F. Girolamo Savonarola* (Prato, 1846). Thus, here, *Scelta*, p. 37; *Sermoni*, p. 556.

52. *Scelta*, p. 37; *Sermoni*, p. 556.

53. *Scelta*, pp. 37–38; *Sermoni*, p. 556.

54. *Scelta*, p. 49; *Sermoni*, p. 570.

55. "That saying was common that former times had woodden Chalices and golden *Preists*; but they golden Chalices and woodden *Preists*" (*Works*, III, 25). Will T. Hale, editing *Of Reformation* (New Haven, 1916), p. 124, traces the epigram to St. Boniface (c. 740) and Camden.

56. *Scelta*, p. 35; *Sermoni*, p. 554.

57. *Scelta*, pp. 51–52; *Sermoni*, pp. 572-73.

58. *Sermoni*, p. 579. Villari makes an interesting misquotation at this point. In his *La Storia di Girolamo Savonarola e de' suoi tempi* (Florence, 1930), I, 200, professing to be quoting pp. 578–79 of the Prato, 1846 *Sermoni*, he has, instead of "Non ti maravigliare," etc., the following: "Ne' vi scandalizate, o fratelli, di queste parole, ma anzi, quando vedete che i buoni desiderano il flagello, egli è perchè essi desiderano che sai, desiderano che sai scacciato il male, e prosperi nel mondo il regno di Gesù Cristo benedetto. A noi oggi non resta a sperare altro, se non che la spada del Signore s'avvicini presto alla terra." These words occur nowhere in the sermon, and a check of the 1528 and 1544 editions in the Library of Congress reveals no textual variations here. I

have not seen the 1539 edition, but it is clear that Villari (as if under the spell of "Lycidas," since "s'avvicini" can—in fact does—turn up in translation as "smite" !) has gone astray, inexplicably.

59.   *Scelta*, p. 36; *Sermoni*, p. 555. He goes on to explain: "La qual punizione bene è significata per la destra, perchè la destra ferisce e percuote più fortemente che la sinistra" (*Sermoni*, p. 555). Three years later his note was similar: "Io vi dico che voi facciate penitenzia, e se voi non la farete, io vi anunzio due grandissimi flagelli: uno in questo mondo, el quale non potrete compare, cioè le tribulazioni che vengono, perchè il Signore Idio accelera presto: io vi dico che viene. L'altro flagello sarà chè anderanno nello inferno" (*Prediche Italiane ai Fiorentini*, III, part 2, pp. 567–68).

60.   On this word and its derivatives in Milton's poetry, see Elizabeth Holmes, "Some Notes on Milton's Use of Words," *Essays and Studies by Members of the English Association*, 10 (1924), 115–17.

61.   *Paradise Lost*, 1.46. It is the fall of pride, too.

62.   *Works*, III, 47. Theodore H. Banks, *Milton's Imagery* (New York, 1950), p. 246, takes it that Milton is thinking of the House of Pride (*Faerie Queene*, 1.4.4–5), but that is not a specifically ecclesiastical structure.

63.   John Reesing in *Milton's Poetic Art: A Mask, Lycidas, and Paradise Lost* (Cambridge, Mass., 1968), pp. 31–49. Those smitten with the conceit that there is automatically progress in these studies, that later articles are necessarily an improvement over earlier, should read this and an essay that is akin to it but ignores it, Kathleen M. Swaim, "Retributive Justice in 'Lycidas': The Two-Handed Engine," *Milton Studies*, II (1970), 119–29. Both bandy about the fashionable word "conflation," which turns out to be a synonym for confusion. Reesing skips about to more than a score of places in the Bible and for the "engine" tries to "conflate" rod, staff, scepter, sheephook, crosier (although "ever since 1552 all mention of the crosier had been omitted from the Anglican Ordinal and from every other part of the Prayer Book," p. 39). Being very open-minded, Reesing finds Thompson's Jack o' th' Clock theory (see above, n.12) also "suggestive" (p. 168). He pays no attention to my previously published objection to St. Peter and his instruments on the basis of "that" not being "this" (above, n.11). Swaim, who announces in her first sentence her distaste for "a precise equivalent," circumvents the "that" problem by saying, (p. 123) "St. Peter begins speaking with line 113, and it is not clear precisely where his speech ends—whether, that is, it ends with line 118 or with line 131." To how many others is it or has it ever been "not clear"? If Swaim were right, the poem, besides being explicit about the new speaker, would have had to shift into the plural at 132: "the dread voices are past." Ultimately Swaim opts for uncertainty as to who the original speaker is: "I suggest that the Pilot image may be another example of conflation. . . . here Peter and Christ" (p. 128, n.10). Swaim "conflates" for the engine "th'abhorred shears," the keys, the sheephook, the crosier, the cross, and the shears of "the shearers feast" (line

117). It is only fair to repeat that she did this apparently without the help of Reesing, who, with engaging candor, states, "a friend . . . did me the favor of reading an earlier version of this essay and was not persuaded" (p. 41).

64. Philip Rollinson, "The Traditional Contexts of Milton's 'Two-Handed Engine,'" *ELN*, 9 (1971), 28-35; Karl E. Felsen, "The 'Two-Handed Engine,' a Balanced View" (coming in 1975 *MQ*). While Felsen (a graduate student at the State University of New York at Albany) keeps to the scales, Rollinson goes in for conflation: "The two-handed engine refers metaphorically to Michael's scales (the two containers closely resemble two extended hands) which determine the fate of all men at the Last Judgement. The smiting refers to Michael's sword which immediately after the weighing of good and bad deeds consigns the damned to hell" (p. 28-29).

65. Ed. John Plummer (New York [1966]), 49. Cf. 58, "Fear of the Lord."

66. *Diary of Walter Yonge, Esq.*, Camden Society Publications, 41 (London, 1848), p. 70. John Chamberlain showed the attitudes on both sides:

> The papists geve out yt was a great blessing for them that perished, because their dieng in this manner is a *supersedeas* from Purgatorie and that they are gon directly to heaven, and their priests will not allow yt to be called or thought a judgement, but only a worke of God. A number were hurt, maymed, and lost their limmes which found little helpe or comfort at first, our people beeing growne so sauvage and barbarous that they refused to assist them with drincke, *aqua vitae*, or any other cordialls in their necessitie, but rather insulted upon them with taunts and gibes in their affliction as they were caried away all that evening and the night following, (for the mischaunce fell about fowre a clocke in the afternoone about the middle of their sermon) and even in Cheapside where they shold be more civill, they were redy to pull and teare them out of the coaches as they passed to their lodgings or to the surgeans. . . . [*Letters*, ed. Norman E. McClure (Philadelphia, 1939), II, 520-21]

67. In his *Parerga* (London, 1632). The poem occupies pages 10-13 and the following lines are also of particular interest:

> Exsurgit ipse Dominus, & causam suam
> Coepit tremenda vindicare dextera.
>   . . . extemplo crepat
> Tecti ruentis machina, imminentia
> Tabula collabuntur in subitae neci
> Devota capita, serus attonitus tremor
> Urget, ruina molis & fractae trabis
> Idololatras pondus elidit grave.

68. *Works*, ed. F. L. Lucas (New York, 1937), IV, 42, and note, 57.
69. Quoted in Elkin C. Wilson, *England's Eliza* (Cambridge, Mass., 1939), p. 144.

70.   Quoted in J. S. Brewer's edition of Thomas Fuller's *The Church History of Britain* (Oxford, 1845), V, 544. Curiously enough, Milton himself as historian dealt with such an incident: "A general Councel both of Nobles and Prelates, was held at *Caln* in *Wiltshire*, where while the dispute was hot, but chiefly against *Dunstan*, the room wherin they sat fell upon thir heads, killing some, maiming others, *Dunstan* only escaping upon a beam that fell not, and the King absent by reason of his tender age. This accident quieted the controversie, and brought both parts to hold with *Dunstan* and the Monks" (*Works*, X, 249-50).

71.   *The Fatall Vesper* .... *in the Black-Friers* (London, 1623, STC 6015) (no pagination). This short and relatively mild account ends, "Repent, repent for by these wonderfull signs and tokens it doth appeare most clearely that the kingdome of heaven is at hand."

72.   *Life of John Milton*, 3rd ed. (London, 1822), p. 161n.

73.   From here to the end of the paragraph, I am quoting my *Yet Once More: Verbal and Psychological Pattern in Milton*, p. 152. In a note, ibid., pp. 191-92, I remarked, "Under the doctrine of divine providence, men were accustomed to see, or to expect, the hand of God, or the sword of God, whenever anything extraordinary happened or catastrophic punishment of conspicuous sinners was hoped for." For instance, the prevalence of the plague in the year of "Lycidas" moved young Andrew Marvell at Cambridge to express himself as follows, in his "Ad Regem Carolum," a "Parodia" on Horace (*Carm.* 1.2) (published in *Sunodia Musarum Cantabrigiensium*, 1637). First he referred to God's hand:

> Jam satis pestis, satis atque diri
> Fulminis misit Pater, et rubenti
> Dextera nostras jaculatus arces
>   Terruit urbem.

Then, in the sixth stanza, he referred to God's sword:

> Audiit caelos acuisse ferrum
> Quo graves Turcae melius perirent;
> Audiit mortes vitio parentum
>   Rara juventus.

74.   If not from Elegia III (1626), 5-8:

> Dum procerum ingressa est splendentes marmore turres
>   Dira sepulchrali Mors metuenda face,
> Pulsavitque auro gravidos et iaspide muros,
>   Nec metuit satrapum sternere falce greges.

75.   Repeating the phrase I used of my haemony conjectures, above, p. 85.

VI

New Objections to a Pre-Restoration Date
for *Samson Agonistes*

That great heretic in Milton studies the late William Riley Parker performed a service by shaking up prejudices. We could not cling to old preconceptions merely because they had fitted comfortably, like well-worn slippers. There would have to be an examination of evidence. But what a shock each time Parker came up with something new! What a shock to be told that Milton (or a never-corrected printer) had misdated his own poems.[1] What a surprise to find in volume XVIII of the Columbia Milton[2] a third poem on Hobson, conjectured by Parker to have gone unacknowledged by its author. What a divorce from poignancy to replace Katherine Woodcock with Mary Powell as "my late espoused saint."[3]

I, for one, bridled at that—and finally bridled in print. I had to admit there were five or six plausible reasons why the wife came "veiled"[4]—not only because Milton had never in actuality seen her. I had to realize that my easy modern interpretation of "late" as an adjective meaning *deceased* was wrong because redundant. (Not that Henry King minded being slightly redundant in "The Exequy"—"Accept, thou shrine of my dead saint"—but a glance at a concordance showed Milton's practice to have been different.) I switched to "late" as adverbial: "late espoused" means "lately

129

married" (and *that* eliminates Mary Powell). To get accustomed to the usage, I quoted[5] from an anonymous play of
c. 1600: "As sadly as the late espoused man / Greeves to
Departe from his new maried wife. . . . " I did not see that
discussing which wife had fulfilled eighty days of purification
as prescribed in Leviticus 12:5 could decide anything,
"because it is impossible to tell whether 'as whom,' 5, does or
does not introduce a condition contrary to fact."[6] I pointed
out that all the emphasis on purity fitted the second wife's
Christian name, which is Greek for "pure."[7] It was absurd to
hold that the poet, in the midst of tenderly showing how
much he missed his wife, got in a thrust about "the impurity
of her body" (as a Parker supporter[8] puts it). In sum, I
refuted Parker to my own satisfaction, as did others.

Then came, in 1949,[9] another blow, the placing of *Samson
Agonistes* years before the Restoration, before, even, Milton's
blindness, partly on the curious theory (the New Criticism
was then in its heyday) that the drama could not afford to be
as autobiographical as it sounded. Parker mused (italics his),
*"The marvel is that the drama was ever printed, even as late
as 1671."*[10] "What shall we be hearing next," I remember
asking my students,—"that *Paradise Regained* was written
before *Paradise Lost*?" I was joking. Parker was not. He put
forward that theory too[11] (the need to refute which strikes
me as less urgent).

Undeterred, I committed in public "the autobiographical
fallacy," as many have done before and since. One paragraph
of a short preface to *Samson Agonistes* read:

> Self-identification must have lent its heightening or deepening
> force. The parallels are numerous—a champion of his people, "my
> breeding ordered and prescribed / As of a person separate to
> God, / Designed for great exploits" (30–32), who, betrayed by a
> wife from the enemy side, languishes blind and helpless in the midst
> of a ruined cause. It is almost too easy to see Mary Powell Milton in
> Dalila (as in Eve), and correspondences present themselves between
> Harapha and Salmasius, Milton's own father and Manoa, one chosen
> but relapsing people and another. Lines 693–96 look like a topical
> allusion; 697ff. come from a gout-sufferer; 566–71 corroborate

Richardson's picture of "Milton sitting in an elbow chair, black clothes and neat enough, pale but not cadaverous, his hands and fingers gouty and with chalk stones. Among other discourse he expressed himself to this purpose: that was he free from the pain this gave him, his blindness would be tolerable."[12]

In the same year as the above, 1961, there came out E. Sirluck's[13] point-by-point rebuttal of Parker's 1949 article and 1958 postscript. It remains the fullest refutation to date. Parker never replied to it.[14] But not everyone agreed (we can never expect that) with Watson Kirkconnell[15] that the position of Parker (and Allan H. Gilbert) had "been completely demolished." John Carey[16] asserted that "Sirluck's attempt . . . to counter Parker's theory leaves it in the main unimpaired." Thus, the best British annotated edition since Verity places *Samson Agonistes* before *Paradise Lost*. Parker's former student John Shawcross had offered the same arrangement in 1963,[17] which, however, he withdrew in 1971, "not because I have altered my belief concerning its date of composition, but because its former position isolated some of the minor poems from others, creating a frankly odd arrangement. It is perhaps best to place the three major poems together, and the standard placement of *Samson Agonistes* last allows one to contrast it effectively with *Paradise Regain'd* in interpretation and form. The dating of the three major poems is, in any case, particularly uncertain and has been frequently challenged."[18]

Although Parker did not formally answer Sirluck, he continued to maintain his heresy in his big biography of 1968, making some new points, as he also did in a February 7, 1961, talk that was published posthumously in 1971.[19] I wish therefore to offer some supplementary material under numbered headings.

1. The Unreliability of the Anonymous Biographer and Edward Phillips. Neither says that *Samson Agonistes* was written before the Restoration, hard as Parker worked to twist such message from them. To erect a superstructure on their slippery prose and inaccurate chronology is to build on sand. If we were to follow the Anonymous Biographer, *Animadversions* comes after *Church Government, Tetrachordon* after *Colasterion*, and *Areopagitica* after both. Mary Powell returned "when Oxford was surrendr'd"[20] (June, 1646): in fact, she was already pregnant in her husband's house in the Barbican. In the Anonymous Biographer's only mention of *Samson Agonistes*, he is not pretending to any information, I submit, except that it was published after the Restoration. In a one-sentence paragraph he wishes to take account of all Milton's works between *Pro Se Defensio*, 1655 (the title of which he gets wrong) and the poet's death in 1674. Up to the colon he refers to the Latin Thesaurus, *Paradise Lost*, and *De Doctrina Christiana*. Then, in his haste to cover ground, he commits a zeugma, which I correct with square brackets: "All which, notwithstanding the several Calamities befalling him in his fortunes, hee finish'd after the Restoration: As also [he published] the *Brittish history* down to the Conquest, *Paradise regaind, Samson Agonistes,* a Tragedy, *Logica & Accedence commenc'd Grammar* & had begun a *Greek Thesaurus.* . . ."[21] The Anonymous biographer intends merely to list works in order of publication, though, as usual, he gets the order wrong: he should have put the Latin Grammar (1669) first. If this source is telling us anything, it is that *Samson Agonistes* belongs "after the Restoration."

As for Edward Phillips, it is amusing to read Parker's own indictment of his accuracy in the preface to *Milton*: " . . . There are big gaps in his knowledge. . . . Moreover, he is extraordinarily careless about dates; he mentions only four in his entire biography, and three of them are wrong. . . . One wishes that he inspired more confidence as an historian."[22] So this is the source we must pay attention to when he says, "It cannot certainly be concluded when he wrote his excellent Tragedy entitled *Samson Agonistes*, but sure enough it is that it came forth after his publication of *Paradice lost*, together with his other Poem call'd *Paradice regain'd*, which doubtless was begun and finisht and Printed after the other was publisht, and that in a wonderful short space considering the sublimeness of it. . . . "[23] Sirluck replies, "If Edward Phillips thought *S.A.* written before *P.L.*, why did he not say so?"[24] If the earlier biographer regretted that Milton had "no better a Pen to celebrate his Memory,"[25] so Phillips mourned (and also rightly) the lack of "a well–informed Pen."[26] Edward Phillips is one of those casual journalists who let one word beget another–or the same. In this area of his manuscript, for instance, he went facilely from one "doubtless" to another. Immediately before he wrote, "It cannot certainly be concluded," he had written, "where at present is uncertain" (referring to the location of the "Character of the Long Parliament" of the *History of Britain*). Staring at his manuscript, its last clause, he got to thinking that he did not know, within a range of years, when *Samson* was written. (Unfortunately, we have no Thomas Ellwood to give us an anecdote about that–which some modern heretics would then disbelieve anyway.) Such mild doubt also expressed and not checked for the (narrow) range of the antiprelatical tracts, hardly encourages sensational conclusions: there is no invitation to leave the first decade of Charles II at most. Phillips, like all lazy persons, is easily impressed by contrasting industry: thus his "wonderful short space" for the composition of *Paradise Regained*, about which Parker also makes much. It is a compliment both conventional and sincere. The next-to-last relation in the Life is about how fast Milton worked. As for 1653, the year of Salmasius's death, which Parker and Shawcross assign for the revision of *Samson*, Phillips explicitly records his belief that Milton, for a change, did nothing: "And now I presume our Author had some breathing space; but it was not long. . . ."[27]

2. *The Links between* Samson Agonistes *and* Paradise Regained. If we may be allowed to conclude, contra Parker and Shawcross, that all of *Paradise Regained* was written after *Paradise Lost*–that Milton was not being disingenuous in presenting *Paradise Regained* as a sequel and that Ellwood was not lying in telling of its composition after 1665–then *Paradise Regained* points to a late date for *Samson* on account of connections between them. The first connection,

not at all to be slighted, is their joint publication in 1671.
They belong together, as the Old Testament belongs with the
New. They have, for the most part, a common severity of
style and outlook. *Paradise Regained* is statistically close to
drama, with only 508 lines out of 2070 not in dialogue or
soliloquy. Both poems deal with the problems of faith,
obedience to God, and redemption: Samson under the old
dispensation, Jesus as the embodiment of the new. The two
principals are seen resisting various common kinds of temptation. Hebrews 11:33 puts Samson among those "who
through faith subdued kingdoms."

Although the brief epic does not refer to Samson, there is
what sounds like a covert or unconscious allusion in book 1,
410–15:

> . . . Thou com'st indeed,
> As a poor miserable captive thrall,
> Comes to the place where he before had sat
> Among the Prime in Splendour, now depos'd,
> Ejected, emptyed, gaz'd, unpityed, shun'd,
> A spectacle of ruin or of scorn . . . .

Are we not put in mind, to borrow a pun from Northrop
Frye[28] (and perhaps Milton), of "the gaze of Gaza"? The
opening soliloquies are interchangeable to some extent. "O
what a multitude of thoughts at once / Awakn'd in me swarm
(*P.R.,* 1.196): this could be Samson, who does complain of
"restless thoughts, that like a deadly swarm / Of Hornets
arm'd . . . rush upon me thronging" (19). "Retiring from the
popular noise, I seek / This unfrequented place" (16)–the
desert? "O wherefore was my birth from Heaven foretold"
(23)–by Gabriel? Each recalls a youth of very special
promise. "Christ is led by 'some strong motion' [1.290] into
the wilderness and Samson to the destruction of Dagon's
temple by 'some rouzing motions' [1382] which he feels
within himself."[29] The former gives Greece credit for "Arts"
(4.338), but says that "*Sion's* songs" (347) precede in every
sense: that amounts to virtually a blurb for *Samson
Agonistes.*

The subordinate print and phrasing on the common title page, "To which is added *Samson Agonistes*," may give the impression of something that had been lying around for years and was taken out of a drawer "to fill up the space" (as the publisher Brabazon Aylmer said of the addition of the *Prolusiones* to Milton's *Epistolarum Familiarium*). But why then was not *Paradise Regained* published sooner (of which more at the close)? The probability is that *Paradise Regained* is being featured as the sequel to *Paradise Lost* and Samson quite properly subordinated to Jesus. One speculation is that "the traditional conception of Samson as a type of Christ probably helped Milton to choose this story to follow" its predecessors.[30] If, however, there were a gap in time between the two jointly published works, would that not have been stated, just as, two years later, when *Of Education* was included in the 1673 *Poems*, there was added the explanatory note, "Written above twenty years since"?

3. The Argument from Rhyme. Parker's contention is that the note on "The Verse" to *Paradise Lost*, attacking rhyme, precludes *Samson* from having been composed in *"the years immediately preceding or immediately following"* 1668.[31] Sirluck's principal answer[32] is that *Paradise Lost* has some rhyme. There are points to be added: (*a*) Milton's original intention did not include having a note on "The Verse." No doubt to his irritation, he was asked for one by the publisher S. Simmons after conventional and unperceptive readers inquired "why the Poem Rimes not." If we do not see that he was writing as the partisan of the moment and in over-reaction and in distaste for what was being produced for the Restoration stage, we shall have him condemning his own 1645 *Poems* that he was willing to republish and add rhymed poems to in 1673. (*b*) As Parker concedes, "there is not much" rhyme in *Samson Agonistes*—154 lines out of 1758, or about one-eleventh. This hardly makes *Samson Agonistes* a rhymed poem. (*c*) Parker quotes one sentence from A. W. Verity: "Milton's occasional use of rhyme in the play is not easy to explain." Parker ought to have finished quoting, for Verity goes on to give explanations. "In some instances the rhyme is probably accidental: in others (cf. ll.1010 *et seq.*) it may be intended, as Professor Percival suggests, to express contempt. In the choruses it serves to emphasize their lyrical character, and Milton may mean it to compensate, in some degree, for their lack of division into strophe, antistrophe and epode."[33] The Verity-Percival suggestion is, I take it, that in such a place as 1010ff. we have Milton's "Fit of Rhyme Against Rhyme"—a very interesting idea, which connects with two recent articles that find the chorus treated ironically.[34] Our author's satiric bent is not to be underrated. He may be slyly illustrating, by his "jingling," the same "contempt" expressed in his 1668 note, making that year a totally likely one for *Samson*.

4. *Specious Evidence.* In his biography Parker gives eighty quotations from *Samson Agonistes* that parallel Milton's prose works of the 1640s.[35] In my *Yet Once More: Verbal and Psychological Pattern in Milton,*[36] I give hundreds of verbal parallels between works that are many years apart (e.g., *Comus* and *Paradise Lost*). I called the parallels method of dating "specious" and commented, "There is no span of years within his productive lifetime across which Milton will not and does not reach to borrow from himself."[37] In a paperback edition[38] I gave about forty phrases *Paradise Lost* and *Samson* share, and I could give at least ten of some interest for *Paradise Regained–Samson,*[39] including a whole cluster around "Tyrannic power" (1.219; 1275)—"heroic," "quell," "the earth," "brute," "truth," but I have to say that not enough is demonstrated. Parker's evidence can be used against him, for he has seized a two-edged sword. The majority of his parallels are with the divorce tracts. The following,[40] for example, is most impressive:

> What e're it be, to wisest men and best
> Seeming at first all heavenly under virgin veil,
> Soft, modest, meek, demure,
> Once join'd, the contrary she proves, a thorn
> Intestin, far within defensive arms
> A cleaving mischief, in his way to vertue.... [1034–39]

the best and wisest men (*Tetrachordon*, 4.87)
the bashfull mutenes of a virgin. . . the sober man
honouring the appearance of modesty, and hoping well
of every sociall vertue under that veile (*Doctrine and*
Discipline of Divorce, 3.394-95)
the sequestr'd and vail'd modesty of that sex (*DDD*, 3.502)
a thorn in his heart (*Tetr.*, 4.93)
a begirting mischeif (*Tetr.*, 4.173)
a familiar and co-inhabiting mischiefe (*DDD*, 3.381)
in the glorious way to high vertu and matchless deeds (*Bucer*, 4.17)

Mary Powell being behind the divorce tracts, Parker has provided stunningly detailed reasons to believe she also haunts *Samson Agonistes*.

Another piquant argument is that "In *Paradise Lost*, IX. 1060–1, 'Dalilah' is mentioned as a harlot; in *Samson Agonistes* (e.g., 321, 537) 'Dalila' is Samson's lawful wife."[41] Why did Parker give as reference line 537, which says nothing about "wife": rather, the passage is remarkably parallel with *Paradise Lost*:

At length to lay my head and hallow'd pledge
Of all my strength in the lascivious lap
Of a deceitful Concubine who shore me
Like a tame Weather. . . [*S.A.*, 535–8]

So rose the *Danite* strong
Herculean Samson from the Harlot-lap
Of Philistean Dalilah, and wak'd
Shorn of his strength. [*P.L.*, 9:1059–62]

If Parker has demonstrated anything, he has pointed to the closeness of *Paradise Lost* (its latter part) and *Samson Agonistes*. Recent critics have called the last three poems "a trilogy."[42] Hanford about fifty years ago remarked, "The desire expressed in the introduction to Book IX of *Paradise Lost* to sing 'the better fortitude of patience and heroic martyrdom,' is fulfilled by the portrayal of a divine pattern in *Paradise Regained. Samson Agonistes* is its nearest possible fulfillment in the life of mortal man."[43]

It is supposed to be significant that "In *Paradise Lost*,
1.422, 438, Milton shows that he knows 'Ashtaroth' to be a
plural form and 'Astoreth' a singular; in *Samson Agonistes*
1242 'Astaroth' is treated as a singular, as in *Nativity* 200
(and *Paradise Regained*, 3.417)."[44] This is a game that two
can play. In *Of Reformation* (*Works*, III, 60) occurs the
phrase "the wings of those his Cherubins, that fanne his Mercy-
seat." "Cherubins" adds a plural to a plural: was Milton's
Hebrew faulty in 1641? He knew better when he wrote in the
Nativity Ode of "The helmed Cherubim / And sworded
Seraphim" (112). Therefore, "On the Morning of Christ's
Nativity" (1629) is later than *Of Reformation*![45] These are
the caprices of an author or his printer, duplicated by
Milton's first annotator Patrick Hume. Hume's *Annotations
on Milton's "Paradise Lost"* (1695) show (1:422, 438) that
he knows Ashtaroth to be "Plur." and Astoreth to be singular: "An Idol of the *Phoenicians*." But a few lines further
down, 444, speaking of Solomon, he says, "Of his adoring
Asteroth the Goddess of the *Sydonians,* consult 1 *Kings*
2"—getting everything wrong, including the biblical chapter,
that he had right before. What is to be made of this? Nothing.

"Melpomene, the muse of tragedy, appears (with seeming
inappropriateness) in a corner of the portrait published with
the 1645 Poems."[46] So does Clio, for whom would be better
substituted Euterpe or Thalia.[47] Milton may no more have
approved the selection of those corner figures—Melpomene,
Erato, Urania, Clio—than he approved Marshall's engraving of
himself, but in any case Parker is demonstrably wrong about
the "inappropriateness" of Melpomene. She properly appears
(booted but significantly without her usual tragic mask) because of the funeral poems. (She could also be there because
she and her "Scepter'd Pall"—clearly pictured—are mentioned
in "Il Penseroso," 97–98.) This muse was not invoked only
for tragedy: Horace invokes her in his ode on the death of
Quintilius Varus, Virgil's friend: "Praecipe lugubres / Cantus,
Melpomene" (*Car.*, 1:24, 2-3). Instead, we are asked to believe that the poet as yet unknown to fame is cryptically
alerting—in the upper left-hand corner—the fit audience (and
they would be few indeed!) that he is at work on a tragedy!

How about Clio (bottom right-hand corner) as a hint at those never-finished histories, *Moscovia* and *Britain*?[48] If ever there was a case of stringing up zeros in the hope of making a sum!

"Milton's tragedy, like his anti-prelatical tracts, is almost devoid of theology. . . . Its severe avoidance of theology (the Fall, original sin, the Devil, Hell, even the concept of immortality) is . . . difficult to explain."[49] Parker is longing for *Paradise Lost*, which had already been published. The Old Testament does not have "the concept of immortality," as Milton pointed out in his *Christian Doctrine (Works*, XVI, 111–15). The first three chapters of Genesis exist in isolation, and their subject is never returned to in the Old Testament. Decorum, which is "the grand master-piece to observe," [50] forbade injecting Christian theology into the poem. "The author of *Samson Agonistes* eschews almost every opportunity to assume or express a theological position,"[51] because there *were* no opportunities. Parker is often plumping for an impersonal Milton, who, if he has a misogynistic passage, is not voicing his own view but what is appropriate to the literary situation. But now we are asked to be puzzled because the same author avoided gross anachronisms and managed to keep his religious beliefs, however deeply and passionately held, out of a poem where they did not belong. According to argumentative convenience, Parker veers between an objective Milton—a good dramatist—and a subjective one, an uncontrolled egotist and didactician.

5. *Topical Allusions.* In his 1961 lecture[52] Parker objected to finding lines 692–94 topical, since they fit the Old Testament and even the *Iliad*. But why did he not go on one line more, to the reference to "unjust tribunals, under change of times" (695)? This fits the royalist vengeance on both the living and the dead (including the execution of Milton's friend Sir Harry Vane on June 14, 1662)—and it fits nothing else that one can think of. Parker protests that "Cromwell, Bradshaw, and Ireton were never victims of the 'hostile sword of heathen and profane.' " True, but Vane was beheaded (the ax is a modification of the sword), and his sentence (commuted

at the last minute on the plea of relatives) was to be hanged, drawn, and quartered and share the fate of regicides, "thir carkasses To dogs and fowls a prey." Vane on the scaffold "hoped they would be civil to his body when dead." To a Puritan, Cavaliers and Catholics were sufficiently "Heathen and profane," and the hostility was mutual. Charles II had a particular resentment against this heroic idealist and failed to keep his word to spare his life. The king wrote Clarendon, "If he has given new occasion to be hanged, certainly he is too dangerous a man to let live, if we can honestly put him out of the way."[53] His trial, of course, was far from "honest." He met his end with dignity. Milton's sonnet to him could, needless to say, have only the underground and anonymous publication it received in *The Life and Death of Sir Henry Vane* (1662). It is possible that Milton would have liked to have got in many more hits at the regime, but, like a playwright under James I and Elizabeth I, he had to be careful with his topical allusions.[54]

I believe that Milton had Vane (as well as himself) in mind in the preceding verse paragraph, when he wrote of God's countenancing the downfall of

> such as thou hast solemnly elected
> With gifts and graces eminently adorn'd
> To some great work, thy glory,
> And people's safety, which in part they effect. [678]

The first two lines echo God's declaration in *Paradise Lost* (3.183): "Some I have chosen of peculiar grace / Elect above the rest." But the author, because it is not Anno Domini, the year of grace, has to change "grace" to "graces"—a considerable diminution but still a clear pointer of what he would have said if he had been as poor a dramatist as Parker asked for. "To some great work, thy glory": Samuel Pepys, from whom I have already taken one quotation from Vane's last words, also recorded under that execution date of June 14, 1662, the doomed man's declaration that "he never did, to this day, any thing against his conscience, but all for the glory of God." "People's safety" is also suspect. The standard expression is "public good" (the Roman "pro bono publico"). That is what Milton used elsewhere, including this poem (867; *Paradise Regained*, 1.204; *Works*, IV, 63; V, 129, 237; VI, 160, 265). In switching to "people's safety" he would be alluding to his own and others' last attempts in October, 1659, to prevent a return to single–person government. Under date of October 20 the blind man dictated "A Letter to a Friend, Concerning the Ruptures of the Commonwealth" (the friend very likely Vane).[55] To quote Parker, "Six days later a new supreme senate, a Committee of Safety so called, was created by the army officers at Wallingford House, and among its twenty-three members were some whom Milton himself would have chosen, men of experience and integrity. They were agreed, moreover, on government without a single person."[56] Vane was invited to join the Committee of Safety, and though he refused, he was associated in the public mind with Lambert and the other army ousters of the Rump. On Vane's downfall in January, 1660, he was jeered in a ballad, "Sir Harry Vane's Last Sigh for the Committee of Safety."[57] Milton referred to the Committee in *Proposalls of Certaine Expedients (Works,* XVIII, 3). "Great work, . . . which in part they effect": Bishop Newton caught this long ago as a reference to "the Heads of the Independent Enthusiasts" and what they did and did not accomplish: "the overthrow of the monarchy, without being able to raise their projected republick."[58]

6. *Suspicion of Autobiography.* Parker is embarrassed at the possibility of connections with Milton's post-Restoration situation, although he freely speculates on "the pertinence of the Samson story for Milton in the period 1647–1653." [59] We are allowed a bit of autobiographical impulse but not much: approaching blindness rather than actual blindness, some reasons to be discouraged but not too many, a faint whiff of personal marital discord, but Heaven spare Mary Powell each and "every ugly suspicion that crawls into print."[60] I never crawled into print against Professor Parker about Milton's first marriage (and I shall not now), but I did

correspond with him about Milton's unhappy 1647 letter to
Dati: Parker was very insistent that a man can be living with
his in-laws and disliking them, without irritation spilling over
onto the wife, and he challenged me to asseverate that Milton
would take back and have children by a woman he did not
love.

Such a monolithic view of love and life does not allow
even transient dissatisfactions or melancholic moods. I must
say I find the following special pleading unrealistic: "But
what of Samson's great speeches on blindness, those passages
in the tragedy which cry with acute awareness of horror? In
simple truth we cannot tell when these passages were written,
but we can believe that they have about them the eloquence
and conviction of newly-met reality. If Milton composed
them after he had won his struggle for serenity, he was
torturing himself for art and risking a dangerous spiritual
relapse."[61] So Milton won, once and for all, and no matter
what new pressures, "his struggle for serenity," around 1654,
and that was that? He kept it for twenty years until he died,
with never a doubt, never a waver? This is an inhuman
conclusion, belied by the personal passages in *Paradise Lost*.
Richardson's report, backed as it is by 7.25ff., has the ring of
truth: "He was in Perpetual Terror of being assassinated,
though he had Escap'd the Talons of the Law, he knew he
had Made Himself Enemies in Abundance. He was So
Dejected he would lie Awake whole Nights."[62]

Also, I believe that this poet, being great (something that
transcends playing it safe and discreetly: discretion can be
left to professors), *would* torture himself for art. He would
torture himself for and with ultimate release, "calm of mind,
all passion spent." *Samson Agonistes* was his release, his
catharsis.[63] He has told us so in his preface, which immediately gets as medical as Burton (who himself had declared,
"I write of melancholy, by being busy to avoid melancholy"[64]). "Things of melancholic hue and quality are us'd
against melancholy." For this homeopathic theory not being
confined to readers and viewers of tragedy, but applicable
also to the author thereof, we need not go outside Aristotle's

Poetics: "Given the same natural qualifications, he who feels the emotions to be described will be the most convincing; distress and anger, for instance, are portrayed most truthfully by one who is feeling them at the moment."[65]

Parker may blush for Milton's being personal, but Milton did not blush. He did not hesitate to inject himself into his writings: Diekhoff's compilation *Milton On Himself*[66] comes to 270 pages. As early as 1642 he put into print his marital preference: "I . . . would choose a virgin of mean fortunes, honestly bred, before the wealthiest widow."[67] In the divorce tracts he strove for impersonality (perhaps not altogether successfully), as the sine qua non of persuasive argument. But his was too strong an individuality to remain suppressed for long.

In the midst of a strong argument, Parker does admit the possibility of Milton's having "a disturbing thought" en passant. "If there was one attack which Milton probably resented above all others, it was the widespread idea, published and talked by royalist sympathizers, that his blindness had been God's punishment upon him for misdeeds. If such a disturbing thought ever crossed Milton's own mind (and it may have!), he would certainly not have put it on paper to comfort his enemies; on the contrary, in his second and third *Defences* (1654–1655) he is at great pains to prove that it simply cannot be true. Yet Samson's blindness, as Milton repeatedly makes clear, was God's punishment for disobedience and loss of virtue."[68] To oppose this it is not necessary to speculate whether Milton ever really regarded himself, even momentarily, as a reprobate. The only necessary question is whether he was ever pressured to feel like one. He himself said that an unhappy husband (free of anything comparable to Milton's later misfortunes) could have such a feeling: "The continuall sight of his deluded thoughts without cure, must needs be to him, if especially his complexion incline him to melancholy, a daily trouble and paine of losse like that which Reprobates feel."[69] Some of the time it would be true of the author what Arnold Stein says of Samson: "He is not questioning God's will but *must* give expression to his pain."[70]

If an excess of biographical speculation leads to vulgarity, the penalty of overinsisting on impersonality is a failure to appreciate the real feeling in the poem. All that Parker could see in the stasimon beginning, "Many are the sayings of the wise / In antient and in modern books enroll'd; / Extolling Patience as the truest fortitude" (652) was "platitudes about patience."[71] The author of a 1963 article, finding parallels and with them breadth and depth, is less bored: "But, as noted earlier, almost identical praise of patience as the highest fortitude is to be found in other passages clearly representing the poet's own views. To these might surely be added that personification of Patience who replies to prevent the murmur of the near-despairing Milton writhing in blind isolation from God's purposes for his life. These instances are not platitudinous; neither then are likely to be the words offered by Samson's countrymen at the point of his greatest despair. In some sense, the choral passage must represent the poet's own Christian belief."[72]

To proceed to specifics, why did Milton invite personal speculation by making Dalila Samson's wife (contrary to the biblical account)?[73] Why does the chorus say, after her departure, "Yet beauty, though injurious, hath strange power, / After offence returning, to regain / Love once possest" (1003)? This is not pertinent to Samson, who could not be moved by Dalila's "beauty" because he could not see it. It is hard not to recall Mary Powell Milton's sudden reappearance after her desertion (and Eve's similar contriteness, 10.910ff.), when, by Phillips's account,[74] her husband "was surprised to see one whom he thought to have never seen more, making Submission and begging Pardon on her knees before him."[75] It is Parker himself who in his biography speculates, "Such beauty as she had, such freshness and youthful vitality, must now, between seventeen and twenty, have flowered most perceptibly."[76]

Why does Milton invent the episode of Harapha, which markedly lowers the tragic tone? Salmasius was not a warrior, but Harapha does not fight, either: he is just a word man, "Tongue-doughty Giant" (1181), "a rougher tongue"

(1066).[77] Samson defeats him with words, tongue to tongue, even as Milton in 1660 proudly recalled that controversial Latin triumph: "Nor was the heroic cause unsuccessfully defended to all Christendom, against the tongue of a famous and thought invincible adversarie" (*Ready and Easy Way, Works,* VI, 116). The following lines fit perfectly Salmasius's ignominious departure from the court of Queen Christina, after Milton's battering:

> His Giantship is gone somewhat crest-fall'n,
> Stalking with less unconsci'nable strides,
> And lower lookes, but in a sultrie chafe. [1244]

The lines are so appropriate that Parker's *Milton* echoes a key word from them: "Queen Christina of Sweden. . . regally dismissed the crestfallen Salmasius."[78] "His Giantship" (a contemptuous substantive coined by Milton) is a reminder that "Ha Rapha" means "The Giant" in Hebrew.[79] Salmasius was the swollen and strutting giant among Continental scholars, whom Milton deflated, and Salmasius's book, running as high as 720 pages depending on the edition, was a dead and dreary ponderosity, a vast heap of misapplied pedantry. It would be hard to think of four words that better summed it up than "bulk without spirit vast" (1238). The Praefatio to the *Pro Populo Anglicano Defensio* characterizes Salmasius in the first sentence: "profusus verborum, vacuus rerum" (*Works,* VII, 2). It soon gets very close to "bulk without spirit vast": "moli tanta libri inconcinna" (VII, 22, and at the end of the book, "acervum cum satis magnum in fine congesseris"). What is further interesting (none of this has been pointed out before) is that in the Praefatio Salmasius struts and frets upon a stage: so Milton repeatedly presents him, beginning with "coryphaeo" (VII, 4). Harapha has often been seen as a miles gloriosus.[80] So Salmasius was like a Terentian soldier, "veluti miles ille Terentianus" in hiding behind the mass of his book (as Harapha was invited to cover himself with armor, 1119ff.). The French hireling was exceedingly *gloriosus*: "superbia et fastidio, ut ferunt,

supra modum turget" (VII, 22). Samson called Harapha a
"coward" (1237), as Milton did Salmasius, "homo
ignavissime" (VII, 36). The latter used tragic terms for the
king's downfall. Milton uses sarcasm: "Perorans plane
tragicus es" (VII, 40); "Sed pergit iste noster ampullari, et
mirabiles tragoedias fingere" (VII, 18). We are hearing the
bombast of an actor, "ovantem" (VII, 10), "prodit histrio in
proscenium" (VII, 14), "resume nunc quam suscepisti
personam" (VII, 286).

As a final touch we have,

I dread him not, nor all his Giant-brood,
Though Fame divulge him Father of five Sons
All of Gigantic size. . . .[1247]

By an odd coincidence, Salmasius had five sons, all of some
little accomplishment.[81] Claude the Younger supervised the
publication in 1660 of his father's *Responsio* to Milton,
posthumous and fragmentary. In 1674 Andrew Marvell associated Milton with Samson pulling down the temple.[82] In
1694 Edward Phillips compared Milton versus Salmasius to
David versus Goliath (Harapha's son, 1249).[83] This is the sort
of readers best qualified to know what was under the surface
of *Samson Agonistes.*

Like Samson, Milton came late in their life to his parents,
his father being about forty-six, his mother about thirty-six
when he was born. Manoa remarks, "I pray'd for Children"
(352). Why the plural, which fits the elder Miltons, not the
Book of Judges? The large part played by Manoa, which has
no more biblical authority than making Dalila Samson's wife,
amounts practically to allegory, since "Manoa" means "rest,"
and rest is exactly what Manoa offers—and nothing else. He
does not understand his son. Milton's "Ad Patrem" is
addressed to a father who does not understand his son but
who indulged him and bought him time and freedom.[84] J. B.
Broadbent,[85] writing about the innovational rhythms of the
choral odes (e.g., 1268–71), profoundly observed, "These
collisions are characteristic of Milton's work: highly indi-
viduated talent striving to realise itself but anxious all the

time to be authorised by tradition—a filial talent excusing itself to paternal authority." Such was Samson's predicament also. While his enemies argued that he was "Due by the Law to capital punishment" (1225), Milton was "ransomed" from captivity at the Restoration. There was even a dispute about the gaoler's fee. True, Milton's father did not pay it, having died full of years in 1647, but the son continued to live on his "Patrimony" (1482). "Fathers are wont to lay up for thir Sons" (1485).

For more than eight months before he passed away at approximately eighty-four, "locks white as down" (327: I am assuming that the father, like the son, was spared baldness), the elder Milton had had to put up with the horde of Powells that his son had taken in after they became refugees with the fall of Oxford. The mother-in-law was definitely unpleasant, the father-in-law got sick and died before the elder Milton's eyes, there were at least five boys and girls under sixteen, and Mary had given birth to a squalling (in fact defective, though that may not have yet been apparent) baby. It is easy to imagine the father being moved to say to the distracted poet, "I cannot praise thy Marriage choises, Son" (420)—yes, using the plural with sarcastic reference to all the extras that came with the wife.

Manoa, Dalila, Harapha—to restore them to their order in Milton's life and poem—we do not reach the Restoration with them. But we reach Milton late in life with two classes of peculiar reference to Samson involving the gout and old age. The lines

> If these they scape, perhaps in poverty
> With sickness and disease thou bow'st them down,
> Painful diseases and deform'd,
> In crude old age;
> Though not disordinate, yet causless suffring
> The punishment of dissolute days [697]

were glossed by Newton: "This was his own case; he escaped with life, but lived in poverty, and though he was always very sober and temperate, yet he was much afflicted with the gout

and other *painful diseases, in crude old age, cruda senectus,*
when he was not yet a very old man."[86] Something has
happened to Milton since he finished *Paradise Lost* in 1665
with its optimistic preaching that by "the rule of not too
much, by temperance taught" (11.531) one could reach an
untormented old age. The Lord has seen fit to visit him,
"though not disordinate," with "the punishment of [the]
dissolute," the "causless suffring" of the gout, podagra. He
might just as well have been one of "the Sons Of *Belial,*
flown with insolence and wine" (*P.L.*, 1:502) or the
Philistines, "th'Idolatrous rout amidst thir wine" (443),
"Drunk with Idolatry, drunk with Wine, / And fat regorg'd of
Bulls and Goats" (1670). No wonder he gloomily added some
more diseases, including "moaping Melancholie," to *Paradise
Lost* (11.485–87) in 1674.

"Painful diseases and deform'd" (699) fits the gout, as
does "sedentary numness craze my limbs" (571).[87] The reference to "deform'd" and to the immobilizing of the "limbs"
is very specific. Parker's alternative, "a reminder of Job,"[88]
will not do. This is not "sore boils from the sole of his foot
unto his crown" (Job 2:7). Milton's affliction is referred to
by Aubrey, the Anonymous Biographer, Christopher Milton,
and the servant Elizabeth Fisher, but the best medical
description comes from Richardson, who received "from an
Ancient Clergy-man in *Dorsetshire,* Dr. *Wright*" the first-
hand information, already quoted, of those "Hands and
Fingers Gouty, and with Chalk Stones" and the poet's
mention of "the Pain This gave him,"[89] which, indeed, was
so much on his consciousness that it even registered in his
metaphors. Samson's thoughts "Exasperate, exulcerate, and
raise / Dire inflammation which no cooling herb / Or
medcinal liquor can asswage" (625).[90]

What indeed has that legendary strong man, still in the
prime of life, to do with disease of any sort? And, for my last
point, why does "old age" keep getting mentioned
(572,700,925,1487, and only once before in Milton's poetry,
P.L., 11.538)? And there is the significant combination
"decrepit age" (69). The standard assumption is that Samson,

who had "judged Israel in the days of the Philistines twenty years" (Judges 15:20), was about forty. Milton was not one to consider forty old:[91] in fact, he had called Vane, at thirty-nine, "young in years." Samson refers to himself as being "in my flower of youth and strength" (938). Yet there are the contravening passages befitting a man in his sixties, who not only has the gout but insomnia (459,629), and whose "genial spirits droop" (594), despite the fact that he has been getting back his strength. As I commented recently in a different connection, "Of course it is partly his helpless blindness (1489) and partly his hopeless frame of mind and the way he keeps looking back over his past, but he seems a fit candidate for an old folks' home."[92] Milton's present condition has been superimposed upon Samson.

"From under ashes into sudden flame" (1601)—Milton in his "dramatic poem" (as it is labeled on its separate title page) triumphs over adversity and adversaries in the catharsis of art.

The indications are—virtually *all* the indications are[93]—that the centuries of commentators and biographers have not been wrong in their common-sense assumption that *Samson Agonistes* is a late work, belonging to the years just preceding its publication. The forward limit would be July 2, 1670, when the book was licensed. Edward A. Block, author of "Milton's Gout,"[94] takes as the *terminus a quo* August 15, 1666, when the poet, in his last extant letter, wrote to Peter Heimbach that he was well.

However, the time can be plausibly narrowed to 1668–70, on the following basis. Ellwood seems to be telling us that *Paradise Regained* was shown to him in manuscript by 1667.[95] Milton might have delayed publication of the shorter epic to see how the long one, just out or about to come out, would fare with the public. But why would he wait more than a year? A reasonable conjecture comes from Allan H. Gilbert.[96] "The publisher of that short epic, like the bookseller who issued *Moscovia*, 'hop'd to have procured some other suitable Piece of the same Author's to have joyn'd with it.' " But that had to wait, not as Gilbert and Parker think, upon digging out of a drawer an old work (which even in the most cluttered circumstances can scarcely take a week), but upon the composition of a new work suitable for joint publication. *Paradise Regained* went to press as soon as *Samson Agonistes* was ready. Indeed, what the Errata calls "the latter Poem" was still being worked on in 1670. "There is evidence that Milton not only supervised the printing of the 1671 edition with care but perhaps actually made an addition to *Samson Agonistes* while the work was going through the press. Lines 1527–35 appear at the end under the heading 'Omissa.' The passage in the main body of the text seems coherent without them, and they may well be an afterthought designed to introduce the element of irony into the situation at this point."[97] That the lines were an addition and not something that the printer had accidentally dropped from the manuscript (the Omissa are on a separate page from the Errata) is demonstrated by the fact that they resulted in an inconsistency, which the author did not have time to consider. It had been Manoa's original idea that Samson's vision might be miraculously restored (583–89) and he comes back to this hope at 1503. But when the chorus hypothesizes that God has indeed wrought this miracle, Manoa, for no reason given, voices skepticism: "He can I know but doubt to think he will" (1534) and "That were a joy presumptuous to be thought" (1531).

A pre-Restoration conjecture is gratuitous and against the grain and a futile exercise in skepticism for skepticism's sake that rapidly turns into a new faith, the more stubbornly clung to the more it is assailed. One can only exclaim, "O dark, dark, dark, amid the blaze of noon!" It is in the highest spirit of scholarship to try on something for size, but also to discard it when it does not fit. Admittedly, we get bored with the obvious. We desire to say something new. It is a hazard of the profession.

NOTES

1.   W. R. Parker, "Some Problems in the Chronology of Milton's Early Poems," *RES*, 11 (1935), 276–83; "Milton's Fair Infant," *TLS*, Dec. 17, 1938, 802; "Notes on the Chronology of Milton's Latin Poems," in *A Tribute to George Coffin Taylor,* ed. A. Williams (Chapel Hill, 1952), pp. 113–31.

2.   Pp. 359, 590–92 (New York, 1938). This edition, 18 vols., I quote for the prose (except at n. 69). For the poetry I use Frank A. Patterson (ed.), *The Student's Milton* (New York, 1933).

3.   Parker, "Milton's Last Sonnet," *RES*, 21 (1945), 235–38.

4.   I gave five in "The Veiled Face of Milton's Wife," *NQ*, n.s. 1 (1954), 245–46. A sixth would be the influence of the traditional representation of the Anima Rationalis, as in Ripa's *Iconologia*, 1603, p. 21, as cited and translated by Edward A. Maser (ed.), Cesare Ripa, *Baroque and Rococo Pictorial Imagery: The 1758–60 Hertel Edition of Ripa's "Iconologia" with 200 Engraved Illustrations* (New York, 1971), plate 5: "The personification of the Soul is a female figure draped in white, the color of purity, the color which is supposedly not made up of any other colors, just as the soul is not composed of anything earthly. Her head is covered with a transparent veil, since the soul, according to St. Augustine, *De definitione animae*, is invisible to human eyes. Through the veil, the woman is seen to be beautiful, since God, the source of all beauty and perfection, created man in His own image."

5.   *A Milton Dictionary* (New York, 1961), p. 312.

6.   Ibid., p. 311. "Moreover, the speaker's wife is a Christian figure, and therefore could not be saved by the old Law any more than by the force of Hercules" (Marilyn L. Williamson, "A Reading of Milton's Twenty-Third Sonnet," *Milton Studies,* 4 (1972), 143).

7.   "The Veiled Face of Milton's Wife," p. 246.

8.   John T. Shawcross, "Milton's Sonnet 23," *NQ*, n.s. 3 (1956), 203.

9.   Parker, "The Date of *Samson Agonistes*," *PQ*, 28:145–66. Also Allan H. Gilbert in the same issue, 106: "The tragedy is essentially an early work, following soon after the making of the notes in the Cambridge Manuscript."

10.   Ibid., 150.

11.   Beginning with "The Date of 'Samson Agonistes': A Postscript," *NQ*, n.s. 5 (1958), 202, and continuing in *Milton: A Biography,* 2 vols. (Oxford, 1968), pp. 616, 1139–42.

12.   Le Comte (ed.) *"Paradise Lost" and Other Poems* (New York, 1961), p. 345.

13.   As an appendix to "Milton's Idle Right Hand," *JEGP*, 60.733–81. (The Parker and Sirluck articles are reprinted in Ralph E. Hone (ed.), *John Milton's "Samson Agonistes": The Poem and Materials for Analysis,* San Francisco, 1966, pp. 218–57.) Dating by metrical analysis has been attempted with opposing results: Ants Oras, "Milton's Blank

Verse and the Chronology of His Major Poems," *SAMLA Studies in Milton,* ed. J. Max Patrick (Gainesville, Fla. 1953), pp. 128–97; also in *Blank Verse and Chronology in Milton,* University of Florida Monographs, Humanities no. 20 (Gainesville, Fla. 1966), finds for the traditional view. Shawcross backs Parker with "The Chronology of Milton's Major Poems," *PMLA,* 76 (1961), 345–58. George M. Muldrow, *Milton and the Drama of the Soul* (The Hague, 1970), appendix: "A Note on the Probable Date of *Samson Agonistes*" pp. 240–62, supports the usual date finally on the basis of changes in *De Doctrina Christiana* made after Jeremie Picard left Milton's employ as his amanuensis in 1661.

14.   Except obliquely in the restatement of his position in *Milton,* pp. 903-17, e.g., "That *Paradise Lost* contains occasional rimes (perhaps as many as 160 out of 5,282 possibilities) is irrelevant" (p. 904).

15.   *That Invincible Samson: The Theme of "Samson Agonistes" in World Literature with Translations of the Major Analogues* (Toronto, 1964), p. 179, n. 4.

16.   Editor with Alastair Fowler of *The Poems of John Milton* (London, 1968), p. 332.

17.   Ed., *The Complete English Poetry* (New York). A reviewer declared, "I might as well say at the outset that I simply refuse to use an edition" with such a placing (William G. Madsen in *College English,* 27 (1966), 513). Both this edition and Shawcross's 1971 edition date *Samson* "1646–48?; revised, 1653 or later?"; *Paradise Regained,* "c. 1646–48?; revised or, according to some critics, written after 1665." "Some critics" is probably the biggest understatement since "I cannot praise thy Marriage choises, Son" (*S.A.,* 420).

18.   *The Complete Poetry of John Milton* (New York), p. v.

19.   "The Date of *Samson Agonistes* Again," in *Calm of Mind: Tercentenary Essays on "Paradise Regained" and "Samson Agonistes",* ed. J. A. Wittreich, Jr. (Cleveland, 1971), pp. 163–74.

20.   *Early Lives of Milton,* ed. Helen Darbishire (London, 1932), p. 22. Parker in 1949 did not say what text of the early lives he was quoting: it was not this one.

21.   Darbishire, p. 29.

22.   P. xiii.

23.   Darbishire, p. 75.

24.   P. 776.

25.   Darbishire, p. 32.

26.   Ibid., p. 50.

27.   Ibid., p. 70.

28.   "Agon and Logos: Revolution and Revelation," in Balachandra Rajan (ed.), *The Prison and the Pinnacle* (Toronto, 1973), p. 150.

29.   Rajan, "To Which Is Added Samson Agonistes," op. cit., p. 104.

30. Geoffrey and Margaret Bullough (eds.), *Milton's Dramatic Poems* (London, 1958), p. 46.

31. "The Date of *Samson Agonistes*," p. 149.

32. Pp. 776–7.

33. A. W. Verity (ed.), *Milton's "Samson Agonistes"* (Cambridge, 1892), p. lxvi. (In Hone, p. 159.)

34. Roberts W. French, "Rhyme and the Chorus of *Samson Agonistes*," *Laurel Review*, 10 (1970), 60–67; Louis L. Martz, "Chorus and Character in *Samson Agonistes*," *Milton Studies*, 1 (1969), 115–34. Arnold Stein found 1010ff. "Miltonic light verse" (*Heroic Knowledge: An Interpretation of "Paradise Regained" and "Samson Agonistes"* [Minneapolis, 1957], p. 177).

35. *Milton*, pp. 911–17.

36. (New York, 1953; repr. ed., 1969.)

37. Ibid., p. 60.

38. Cited above, n. 12.

39. *Yet Once More*, pp. 66–67.

40. *Milton*, pp. 914–15.

41. Ibid., p. 908. Under date of July 22, 1964, Parker circulated among Milton scholars specific questions in connection with his editing of the forthcoming *Variorum*, of which one was, "Why does Samson call his wife a concubine?" I would answer, "Because he feels that she has acted like one, a bought woman."

42. E. L. Marilla, *Milton and Modern Man* (University, Alabama, 1968), p. 76; Arthur Barker, *The Prison and the Pinnacle*, p. 16.

43. James Holly Hanford, *"Samson Agonistes* and Milton in Old Age" (1925), in *John Milton: Poet and Humanist* (Cleveland, 1966), p. 274.

44. *Milton*, p. 908.

45. The same game can be played with Shakespeare. When the ignorant man from Stratford wrote *Hamlet*, he thought "Baptista" a feminine name (III.ii.249, "his wife, Baptista" in the play-within-the-play). When he wrote *The Taming of the Shrew* he knew better. Therefore, *The Taming of the Shrew* is later than *Hamlet*.

46. *Milton*, p. 906.

47. But Milton refers to Clio three times in his Latin poetry (Eleg. 4, 31; "Ad Patrem," 14; "Mansus," 24), "in a traditional way, as the prime and general representative of poetry; she had acquired that function because, from Hesiod (*Theog.* 77) onward, she commonly came first in lists of the Muses." Douglas Bush, *Variorum Commentary*, I (New York, 1970), 241.

48.   Again I am joking where Parker was not: "There are Clio and Urania to symbolize the interest in history and natural science reflected in both *Of Education* and Milton's private studies" (*Milton*, p. 296).

49.   *Milton*, p. 907.

50.   *Of Education, Works*, IV, 286.

51.   *Milton*, p. 909. He does have St. Paul's antinomianism. See Samuel S. Stollman, "Milton's Samson and the Jewish Tradition," *Milton Studies*, III (1971), 185–200. I will not answer Parker by joining the typology craze, under the sway of which it becomes obligatory, for instance in the first paragraph of an essay on Samson and Manoa, to give vent to such solemn nonsense as: "The interactions suggest the workings between the Eternal Father and His Son, albeit obliquely, and between Adam, as first father, (and having failed to cope with a Latin tag: "*in media res*" [sic]), and all mankind as his posterity." Having said this, the writer then wisely forgets about it and even, on the same page, contradicts it: "Samson is no Christ figure." F. Michael Krouse started it all by making the fallacious assumption, without a shred of internal evidence, that because some of the biblical commentators found Christ in Samson, Milton *must be* intending the same connection (*Milton's Samson and the Christian Tradition* (Princeton 1949), pp. 118ff.). Many are those who have tripped down (or up) that pious path since. A recent typological article begins, with a typical blast of discovery, "In spite of its format *Samson Agonistes* is really a dramatic poem rather than a drama;[1]" I turned to the note wondering if there would be cited the separate title page of 1671, which says, "A Dramatic Poem." But no, the reference is to another article by somebody else, who, it turns out, is not aware of this fact either, but cited in his turn seven other articles and books. These typology articles are loftily above facts; they feed on air, like the chameleon, and on one another.

52.   *Calm of Mind*, p. 168.

53.   David Masson, *The Life of John Milton* (New York, 1946), VI, 231.

54.   Masson and Tillyard give Milton much credit in this regard. "It is impossible to point out a single particular in which, having chosen for his subject the Biblical story of Samson's dying revenge, he has over-strained it for a personal purpose." Having said this, Masson then goes on to the "personal" (VI, 670–8). E. M. W. Tillyard, *Milton* (New York, 1930), pp. 329–30: "As a political manifesto Milton must have enjoyed writing *Samson Agonistes*. It is nothing less than stark defiance of the restored government and a prophecy that it will be overthrown. And yet there is scarcely a word in the play that could not be referred quite plausibly to the story of Samson as narrated in the Old Testament. The controversial side of Milton's nature must have got rich satisfaction." Since Tillyard wrote, the "political" approach to *Samson Agonistes* has not been in fashion, but see Mary Radzinowicz, "*Samson Agonistes* and Milton the Politician in Defeat," *PQ*, 44 (1965), 454–71, which was inspired by William Haller, "The Tragedy of God's English-

man," in J. A. Mazzeo (ed), *Reason and the Imagination: Studies in the History of Ideas, 1600–1800* (New York, 1962), pp. 201–11.

55.   Masson, *Life*, V, 618.

56.   *Milton*, p. 537.

57.   *DNB*, XX, 126. I do not wish to push Milton's rather conventional phrases too hard, for they can have a wide applicability. "Public safety" occurs in *The Tenure of Kings and Magistrates* (*Works*, V, 10); cf. "the general safety," *P.L.*, 2.481. "Thy glory" (*S.A.*; cf. *P.L.*, 12.477) or "the glory of God" (Vane) is a standard appeal: see *OED*, s.v. "glory," 2 b. Both "the glory of God" and "people's safety" were slogans of the Revolution of the 1640s. Henry Parker wrote in 1642 that the "paramount law that shall give law to all human laws whatsoever . . . is *salus populi*." *A Representation of the Army*, 1647, stated, "Nor is that supreme end, the glory of God, wanting in these cases to set a price upon all such proceedings of righteousness and justice." (I derive these quotations from *Puritanism and Liberty*, ed. A.S.P. Woodhouse [Chicago, 1951], pp. [91] and 405.) But my point is that these phrases become connected with the downfall of Vane. The *Samson Agonistes* passage refers to elect but discountenanced leaders.

58.   Thomas Newton (ed.), *The Poetical Works* (Dublin, 1754), III, ad loc., or in the variorum editions of Henry John Todd, e.g., *Poetical Works* (London, 1801), IV, 414. To return to *The Life and Death of Sir Henry Vane, Kt.*, attributed to George Sikes, Milton must have had at least portions of it read to him, since pp. 93–94 contained his sonnet, followed by a commentary on it on pp. 94 and 98. There are parallel attitudes certainly worth a footnote, including a comparison with Samson (first mentioned on the first page) on p. 119: "He has more advantaged a good CAUSE and condemned a bad one, done his honest Countrey-men more service, and his enemies more disservice by his death, (as *Sampson* served the *Philistines*) then before in all his Life, though that also were very considerable." Cf. *S.A.* 1660–68, "Living or dying thou hast fulfill'd," etc. With 1745–48, ending "ever best found in the close," compare p. 142, "What work God will suffer to be made by any instruments of cruelty amongst us . . . he himself best knows. But that God will send deliverance in the close. . . I am. . . confident." On the scaffold, according to "A Letter from a Person of Quality" (p. 162), "he strove to make the People in love with that Freedom, they had so lavishly and foolishly thrown away," in contrast to, Sikes says, "teachers and professors" who "have been the meanes of betraying the whole Nation afresh, and rolling all back again into more insufferable bondage than ever" (p. 20). Cf. *S.A.* 268–74, the last two lines—"Whom God hath of his special favour rais'd / As thir Deliverer"—corresponding to "He was one of the peculiar Favourites of Heaven" (p. 96). The idea of betrayal is very prominent: "All is vanished, save a few faithful, chast-spirited men, who for being true to their trust, steadfast in their Covenant and undertake, have been and are daily delivered up *as Lambs for the slaughter*, by their apostatized friends" (p. 71). "He was for several years rejected, persecuted, &

imprisoned by his apostatized friends (that had gone to the house of
God in company with him) who at length to compleat their persecuting
work upon him, delivered him up, to be hunted to death by his
professed foes, enemies of all righteousness, Gods and mans too"
(p. 105). "Thus treacherously was this steddy witness of the true
Liberties of Christs Kingdom and his native Countrey, handled by those
that for many years had joyned with him in the profession of the same
righteous CAUSE, against sacrilegious and tyrannical domination in
Church or State" (p. 106). The last page (162) reads: "He was great in
all his Actions, but to me he seemed greatest in his Sufferings, when his
Enemies seem to fear, that He alone should be able to acquaint them
with a Change of Fortune."

59.   "The Date of *Samson Agonistes*," p. 164.

60.   Ibid., p. 165; *Milton*, p. 318.

61.   "The Date of *Samson Agonistes*," p. 163.

62.   Darbishire, p. 276. A. S. P. Woodhouse might have quoted this in
connection with his hypothesis of a date for *Samson* less radically early
than Parker's, but still, I give reasons to believe, too early: "the year
following upon the Restoration, between May 1660 and May 1661"
(*The Heavenly Muse: A Preface to Milton* (Toronto, 1972), p. 294).
Woodhouse himself undermines his first hypothesis with his eloquent
presentation of a second: "Though Masson recognized no such
necessity, it is, indeed, possible to devise an hypothesis which would
permit us to regard *Samson* as Milton's last poem: namely, that unlike
Paradise Regained, it was the product, not of Milton's normal state of
mind, but of one of those periods of depression, of retrospective and
introspective brooding, which must, as old age came on and physical
powers waned, have beset any man in Milton's situation: his world in
ruins about him, and himself old and ailing, blind and essentially alone.
In such a mood the certainties of *Paradise Regained* would recede and
the paradise within have to be struggled for again" (ibid., p. 295).

63.   After writing the above I came upon the following in Muldrow,
p. 253: "The theory of catharsis advanced in the preface to the drama
could have worked as well for the poet as for his audience." I should
have expected this to have been said often. For some psychoanalysis see
Donald Greene, "The Sin of Pride: A Sketch for a Literary Explora-
tion," *New Mexico Quarterly*, 34 (1964), 21-22.

64.   Robert Burton, *Anatomy of Melancholy*, Everyman's Library, I,
20.

65.   Ingram Bywater translation, ch. 17 (1455a), *The Student's
Oxford Aristotle*, ed. W.D. Ross, VI (London, 1942).

66.   (Oxford, 1939).

67.   *Apology for Smectymnuus, Works*, III, 342.

68.   "The Date of *Samson Agonistes*," p. 150.

69.   *The Doctrine and Discipline of Divorce*, 1st ed., 1643, in J. Max
Patrick (ed.), *The Prose of John Milton* (New York, 1967), p. 148.

70. *Heroic Knowledge*, p. 141.

71. Parker, *Milton's Debt to Greek Tragedy in "Samson Agonistes"* (Baltimore, 1937), p. 39.

72. William O. Harris, "Despair and 'Patience as the Truest Fortitude' in *Samson Agonistes*," originally *ELH*, 30 (1963), in *Critical Essays on Milton from "ELH"* (Baltimore, 1969), p. 286. I have changed "murmer."

73. This was not an unheard of view among the Christian biblical commentators, but naturally a minority one. See Krouse, p. 76. The rabbis made her the wife (Stollman, p. 189). I do not deny aesthetic reasons for the change. "Milton gives his hero tragic dignity by having him wed, with the idea of serving God, the cause of his downfall" (Parker, *Milton*, p. 318). "By making her his wife instead of the mistress . . . Milton intended to stress the depth of her treason and of Samson's infatuation." Merritt Y. Hughes (ed.), *Complete Poems and Major Prose* (New York, 1957), p. 534. But the notorious "divorcer" was certainly inviting speculation, the more so as the first wife, the woman of Timna, is made to sound divorced rather than dead: "She proving false, the next I took to Wife" (227). Samson also "divorces" Dalila. See Dayton Haskin, "Divorce as a Path to Union with God in *Samson Agonistes*," *ELH*, 38 (1971), 358–76.

74. Refused admission into the text of Parker's *Milton*: see p. 927.

75. Darbishire, p. 66.

76. *Milton*, p. 298.

77. For clarity I have modernized "tongue-doubtie."

78. P. 409. The index volume to Masson's *Life*, VII, 205, 1st column, top, uses "crestfallen" in the same connection.

79. In *A Milton Dictionary*, p. 281, I stated that Salmasius rendered his *Defensio Regia* "in French under the megalomaniac pseudonym of 'Claude Le Gros' "—which would make a neat, if recondite, connection here. My authority for the pseudonym was the unsigned article on Salmasius in the eleventh edition of the *Encyclopedia Britannica*—and ultimately Eug. and Em. Haag, *La France protestante* (reprinted Geneva, 1966), IX, 168, where the name is expanded to Claude Legros de Saint-Hilaire. Salmasius *was* his own translator' *Apologie Royale Povr Charles I. Roy D'Angleterre* (Paris, 1650). (See F. F. Madan, "A Revised Bibliography of Salmasius's *Defensio Regia* and Milton's *Pro Populo Anglicano Defensio*," *The Library* [London], 9, 5th ser. [1954], 109.) But I became suspicious when none of the bibliographical entries listed the pseudonym. Alison M. Gee of the British Museum staff, having examined for me their copy of this rare book, writes: "The name Charles [sic] Le Gros does not appear on the title-page as translator, nor is there any reference to him in the rest of this work." What was the origin of this potentially interesting mistake? At the right European library it might be possible to find out.

80. Daniel C. Boughner, "Milton's Harapha and Renaissance Comedy," *ELH*, 11 (1944), 297–306.

81.   Haag, IX, 161.

82.   "On *Paradise Lost*," prefatory poem to the second edition, ll.5ff.:

> the Argument
> Held me a while misdoubting his Intent,
> That he would ruine (for I saw him strong)
> The sacred Truths to Fable and old Song
> (So *Sampson* groap'd the Temples Posts in spight)
> The World o'rewhelming to revenge his sight.

With reference to Marvell's comment on the behavior of Charles I on the scaffold, "He nothing common did or mean / Upon that memorable scene," ll. 57–58 of "An Horatian Ode upon Cromwell's return from Ireland" (written in June, 1650), had Marvell read in manuscript and was he answering the second sentence of Milton's *Pro Populo Anglicano Defensio*, which begins, "Dicam enim res neque parvas, neque vulgares"? I finish quoting the sentence and add Samuel Lee Wolff's translation (*Works*, VII, 2–5): "Regem potentissimum, oppressis legibus, religione afflicta, pro libidine regnantem, tandem a suo populo, qui servitutem longam servierat, bello victum; inde in custodiam traditum; et cum nullam omnino melius de se sperandi materiam vel dictis vel factis praeberet, a summo demum regni Concilio capite damnatum; et pro ipsis Regiae foribus securi percussum." "For I shall relate no common things, or mean; but how a most puissant king, when he had trampled upon the laws, and stricken down religion, and was ruling at his own lust and wantonness, was at last subdued in the field by his own people, who had served a long term of slavery; how he was thereupon put under guard, and when he gave no ground whatever, by either word or action, to hope better things of him, was finally by the highest council of the realm condemned to die, and beheaded before his very palace gate." Milton's recommendation of Marvell to Bradshaw on February 21, 1653, has the tenor of new and slight acquaintance, but their enemies dated their friendship back to *Eikonoklastes* (1649): see Pierre Legouis, *Andrew Marvell: Poet, Puritan, Patriot* (Oxford, 2nd ed., 1968), p. 93. A possibly not unusual litotes is not much to build on, but I deem the question worth raising, in passing.

83.   "Our little *English David* had the Courage to undertake this great *French Goliah*, to whom he gave such a hit in the Forehead, that he presently staggered, and soon after fell" (Darbishire, p. 70). On the Goliath-Harapha resemblance, see John M. Steadman, *Milton's Epic Characters* (Chapel Hill, 1968), pp. 185–93.

84.   Both fathers realize the power of money: we go, so to speak, from "gazas" ("Ad Patrem," 94) to Gaza.

85.   *Milton: "Comus" and "Samson Agonistes"* (Great Neck, N.Y., 1961), p. 37.

86.   Newton, ad loc. (see note 58).

87. Edward A. Block, in his otherwise comprehensive article, "Milton's Gout," *Bulletin of the History of Medicine*, 28 (1954), 201–11, misses this line.

88. *Calm of Mind*, p. 169.

89. Darbishire, 203–04.

90. I quote a standard reference book: "Inspection shows the cardinal signs of an acute inflammatory response resembling an infection, with swelling, warmth, redness, and exquisite tenderness." *The Merck Manual of Diagnosis and Therapy*, 12th ed. (Rahway, N.J., 1972), p. 1102.

91. See "Milton versus Time," in my *Milton's Unchanging Mind* (Port Washington, N.Y., 1973), pp. 5–68.

92. Ibid., p. 46.

93. Parker's strongest point, in my view, reads: "There is. . . a tantalizing sentence in the preface in which Milton speaks of the stage and says, parenthetically: 'to which this work never was intended.' Why didn't he say: 'to which this work is *not* intended'? It could not have been intended for the stage in the period 1642–1660" (*Calm of Mind*, p. 164). Milton's temporal adverbs can be troublesome. There is "yet once more" in the sonnet to his wife. There is the almost algebraic "For never but once more was either like / To meet so great a foe" (*P.L.*, 2.721). There is the reference in the preface to *Samson* to "*Aeschulus, Sophocles,* and *Euripides*, the three Tragic Poets unequall'd yet by any," which Walter Savage Landor regretted "because it may leave a suspicion that he fancied he, essentially undramatic, could equal them, and had now done it; and because it exhibits him as a detractor of Shakespeare" *Imaginary Conversations*, "Southey and Landor: Second Conversation," in *Works* (London, 1846), II, 160. To get back to "never was intended," Milton must mean that ever since he first contemplated a Samson drama and made entries for one in his notebook, c. 1640, he never intended that it be for the stage, Puritan (they closed the theaters), or Restoration.

There is nothing to Parker's contention that Edward Phillips borrowed material from *Samson* (in manuscript) for the third edition of his *The New World of Words* (1671). *Milton*, p. 1142; "Milton's Harapha," *TLS*, January 2, 1937, p. 12. This has been disposed of by Geoffrey M. Ridden, "Milton and Phillip's [sic] *New World of Words,*" *MQ*, 7 (1973), 29–32.

94. P. 209.

95. "Ellwood's account implies, but does not explicitly say, that he saw a manuscript of *Paradise Regained* not long after the conversation at Chalfont" (1665). Parker, *Milton*, p. 1142.

96. "Is *Samson Agonistes* Unfinished?" *PQ*, 28 (1949), 106. There is also the theory that Milton entirely of his own volition held back *P.R.* until *S.A.* was finished (Alfred Stern, *Milton und Seine Zeit* [Leipzig, 1879], II, Viertes Buch, 120–21).

97. James Holly Hanford and James G. Taaffe, *A Milton Handbook* (New York, 1970), p. 223 (repeated from earlier editions of Hanford's *Handbook*). 1537 was also omitted, and 1536 had been given to the chorus.

VII

Marvell's
"The Nymph Complaining
for the Death of Her Fawn"

The author of one of the more recent articles on Marvell's poem starts a book by quoting James Russell Lowell. "Will it *do* to say anything more about Chaucer?" asked Lowell—and that was over a hundred years ago. "Can anyone hope to say anything, not new, but even fresh, on a topic so well worn?" But Lowell, who was, after all, something of a genius and very much a linguist, wrote anyway, and so do thousands now, who are neither. Sometimes they seem to be moved only by "publish or perish," not realizing that there is such a thing as publishing *and* perishing.

When I was a graduate student at Columbia University thirty-five years ago, the prospect for research in English or American literature was widely regarded, even then, as desperate. How could one hope to say anything new about Chaucer or Shakespeare or Milton or Poe? The bones had been picked over for a century, or several centuries, as the case might be. There was nothing left to do. Even third-rate authors had been mulled over, or mauled over. Even the most diligent and talented aficionados of research were hard pressed, while the average student seeking a bread-and-butter degree, the tired teacher from Texas perspiring through summer session for credits toward tenure or a salary increment, asked professors to find them subjects who were having trouble finding subjects for themselves. Master's Essays had to be written and doctoral dissertations, at Columbia, published. Each was to be "an original contribution to scholarship." One professor solved the problem by having each of his students do a history of English literature for one year. "You do 1597," he said, "and you do 1598. Study every text you can set eyes on that came out that year."

Obviously, this was a temporary expedient that ran out of years. Even if one found a subject with which there was still room to move around, somebody in Iowa was probably already at work on it, and it would be a race against time as to who would be first to come out with it. Horror stories abounded. In 1938 there appeared two definitive works on Thomas Fuller's *The Holy State*. In 1939, on opposite sides of the Atlantic, appeared competing definitive editions of the letters of William Shenstone. The American editor has a poignant and hastily inserted footnote in his preface: "We learn as we go to press, of a forthcoming edition of the letters of Shenstone by Miss Marjorie Williams, a work of which we had long since reluctantly despaired and which we now welcome with renewed interest." Ah, that reluctant despair, how often we gleaners in a cluttered field have known it! In recent years excellent biographers of Southampton and of Keats have known it, the tough competition for the public prize. The preface to a 1971 collection of essays by Miltonists mentions a coincidence of the sort with which scientists (submitting, say, to *Nature*) are quite familiar: "two of us in the same month submitted substantially the same article with the same conclusions to the *Harvard Theological Review*. Even the titles were similar: 'Milton's Arianism Reconsidered' and 'Milton's Arianism.' " I had a gifted colleague interested in doing a life of Henry Vaughan, but deterred by rumors that two ladies in England were sitting on heaps of material gathered for *their* biography of the poet. The ladies died, leaving very little behind them, and so in fact did my friend. I, when it became known that I was doing a life of Donne, was advised in several quarters to cease and desist, because (1) the definitive life had already been done, but the only manuscript of it disappeared after being left in a London taxi; (2) another well-known worker was about to come out with *his* definitive life. My reply was that my book was just to be a short one, not at all definitive.

The conscientious worker is lacerated between pressure to rush into print and a desire to produce careful, mature work. Any little particular "discovery" has to be rushed. One of our best graduate students came to me a while back, a happy gleam in his eye. "I've just realized what the two-handed engine in 'Lycidas' is," he said. "The scales of souls at the Last Judgment." "You're too late," I answered. "That came out in *ELN* last year." I knew how he felt. It had happened to me. For years at Columbia College I had taught The *Aeneid* in one course (Freshman Humanities) and Marvell in another (The Seventeenth Century), and I was well aware of a probably prime inspiration for Marvell's "The Nymph Complaining." At last, because I had additional things to say, I wrote an article early in 1951. While my manuscript was being disapproved of at the first journal I sent it to, *PMLA*, Kenneth Muir came out with *my* Virgilian point in *Notes and Queries*. (On the other hand, Paola Colaiacomo issued from Rome in 1960 an article that reproduced portions of mine in Italian—without quotation marks and without happening to mention, anywhere, my name.[1] I am told this is an honor, of sorts.)

If the pickings had not become so desperately lean, there might be less jealousy over what is *mine* and what is yours. Of course, we are hemmed in more and more with each yearly proliferation of "scholarship," even though universities give up requiring Master's Essays and make more modest demands of doctoral candidates. In 1973 a veteran scholar in a portly book complains that dissertations "are becoming increasingly impressionistic." And what does *he* preen himself on in one of his footnotes? On having looked up a quotation admittedly referred to by someone else forty years earlier: "quoted in full for the first time, I believe, here" ! As original research has become less and less possible, the linguistic equipment for doing it in such a field as the Renaissance has vanished. I recall an article a generation ago on one of the putative neo-Latin sources of *Comus*: the author admitted, without embarrassment, that he had engaged someone to make an English translation for him. How different from the older, legendary stories of Kittredge crossing the Atlantic to check a footnote or the Blake scholar studying Japanese because there were two articles in that language that might, that just might, be helpful. Now it seems that the *Publications* of the Modern Language Association are to be published in no other modern language than English: no longer can a substantial part of the membership be expected to cope with French, or German, or Italian. The will, the very will, to learn much of anything is lacking, which is one reason why a good research book on Milton, such as C.A. Patrides's *Milton and the Christian Tradition* (1966), is such a rarity. No wonder we lose hordes of graduate students to sociology, not just on grounds of "relevance," but because of the obvious appeal of instant research: all you need do, apparently, is distribute a questionnaire among seven secretaries, or five bartenders, or thirty-one freshmen, and presto! you have the material for an article, if not a book.

But one solution to this academic problem in literature has become very conspicuous in the last twenty years or so. This is, give up all pretence of doing research: do literary criticism instead. It beats spending months in the stacks. *Anybody* can do literary criticism. All he needs is an idea or an angle that has not been used before; lacking even that, he can at least carry someone else's idea a bit further.

And that precisely is what we have been having with commentaries on Andrew Marvell's "The Nymph Complaining"—one wild fantasy after another, unencumbered by research. It is not even necessary to spell correctly. Two of the articles mix up "faun" and "fawn," misled by Marvell's seventeenth-century "u" spelling of the latter. After all, when conflation and typology are all the rage, what is the difference? and if we are giving up research and literalness we may as well give up literacy, because what really counts is the inner light, profundity, and spirituality. So one of these writers tells us, as if he were reviewing Debussy, "The lips of the faun communicate something like blood. Is it too much to suppose that this singular image may represent 'the Blood of our Lord Jesus Christ,' presented to the partakers of Holy Communion, one of the most important functions of the Church?" This spelling of fawn is not just a solitary misprint: it runs through the article. And another article goes on in the same way, "The faun here becomes on one level of reading a Christ figure slain by the sins of the world." Spenser and Milton saw Pan as Christ; ignorance has lost track of Marvell's deer, substituting a goat—foot. A third contributor, Ruth Nevo, who *can* spell, finds a pun, identifies Marvell's four-footed fawn with "the lustful offspring of satyrs, half-man, half-beast." But it is also—Miss Nevo has been reading Ficino—"the countenance of God," "the glow of God in the beauty of the creature."

A contributor to *Explicator* leaves, as it were, the SPCA to join the SPCC: the nymph and fawn are "a mother mourning the arbitrary murder of her . . . infant."

All the modern eccentricities and extravagances owe much to a 1940 book. Before 1940 all the commentators were obtuse and blind—and sensible. To deal with the one book, the mother of them all, is in large measure to deal with her unruly and mutually quarreling offspring of the last twenty years.

To all appearances, "The Nymph Complaining for the Death of Her Fawn" is a pastoral delineating with "a pretty skipping grace" and many *concetti* a girl's tender relation with and mourning for her pet that "wanton Troopers riding by / Have shot." The poem, a favorite with anthologists even before Palgrave added a portion of it to *The Golden Treasury* in 1883, undoubtedly has had a goodly number of appreciators, and, of these, none (including T. S. Eliot, who certainly cannot be accused of lack of sensitivity in these matters) had taken it other than literally until the appearance of *Andrew Marvell* by M. C. Bradbrook and M. G. Lloyd

Thomas (Cambridge, 1940). (To be precise, their views first
appeared in a 1939 article.) These critics advanced (pp. 47ff.)
what I venture to call the startling thesis that the poem is an
allegory on the Crucifixion. In the critics' own words, " 'The
Nymph Complaining for the Death of Her Fawn' opens with
straightforward and charming naturalism; it ends by drawing
largely on *The Song of Solomon* and its identification of the
fawn with Christ." Ten years passed without much of a
traceable reaction, one way or another, to this view. Marvell's
standard editor, H. M. Margoliouth, was favorably disposed,
in his review: "I am not convinced that they are wrong. If
they are right, the poem takes on altogether new color and
significance" (*RES*, 17:221; compare Ruth Wallerstein, who
took a middle position, *Studies in Seventeenth-Century
Poetic* [Madison, 1950] pp. 335–36). Margoliouth's attitude
presaged what was to come: it is a better poem if more
meaning can be found in it. The 1950s and 60s produced a
series of allegorical modifications of the Bradbrook–Thomas
thesis. It is not belaboring the obvious, then, to argue that
the poem is *not* about the Crucifixion (*nor* the Church of
England, *nor* the Holy Ghost). It *is* useful to show inci-
dentally what, in so far as the poem has a traceable background, that background is. On the positive side, this essay
will offer more than one reason for believing that the poem is
what Emile Legouis (in Legouis and Cazamian's *History of
English Literature*) calls it, "semi-mythological."

The Bradbrook-Thomas interpretation comes in the form
of an aperçu, we being mostly left to work out the details as
best we can. And, contrary to the implication of the sentence
quoted above, it appears to be the first paragraph of the
poem, not the last, which holds out the best prospect for
such an interpretation:

> The wanton Troopers riding by
> Have shot my Faun and it will dye.
> Ungentle men! They cannot thrive
> To kill thee. Thou neer didst alive
> Them any harm: alas nor cou'd

Thy death yet do them any good.
I'me sure I never wisht them ill;
Nor do I for all this; nor will:
But, if my simple Pray'rs may yet
Prevail with Heaven to forget
Thy murder, I will Joyn my Tears
Rather then fail. But, O my fears!
It cannot dye so. Heavens King
Keeps register of every thing:
And nothing may we use in vain.
Ev'n Beasts must be with justice slain;
Else men are made their *Deodands*.
Though they should wash their guilty hands,
In this warm life-blood, which doth part
From thine, and wound me to the Heart,
Yet could they not be clean: their Stain
Is dy'd in such a Purple Grain.
There is not such another in
The World, to offer for their Sin.

Here are blood, prayers, sin, Heaven's King, and sacrifice. In a Christian poet the combination is certainly provocative, and, if the poem continued in this strain, we should have a right to suspect allegory. It is true that there are already grave theological problems, in such a case. Allowing that the "wanton Troopers" are the slayers of the Savior, can it be said, "Nor cou'd Thy death yet do them any good"? But the main point is that 24 lines in a poem of 122 lines do not make it an allegory, and even the last couplet quoted above (the most provocative of all) fits into place as part of the poem's pattern of hyperbole and conceit, half-Italianate, half-metaphysical, whereby the fawn is magnified, at mankind's—and particularly womankind's—expense. Marvell, whose Eden in "The Garden" is conspicuous for barring Eve (St. Basil and Gregory of Nyssa saw the original man as without sexual passion), is being beguilingly antifeminine in his insistence on how much whiter the fawn is than the nymph:

       And oft
I blusht to see its foot more soft,
And white, (shall I say then my hand?)
NAY any Ladies of the Land.

He has reversed the cliché of his Hobbinol poem: "Nor our Sheep new Wash'd can be / Half so white or sweet as *She*."

He is reacting against the Petrarchan tradition by removing woman from the pedestal, substituting a fawn, and making the woman the wooer. Whereas poets going back to Horace (*Car.*, 1.23) and Ovid (*Met.* 11.771f.) and including Wyatt (the poem commencing, "They flee from me"), had maidens flee men like fawns, Marvell's fawn—and what a sweet revenge it is!—literally as well as figuratively leaves Marvell's nymph far behind (ll. 63–70). The poem, like any good poem, has overtones, but these are not religious: rather, they have to do, as in other of Marvell's poems, with the Eden (or nature) versus civilization issue, the intrusion into the secret garden, the place and time of innocence. Milton was to compare Adam and Eve to "two gentle fawns at play" (*Paradise Lost*, 4.404), menaced.

The second verse paragraph deals, one would think, the deathblow to the Bradbrook-Thomas thesis and all its descendants:

    Unconstant *Sylvio*, when yet
I had not found him counterfeit,
One morning (I remember well)
Ty'd in this silver Chain and Bell,
Gave it to me: nay and I know
What he said then; I'me sure I do.
Said He, look how your Huntsman here
Hath taught a Faun to hunt his *Dear*.
But *Sylvio* soon had me beguil'd.
This waxed tame, while he grew wild,
And quite regardless of my Smart,
Left me his Faun, but took his Heart.

In all common sense—however unfashionable that has become in criticism—does this tone, do these undoctrinal puns, permit us still to believe that the fawn is Christ? And who is Sylvio? The name suggests nothing except a figure in a pastoral poem. Is Sylvio a pagan lover from whom the nymph turned to Christ? In the first place, the two influences were side by side for a time. In the second place, how can Sylvio be said to have been the giver of the fawn ("ty'd in this silver Chain and Bell" !), if the fawn is Christ? It does not work out. It will not bear a moment's thought.

And in the fourth verse paragraph, this is said:

> Had it liv'd long, I do not know
> Whether it too might have done so
> As *Sylvio* did: his Gifts might be
> Perhaps as false or more than he.

How can this be said of the Savior? How can this be said, even if—the only possibility—it is meant to indicate lapse of faith on the part of the Church, the nun, the Virgin or whoever the nymph is supposed to be? Quoting lines 93–98, the Misses Bradbrook and Thomas grant, "It would be difficult to do this now without being blasphemous." But the above inversion is still more dangerous.

Let us grant what must be granted. There is a deer here and a deer in the Song of Solomon: "My beloved is like a roe or a young hart" (2:9). In both works the deer skips (2:8), as young deer are wont to do. Also there are lilies common to both: the biblical "beloved. . . feedeth among" them (2:16); Marvell's does something similar:

> Among the beds of Lillyes, I
> Have sought it oft, where it should lye;
> Yet could not, till it self would rise,
> Find it, although before mine Eyes.
> For, in the flaxen Lillies shade,
> It like a bank of Lillies laid.
> Upon the Roses it would feed,
> Until its Lips ev'n seem'd to bleed:
> And then to me 'twould boldly trip,
> And print those Roses on my Lip.
> But all its chief delight was still

On Roses thus its self to fill:
And its pure virgin Limbs to fold
In whitest sheets of Lillies cold.
Had it liv'd long, it would have been
Lillies without, Roses within.

Where is the crown of thorns here? In their urbanization, or their mysticism, our modern critics perhaps need to be told, as the latest edition, Pierre Legouis's, tells them, that deer actually do eat rose petals. I live on land in Massachusetts that they visit; I do not need a book to inform me of their omnivorousness. Maybe the ability to take Marvell's poem literally is in direct proportion to personal acquaintance with deer (not that books cannot provide a substitute). To carry this further, having known grief (or at least having read about it elsewhere) over a lost pet, of whatever species, would also help and would forestall such remarks as E. H. Emerson's (1955), "If the poem is to be taken literally, we have only the death of an animal as the objective correlative for emotions of the most intense sort," and J. E. Reese's (1965), "Although these allegorical interpretations of the poem have been challenged as strained and superfluous, if one accepts the poem merely as the expression of a young girl's grief for the death of a beloved animal, then there is a considerable discrepancy between the 'tragedy' and the passionate distress of the speaker." Besides, the poem delights, as I have said, in hyperbole, or it presents a frenzy not necessarily permanent. In any case, there is a long literary tradition of (to quote Leo Spitzer, note 2 of article listed below[2]; see also D.C. Allen, "Marvell's 'Nymph,' " *ELH*, 23 [1956], 94–99) "epitaphs for pets (Catullus, Martial, Navagero, Du Bellay, Ronsard, etc.)." That opening paragraph was *as if it were* about the Crucifixion: "the point is that for the nymph, the loss is incomparable, and therefore she uses language which, in the ordinary world, is suitable for a far more important sacrifice and death" (Rosalie Colie, *"My Ecchoing Song"* [Princeton, 1970], p. 131).

Donald M. Friedman would like to adhere to the Brad-brook-Thomas thesis, but, faced with "Lillies without, Roses within," he reluctantly gives up and takes the position I took eighteen years before. "It is comparatively easy to see how this radical vision stems naturally from the preceding ten lines; it is less easy to phrase its relation to the biblical tradition it recalls. I do not think that the line is intended to say anything about the relative value or position of body and spirit. Rather, the conceit is a triumphant final touch to cap a succession of witty variations on themes that are kept throughout the poem suspended between serious and mocking treatments" (*Marvell's Pastoral Art* [Berkeley, 1970], p. 110). One could be an allegorist, if only common sense did not keep breaking through!

Even if Marvell *were* echoing the Song of Songs, there would still be the question of whether he took *that* allegorically, as Milton, perhaps, did not (*Paradise Lost*, 9.442: "not mystic"—glossed by the first annotator Patrick Hume [1695] "not *Typical*"). There were those—William Gouge (1634) was one—who referred to the Canticles "as providing profitable instruction in perfect married love." (See Roland M. Frye, "The Teachings of Classical Puritanism on Conjugal Love," *Studies in the Renaissance*, 2 [1955], 153.) The nymph could be echoing a beautiful amorousness, the same the modern reader finds.

It is most confusing to say, as Bradbrook-Thomas do, that "the whiteness of the fawn. . . is of course symbolic of the Agnus Dei." It is true, a lamb is mentioned:

> Now my Sweet Faun is vanish'd to
> Whether the Swans and Turtles go:
> In fair *Elizium* to endure,
> With milk-white Lambs, and Ermins pure.

But who are the ermines? One imagines that, if Marvell had wished to be so understood, he would have used a lamb instead of a fawn, or if, like Dryden in *The Hind and the Panther*, he had intended something allegorical by his deer, he would have found ways of consistently intimating as much. Instead, he ends, as he began, with a series of conceits:

> First my unhappy Statue shall
> Be cut in Marble; and withal,
> Let it be weeping too: but there
> Th' Engraver sure his Art may spare;
> For I so truly thee bemoane,
> That I shall weep though I be Stone:
> Until my Tears, still dropping, wear
> My breast, themselves engraving there.
> There at my feet shalt thou be laid,
> Of purest Alabaster made:
> For I would have thine Image be
> White as I can, though not as Thee.

What parting shot of doctrine is here? One can discern, at most, an amalgamation of Cyparissus, the youth who so notably grieved for his accidentally slain pet deer (Ovid, *Met.* 10.106ff; Spenser, *The Faerie Queene* 1.7.17), and Niobe. As for white deer, they can be found outside the Song of Solomon. Petrarch himself has one (meaning by it Laura), *Rime* no. 190, the sonnet beginning, "Una candida cerva sopra l'erba." The white roebuck is a commonplace in folk–lore (a fact which Robert Graves publicized in *The White Goddess*). Life itself still furnishes albinistic fallow deer. Marvell could have got both fact and legend from the section on deer in Pliny's *Natural History*: "Sunt aliquando et candido colore, qualem fuisse traditur Q. Sertorii cervam, quam esse fatidicam Hispaniae gentibus persuaserat" (8.117). Lines 66–68, quoted below, reproduce accurately 8.113: "Semper in fuga adquiescunt stantesque respiciunt, cum prope ventum est, rursus fugae praesidia repetentes." Plutarch in his life of that general tells more about the famous white hind of Sertorius, how he feigned it was given him by the goddess Diana and communicated to him divine messages. It is possible that among the "300 head of deer" (Augustine Birrell, *Andrew Marvell* [New York, 1905], p. 31) in the park at Nunappleton was a white fawn. But this is to oppose the extreme of mysticism with the extreme of literalism. Let us say Marvell's fawn is white in sign of beauty, superiority, and innocence. The color and everything else about the fawn are amply accounted for without resort to biblical allegory; on the other hand, there is much, too much, in the poem that mocks any attempt at a theological reading.

Note that it is "troopers" who shot the fawn—which connotes, then as now, soldiers. The *Oxford English Dictionary*, recording no appearance of the word before 1640, states: "The term was used in connexion with the Covenanting Army which invaded England in 1640." It was also used of the Cavaliers. If allegory is our game, why may we not say that the fawn stands for Merry England, mortally wounded in the Civil War?

> For it was full of sport; and light
> Of foot, and heart; and did invite,
> Me to its game . . .
>   It is a wond'rous thing, how fleet
> 'Twas on those little silver feet.
> With what a pretty skipping grace,
> It oft would challenge me the Race:
> And when 'thad left me far away,
> 'Twould stand, and run again, and stay.
> For it was nimbler much than Hindes;
> And trod, as on the four Winds.

Things will never be again what they were in Marvell's youth, not to push further back to the Elizabethans (who got their culture through Italy—Sylvio is an Italian name). This is Marvell's "Farewell, Rewards and Fairies."

Two—or, rather, three—can easily play at this game of letting our thoughts wander. It is not even to be denied, considering the fact of the Civil War and the fact of Marvell's (or any seventeenth-century Puritan's) intimacy with the Bible, that the poet's thoughts *could* have wandered in both these directions, at times, as he wrote. But this is mere psychobiographical conjecture—or autobiographical wool-gathering—rather than defensible interpretation of a poem whose lines are straight and clear, however much fun the frivolity of trying to twist them. Not every fancy or free association that may dart into a reader's head is fair. One reader who was questioned as to the meaning of the poem replied without hesitation that it represented a girl's lament for her lost virginity. The reader went on to substantiate this view in painful detail, beginning with the word "wanton"!

In 1956 Don Cameron Allen (p. 106, n. 32) prophesied that "one of the modern critics is likely to take up the suggestion" (above) that I published in 1952. Lo and behold! in 1967, also in *Modern Philology*, Earl Miner brought in the troopers as lovers and asked, "Have there been passages between the Troopers and her?" Pierre Legouis took issue with this in 1968 (in the bibliographical Appendix, p. 253, to his *Andrew Marvell*, Oxford, 2nd edition) and it is dropped in the redoing of the article in Professor Miner's *The Metaphysical Mode from Donne to Cowley* (Princeton, 1969). It is pleasant to be able to record that there are individuals who have second thoughts. A German translator of the poem speculates on the erotic attraction of "nymphets" for Marvell, which he notes to be the English vice: he mentions Ruskin and Lewis Carroll.

These factitious interests!—the poem does not need to be made more interesting than it is. Let us freely admit, without straining grotesquely for Christian "color and significance," that "The Nymph Complaining for the Death of Her Fawn" is less pious than, say, *The White Doe of Rylstone*. It does not follow, as night the day, that Wordsworth's is the better poem. Heaviness is not all. Poe, in singling out Marvell's poem on the occasion of its appearance in S. C. Hall's *The Book of Gems* in 1836, flatly took issue with the editor by denominating it "poetry of the *very loftiest order*" (*Complete Works*, ed. J. A. Harrison [New York, 1902], IX, 102). And for Poe the poem was lighter than for other readers, since he strangely and characteristically, ignoring Sylvio and the tone of the opening lines, insisted on calling the nymph a "child," "the little maiden." And, indeed, there is something to Rosalie Colie's observation (p. 87), "The girl's innocence is in part communicated by the childishness of some of her sentences" and L. N. Wall's (in Legouis's edition) on "the unusually high proportion of monosyllables, which copies a simple girl's speech" ("*Deodands*," 17, being the great exception).

To come back to those opening lines, the part to which it is proposed to sacrifice the whole, they admit of a pagan interpretation—and that is more what the rest of the poem seems to require. In line 104 "*Diana's* Shrine" is mentioned. The nymph has turned away from men, become a practitioner of chastity and lover of deer, like Diana. Marvell is not likely to be using the word "nymph" just casually to mean girl. Diana was *the* nymph, *nympha nympharum*, and her followers were nymphs. In connection with the opening suggestion of recompense for a slain fawn, one is probably supposed to remember, if anything, not Christ, but the sacred stag which Agamemnon and his party slew (*they* were troopers, on the way to the Trojan War) while hunting in the grove of Artemis at Aulis, and on account of which the goddess exacted the sacrifice of Iphigenia. That such an exchange would be worthwhile in the present case is denied by Marvell's nymph:

> There is not such another in
> The World, to offer for their Sin.

The attitude in the first verse paragraph is, as Grosart noted, similar to Blake's in "Auguries of Innocence": "A Robin Red breast in a Cage / Puts all Heaven in a Rage" and "A Horse misus'd upon the Road / Calls to Heaven for Human Blood," etc. Pity for the stricken deer is shown by Shakespeare (*As You Like It*, II 1.33ff.), Drayton (*Poly-Olbion,* XIII, 147ff.), and Montaigne (*Essais,* 2.11), and the antivenery literature includes More's *Utopia* (II, 6), Erasmus's *Encomium Moriae* (19), Plutarch's *De solertia animalium* (i–ii), and goes back to Pythagoras and the Pythagoreans (see Ovid., *Met.,* 15.75ff.).

My insisting on a relationship between the nymph and Diana has been objected to on the grounds that the former "is the last person who would go to the hunt, who would

destroy the beauty and innocence represented by the Faun."
I see that it is necessary to explain that neither Diana nor any
other decent or legal hunter goes after fawns. "A giant hunter
named Orion boasted that he was about to kill all living
creatures, and Artemis, as Mistress of Animals, very properly
slew him." I quote Charles Seltman's *The Twelve Olympians*
(New York, 1956, p. 136), partly because it has a photo of a
bronze of Artemis (plate 3) as protectress, holding tenderly a
fawn in both hands. Oddly enough, my critic had just mentioned, as I did, "that on at least one occasion Diana was
upset to have a favorite stag killed."

What set the Misses Bradbrook and Thomas off in an
allegorical direction? Was it, perhaps, *another* poem? It was,
judging by the footnote on page 49: "The whole poem may
be related to the death and metamorphosis of Fida's hind in
William Browne's *Britannia's Pastorals* (book 1, songs 4 and
5). Browne's nymph represents religious Faith and the hind,
Truth." This suggestion is not original with these critics—it
goes back to the edition of Margoliouth, who, in turn, is
repeating Robert Poscher, *Andrew Marvells poetische Werke*
(Vienna, 1908, p. 30). Long the only proposal offered for a
source for Marvell's poem, it is not very cogent. The nearest
that Browne's hind comes to being shot by hunters is that a
shepherd's dog barks at it; thereupon, without fear, it walks
up to Fida in a friendly way (song 3), only to be later (song
4) devoured by the man-monster Riot; on which occasion we
are given, not Fida's implorations, but the hind's. The happy
ending has it that from the mangled remains springs up the
maiden Aletheia (observe that Browne, like Dryden, makes
unmistakable *his* allegories).

If we must have a source for the simple situation in
Marvell's poem, we can do better by turning to a more
famous poet than Browne—Virgil. In the seventh book of the
Aeneid, lines 475ff., we are told how the Fury Alecto stirred
up war between the Rutulians and the Trojans in Italy by
causing Ascanius, while out hunting with his men, to wound
mortally, with his arrow, the pet stag of—the name is not
without interest—Silvia. We are provided with details (Browne

offers none) of what this pet, stolen from its mother's udder, meant to the girl, how she had tamed it and adorned its antlers with garlands, and was wont to comb and bathe it. It became accustomed to its mistress's table, "mensaeque adsuetus erili," inspiration enough for Marvell's couplet,

> With sweetest milk, and sugar, first
> I it at mine own fingers nurst.

Moaning and with the blood flowing, the stag finds its way back to its mistress, who reacts as one would expect.

> Silvia prima soror palmis percussa lacertos
> Auxilium vocat et duros conclamat agrestis,

says Virgil. "O help! O help!" cries Marvell's nymph, whose name, if she is to be assigned one, is Silvia rather than Pietà.

In conclusion, I am glad to draw on two distinguished names. Leo Spitzer (note 1 of his article) attacked "the gratuitous belief that an allegorical explanation is in itself of higher quality than a non-allegorical one (whereas the true touchstone of any explanation is whether or not it actually 'explains' convincingly and completely), a belief that in turn may represent an excessive reaction of overcompensation for traditional American qualities which have come to be felt in certain quarters as too pedestrian: good sense, matter-of-factness, realism." Pierre Legouis, who has used his French logic and common sense to prick many of these bubbles, sums it all up in his new Oxford edition: "All the allegorical interpretations of the poem, beginning with Bradbrook-Thomas's in 1940, only testify to the recent tendency to scorn the plain meaning of a text; they overbid one another and are mutually exclusive."

NOTES

1. "Alcuni Aspetti della Poesia di Andrew Marvell," English *Miscellany*, 11 (1960), 75-111. Oddly enough, Miss Colaiacomo does mention (p. 92) "la Williamson," author of "A Reply"—which is a reply to me (see below, n. 2). Readers interested in Italian translation will recognize the following in the (expanded) present essay or my original article (*MP*, 50 [1952], 97-101): "Come si può dire infatti, riferendosi alla morte di Gesù e a coloro che Lo uccisero: '. . .nor cou'd / Thy death yet do them any good.'? E se il cerbiatto è Cristo, chi è mai Silvio? E come si spiega il fatto che Silvio abbia donato il cerbiatto (cioè Cristo) incatenato? Non basta citare i versi: 'There is not such another in / The World to offer for their Sin' per dire che siamo di fronte ad una poesia religiosa che adombra la passione di Cristo" (p. 93). Rather, they are "dell'atmosfera iperbolica, leggermente artificiosa di tutto il componimento" (p. 94). Even when disagreeing with unmentioned me—I become "alcuni"—Colaiacomo goes on translating:

> Non è il caso di considerare questa poesia, come da alcuni è stato fatto, una deliberata reazione, da parte di Marvell, alla stereotipata tradizione petrarchesca che venerava e idolatrava la donna. Si sono volute interpretare le manifestazioni d'affetto della Ninfa per il suo cerbiatto come una cosciente parodia delle sdolcinate lodi e delle profferte amorose che, ormai per convenzione, venivano rivolte alle dame nei canzonieri italianeggianti del tempo. La donna qui non sarebbe più posta su un piedistallo, quasi creatura sacra cui siano dovute venerazione e rispetto, anzi le profferte amorose che era abituata a sdegnare, sarebbe lei stessa, questa volta a farle, e neppure ad un uomo, bensì ad un animale, ad un cerbiatto. Si è voluto vedere nei versi (59-62) un deliberato rovesciamento della posizione tradizionale che già in antico era stata codificato da Ovidio, profondo conoscitore dell'animo femminile. [*Met.* 11.771-72] [pp. 97-98]

"È vero che Marvell usa a volte delle espressioni che possono farlo apparire quasi misigino, come per esempio i versi tanto spesso citati" ("The Garden," 61-64) (p. 98). The *Metamorphoses* and "Garden" references are mine: so are Colaiacomo's citations from Virgil (pp. 94-95), her references to Niobe (p. 94) and Cyparissus (p. 95), to Wallerstein and the review by "Margaliouth" (Colaiacomo's spelling, p. 91), and the quotation about deer from Pliny (p. 95—for which she is credited by Legouis in 1971: see n.2 below).

2. Spitzer's article is "Marvell's 'Nymph Complaining for the Death of Her Faun': Sources Versus Meaning," *MLQ*, 19(1958), 231-43; reprinted in his *Essays on English and American Literature* (Princeton, 1962), pp. 98-115, and in William R. Keast (ed.), *Seventeenth-Century English Poetry: Modern Essays in Criticism* (New York, 1962, 1971). However, Spitzer takes, I believe, an untenable position on the syntax of lines 18ff.: see Pierre Legouis, "Marvell's 'Nymph . . .,': A *Mise au Point*," *MLQ*, 21 (1960), 30-32. My closing quotation from Legouis

comes from his annotations in vol. I to the Oxford, 1971, 3rd ed. of Margoliouth's text, *The Poems and Letters of Andrew Marvell.* The eminently sensible J. B. Leishman also advised "not to search in his poems, as has too often been done in recent times, for all manner of ambiguities and profundities which are not really there." *The Art of Marvell's Poetry* (New York, 1968), p. 99.

The first article to follow mine of 1952 was Karina Williamson, "Marvell's 'The Nymph Complaining': A Reply," *MP*, 51 (1954), 268–71 (both articles are reprinted in the Penguin critical anthology, *Andrew Marvell*, ed. John Carey, 1969). Miss Williamson starts out so winsomely, i.e., that I "was right to expose the flaws" and she continues so moderately, never claiming allegory, that it is rather with the following that I would and do quarrel, in whole or in part: Everett H. Emerson, "Andrew Marvell's 'The Nymph Complaining for the Death of her Faun' " *Etudes Anglaises*, 8(1955), 107–10; Ruel E. Foster, "A Tonal Study: Marvell, 'The Nymph . . . , ' " *University of Kansas City Review*, 22 (1955), 73–78; Werner Vortriede, "Ein Gedicht von Andrew Marvell," *Neue Rundschau*, 72 (1961), 868ff.; Ruth Nevo, "Marvell's Songs of Innocence and Experience," *Studies in English Literature 1500–1900*, 5 (1965), 1–21; Jack E. Reese, "Marvell's 'Nymph' in a New Light," *EA*, 18 (1965), 398–401; Earl Miner, "The Death of Innocence in Marvell's 'Nymph Complaining for the Death of her Faun,' " *MP*, 65 (1967), 9–16; Evan Jones, *Explicator*, 26 (1968), item 73; Geoffrey H. Hartman, " 'The Nymph Complaining for the Death of her Fawn': A Brief Allegory," *Essays in Criticism*, 18 (1968), 113–35.

Appendices

THE NEW CRITIC PAUSES OVER EVA

Lest it be thought I am utterly incapable of swimming with the tide, I offer the following plumbing of the depths of chapter 14 of *Uncle Tom's Cabin.*

All poetry is paradox; so, too, is the only prose worth considering. Stowe loses no time in anticipating this present-day discovery in her introductory description of Eva. "Her form was the perfection of childish beauty, without its usual chubbiness and squareness of outline." Chubbiness suggests roundness: in other words, Eva was not round and square like other children. Her shape is left deliberately indeterminate, for a purpose flashed at us darkly in the next sentence: "There was about it an undulating and aerial grace, such as one might dream of for some mythic and allegorical being." Here is what we are always looking for—myth, myth and symbolism. The physical contour is trivial, beneath contemplation: we care not to know how Eva stands, let her remain unlimned (paronomasia); our quest, rather, is to know what she stands for.

Her name ushers in primitivistic associations: Eve, *das ewig Weibliche* (Goethe, Joyce's Gerty, too), Dante's "ch'è tanto bella" stationed at the feet of Mary, Yeats's Queen Maeve (Ma-Eve, mother Eve). The golden hair—persistently stressed, imagistically wound through this and subsequent paragraphs—of this mythic being is like Blake's golden bowl (James's too). Can love be put in a golden bowl?

What are the auguries of innocence? Why is Eva white and Tom black?

Eva, at present "between five and six years of age," straddles time like twin compasses (Donne). In her diminutive but comprehensive image are subsumed the Jungian, palimpsestic past and foreordained future. "The shape of her head and the turn of her neck and bust were peculiarly noble." We need not take this as a hint of physical precocity (though the anthropometry of New Orleans' female white residents before the Civil War might be worth looking into, were anyone willing to do the research). No, we catch the telltale sign of the telescoped image. Eva looks back to Eve, her forebear and her archetype. She is innocence trembling on an unmentionable threshold. At the same time she looks forward to her future self, virginal in a soiled world.

She always wears white, symbol of nudity. Her relation to the fireman on board the ship is ambiguous. "The fireman, as he looked up from his sweaty toil, sometimes found those eyes looking wonderingly into the raging depths of the furnace, and fearfully and pityingly at him, as if she thought him in some dreadful danger." Tiger, tiger, burning bright, surely! We learn too that "when she tripped fearlessly over dangerous places, rough, sooty hands were stretched involuntarily out to save her." But what kind of salvation is this? Moreover, what right has salvation to be involuntary? And what is the true significance of Tom's rescue of Eva when she falls overboard ("accidents don't just happen") a few paragraphs later? Are these waters, by any chance, the Joycean waters of the womb? (Compare "Lycidas," Milton's only poem, and the Orpheus myth.) The student of French literature will think instantly of Saint–Pierre's Virginie, who, on a similar occasion, preferred to drown. For the significant moment Uncle Tom is a symbol of evil as ineluctable as Moby Dick: "A broad-chested, strong-armed fellow, it was nothing for him to keep afloat in the water." Why *was* it nothing? How can this be said but of a monster of the deep? How, indeed, could the by now blatant pectoral obsession—the syllogism, of which Eva's bust is the major, Uncle Tom's chest the minor—how could this be resolved except by flinging itself, Ahab-like, upon the broad, death-sweet bosom of the largest of mammals? We are to note, too, the unconsciousness of Eva when carried out. She had been called "dreamy" before. The waters of the Mississippi pass into the well of the unconscious. *The deep* (noun or adjective) *well* (adverb or noun) *knows id* (bilingual pun). (I reJoyce to express my detextable debt here to Hugo von Hofmannsthal: "Der tiefe Brunnen weiss es wohl.") Moby Dick floats, externally and internally, logos upon the waters.

But in Eva's case this saturation is the fluminous dawn of love. However, she wears to the last—paradox again—what is at once the dress of the angel and the dress of the bride. In this last respect she is reminiscent of—or would have been, if the novel had come out in time—Miss Havisham in *Great Expectations*. There is also the Kafkaesque rejection of her father; Uncle Tom has replaced him. Both stand ready to plunge in, but only Tom does.

The sociologically-minded reader will have a free association with Eva Peron. Superficially, it may seem extreme to mention her, but extremes meet, do they not? and it is at least a salutary extreme—away from "the intentional fallacy"—which is, you will recall, the surrender to the naive assumption that the author knows what he is doing and has supplied not much more meaning than he intended. The striking fact is that Eva Peron died exactly one hundred years after Eva St. Clare was given literary birth in this book (the cyclical theory, Vico, Toynbee; metempsychosis too, Pythagoras, Plato). This number, one hundred, is certainly not a concidence; it is fraught with symbolism: it is, indeed, the number of cantos in *La Divina Commedia,* 3 X 33 + 1. Bearing in mind that the subtitle of *Uncle Tom's Cabin* is *Life Among the Lowly*, we are now in a position to see that "the lowly" has reference to the damned of the *Inferno*. In addition, "lowly" has geographical over-tones—perhaps one should say undertones—of the South. In the chapter I have been analyzing we meet Eva traveling on the Mississippi in the direction of South America! Both Evas were blonde, and the workers, the *descamisados*, had a curious affection for both. After Eva comes anti-Eva. . . . Every novel is to be considered either as *therapoetics* or as a parable of the times; by "a parable of the times" one must of necessity mean a parable of *our* times.

I had intended to move on from the chapter that introduces Eva, but these hints of themes and sub-themes, this tentative-definitive unraveling of certain strands of form and texture (ambivalence, too), will have to serve as a guide to the rest of the novel. Rapidity of movement, glossy coverage of the large surface, is not characteristic of the new egotism. Yet I had hoped, if time had permitted, to settle, not whether Eva's father is liberal, but whether he is *a* liberal. It is a question that would have taken us not only forward but back. For to discuss the issue in connection with Augustine St. Clare one would be semantically bound to settle the famous (Latin *clarus*, vocative *clare*) St. Augustine first. Was St. Augustine a liberal? And which famous St. Augustine, the African or the Englishman? This, naturally, leads into the colonial question, which is what I wanted to talk about most.[1]

[1]Reprinted from *The Long Road Back* (Boston, 1957; London, 1958), pp. 92–94.

A POSTSCRIPT TO
"THE ENDING OF *HAMLET* AS A FAREWELL TO ESSEX"

A safer and slighter case, ten years later, of inspiration from life might be Prospero and Forman. It has long been known that Simon Forman, the magus and astrologer, attended several of Shakespeare's plays and took notes on them. A. L. Rowse, in three books, has made it seem probable that Shakespeare had at least heard of Forman, because the dramatist's landlady, Mrs. Mountjoy, consulted Forman in 1597 and 1598, as did, between 1597 and 1600, Emilia Bassano Lanier, identified by this historian as the Dark Lady of the Sonnets. But even in his newest book, *Simon Forman: Sex and Society in Shakespeare's Age* (London, 1974), Rowse does not offer any speculation on a possible connection between Forman and Prospero. Forman had died the death that he had forecast, September 8, 1611. *The Tempest* was acted at court November 1, 1611. The name "Prospero" (twice "Prosper") links in meaning with "Fore-man," who worked so hard to get ahead. Forman and Prospero used magic for what they regarded as good only. Did Forman show or talk his "Autobiography," which mentions the dream he had at six of a tempest that was, as it were, his own creation and that he overcame? "Then he should see many great waters like to drown him, boiling and raging against him as though they would swallow him up, yet he thought he did overpass them" (Rowse, op. cit., p. 268). The ousted Duke of Milan was "all dedicated / To closeness and the bettering of my mind" (I.ii.90). So was young Simon: "When his fellows went to play he would go to his book, or into some secret place to muse and meditate, or into the church" (p. 276) . Both were dependent on their magic books (or manuscripts). Caliban reiterates to his fellow conspirators, "Having first seiz'd his books, . . . Remember / First to possess his books; for without them / He's but a sot. . . . Burn but his books" (III.ii.106). Forman was never worse off than when "robbed and spoiled of all my goods and books" (p. 280). That was the year, 1579, when "The very spirits were subject unto me; what I spake was done." Ferdinand and the other ship- wrecked men may wonder, "Where should this music be? i' th' air, or th' earth?" (I.ii.385). Forman would have taken it in stride, since, in 1591, "The 22nd day of March a.m. at 8, we heard music at circle" (p. 287). Prospero forgave; so did the Forman family, according to Simon: "They always love justice and maintain the right, and are utter enemies to injury and oppression, apt to forgive" (p. 300). Trinculo drinks, but the name could be regarded as something of a diminutive of the nickname of Forman's wife, Tronco. Forman, who had no legitimate daughter of his own, was "Father"—two Frances Howards called him that—to many a "wondering" (Miranda) female client. "If by your art, my dearest father. . ." (I.ii.1).

Index

Index

Schmidt, Alexander, 9, 20
Schmidt, Immanuel, 92
Schücking, Levin L., 8
Scoufos, Alice L., 94
Seltman, Charles, 176
Servius Grammaticus, 75
Seward, Thomas, 95, 96
Seznec, Jean, 91
Shakespeare, William, ix, xii, xiii, 3-43,
    45, 46, 49, 53, 56, 62, 63, 90, 97,
    105, 123, 153, 161, 175
Shawcross, John T., 88, 130, 131, 133,
    151, 152
Shenstone, William, 162
Sidney, Sir Philip, 97, 119
Sikes, George, 140, 155-56
Simpson, Evelyn, 47, 59, 66
Sirluck, E., 131, 133, 135, 151
Smith, Sir Thomas, 42
Sophocles, 159
Southey, Robert, 159
Spencer, Theodore, 58
Spenser, Edmund, 13, 18, 74, 87, 88,
    90, 92, 99, 103, 165, 172,
Spillane, Gerald B., 8, 9
Spitzer, Leo, 170, 177, 178
Sprott, S. Ernest, 46, 47, 58, 59
Stampfer, Judah, 65
Starnes, Dewitt T., 91
Stauffer, Donald A., 108, 121, 123
Staunton, Howard, 8
Steadman, John M., x, 74, 92, 99, 158
Steevens, George, 8
Stein, Arnold, 143, 153, 157
Stempel, Daniel, 124
Stern, Alfred, 91, 160
Stevens, D. H., 122
Stollman, Samuel S., 154, 157
Stopes, Charlotte C., 41
Stoppard, Tom, 4
Stow, John, 38
Stowe, Harriet Beecher, 180-82
Strachey, Lytton, 17, 35, 42
Svendsen, Kester, x, 96
Swaim, Kathleen M., 126-27
Swetnam, Joseph, 63
Swinburne, Henry, 62
Symmons, Charles, 119, 128
Sympson, J., 95
Sypher, Francis J., 62

Taafe, James G., 160
Talbert, Ernest W., 91
Tavenner, Eugene, 92
Terence, 145
Theobald, Lewis, 95
Theocritus, 84, 97
Thomas, M. G. Lloyd, 165-73,
    176, 177
Thompson, Claud A., 122, 126

Thou, Jacque-August de, 38
Tillyard, E. M. W., xi, 103, 108, 123,
    154
Tillyard, Phyllis B., xi
Todd, Henry John, 76, 90, 93, 95,
    96, 105
Toland, John, 88
Townshend, Aurelian, 91
Toynbee, Arnold, 182
Tuve, Rosemond, x, 73, 91

Usher, Roland G., 60

Van Doren, Mark, 8
Van Tromp, H., 122
Vaughan, Henry, 162
Verity, A. W., 101, 121, 131, 135-36
Vico, Giovanni, 182
Villari, Pasquale, 124, 125, 126
Virgil, 68, 71, 75, 90, 96-97, 138, 163
    176-77, 178
Visiak, E. H., 108, 123
Vortriede, Werner, 174, 179

Wall, L. N., 175
Wallerstein, Ruth, 166, 178
Walton, Izaak, 46, 47, 51, 56, 57, 59,
    60, 65
Warton, Thomas, 80, 81, 95, 96
Watson, S. R. 92
Webber, Joan, 58
Webster, John, 65, 119, 127
White, Beatrice, 60
White, Richard G., 9
Whiting, George, 73, 91
Wierus, Joannes, 76, 97
Wilkinson, Henry, 123
Williams, Marjorie, 162
Williamson, George, 59
Williamson, Karina, xiv, 178, 179
Williamson, Marilyn L., 151
Wilson, Elkin C., 43, 127
Wilson, J. Dover, xii, 8, 9, 12, 32, 33,
    34, 35, 37, 38, 41, 42
Wind, Edgar, 91
Winstanley, Lilian, 20, 33, 36, 38, 39,
    40, 41
Winwood, Sir Ralph, 43
Wittreich, Joseph A., 93-94, 152, 159
Wolff, Samuel L., 158
Woodhouse, A. S. P., x, xi, 88, 90, 94,
    96, 121, 155, 156
Wordsworth, William, 174
Wright, B. A., 88
Wright, Louis B., xii, 63
Wyatt, Sir Thomas, 168

Yeats, William Butler, 57, 66, 180
Yonge, Walter, 127

Zervos, C., 91